God of My Days

DAILY DEVOTIONALS
THROUGH THE CHRISTIAN YEAR

DAVID BAST

God of My Days
© 2024 by Words of Hope

Published by Words of Hope
700 Ball Ave. N.E.
Grand Rapids, MI 49503-1308
woh@woh.org
www.woh.org

Italics in biblical quotations represents emphasis added by the author.

Cover and interior design by Claudia Elzinga

Words of Hope provides people both near and far with daily access to God's Word.

Printed in the United States of America

16 15 14 13 12 11 10 9 8 7 6 5 4 3 2 1

Introduction

Near the end of Matthew 13, a chapter in which Jesus tells seven different parables about the kingdom of God, he asks his hearers a question.

> *"Have you understood all these things?" They said to him, "Yes." And he said to them, "Therefore every scribe who has been trained for the kingdom of heaven is like a master of a house, who brings out of his treasure what is new and what is old." (Matthew 13:51-52)*

That's an interesting and perhaps somewhat cryptic statement, but it describes perfectly the nature of this one-year devotional, a collection of my devotional writing for Words of Hope. In it, I am bringing out of my treasure something old and something new. To be honest, the treasure I'm mining isn't really mine, it's the Bible's, and what is old in this book far outweighs what is new. But nevertheless, I still hope you find it valuable.

The devotionals published here were written over the course of many years. The earliest date from 1984; the most recent from 2024. When Words of Hope and I began talking about republishing a whole year's worth of devotionals, I discovered that I had plenty of material to choose from. But it didn't begin to cover the entire Bible. I found that I had focused on my favorite books and themes: the person and work of Jesus, the great doctrines of the faith, the Psalms and Isaiah, the gospels and epistles. So if you choose to read it through the whole year, this book will not take you through the whole Bible, but it will allow you to spend time each day thinking about the meaning of Jesus' life, death, and resurrection, and what it is to follow him.

The book is organized around the church's liturgical calendar—the Christian year. When I was growing up in a Reformed church we didn't observe the church year. We did the big days—Christmas, Palm Sunday, Good Friday, Easter, Ascension Day, Pentecost—but seasons like Lent and Advent were *terra incognita*. One of the things I have appreciated in recent years is the way believers from many traditions have discovered the value of paying attention to a calendar that marks Christian seasons and holy days rather than just secular ones. So our year begins and ends with Advent.

A note about how to use this book. Because Advent, Epiphany, and Ordinary Time vary in length each year, I have included extra devotionals in those seasons. In some cases, I have written new devotionals to fill in gaps here and there. If you want to stay seasonal you will have to keep your eye on the Christian calendar (see appendix) and add or subtract readings accordingly. Devotionals for specific days, like Christmas, are noted and you can also find a list of them in the appendix.

I hope you will find that spending a little time each day in the Scriptures and with the Lord in prayer encourages your spirit and builds your faith. And most of all, that it will deepen your love for the one who loved us and gave himself for us.

Amen! Come, Lord Jesus!

Advent & Christmas

Advent & Christmas

The Christian calendar starts each year with Advent. As Christians we live in three dimensions of time: remembering what God has done in the past, looking forward to what he will do in the future, worshiping and serving him in the present. Advent is the season when we think about these three aspects of time. We celebrate Jesus' coming into the world long ago in Bethlehem, we rejoice in his spiritual presence with us now, and we anticipate his return in glory and the consummation of all things.

Advent is a season for thought, reflection, and preparation, when we can take time each day to wait, watch, and welcome Jesus. Advent begins on the fourth Sunday before Christmas, and extends to December 24, Christmas Eve. The season of Christmas follows Advent, starting on December 24 and extending to January 5. During the season of Christmas, Christians rejoice with all creation in the birth of our savior. The world is done with Christmas on December 25, but our celebrations are only beginning.

The devotionals this season are drawn from four series.

* ✳ *Trustworthy Sayings*, published in January 2008, shares "trustworthy sayings" from Paul, things that we can be especially sure of as we face an unknown future.

* ✳ *Christmas*, published in December 2008, shares the Christmas story as told in all four gospels.

* *Waiting, Watching, Welcoming*, published in December 2019, focuses on our response to Jesus in the three aspects of time: past, present, and future.

* *Hearing Jesus*, published in October 2020, explores the first three chapters of the book of Revelation and the vision of Christ in glory and power given to us there.

READ: John 14:15-23

The Third Coming

I will not leave you as orphans; I will come to you. (John 14:18)

The Christian season of Advent is at odds with what our culture has come to call "the holidays." Advent is all about quiet expectation and preparation. People will be increasingly busy during these December days shopping for presents, going to parties, traveling to and preparing for family gatherings. That's great. No one wants to be Ebenezer Scrooge ("Bah, humbug!"). You will probably be doing those things too, but you can also use this season for a deeper purpose.

In Advent, Christians remember that we are waiting. As we worship on these four Sundays, we can identify in a small way with the Old Testament saints who waited long centuries for the Messiah to come. And while we rejoice that God did come into our world in Jesus, we also remember that we are still waiting for another, greater advent, when Jesus will come again to complete the salvation he has begun.

We usually think in terms of those two comings: in the past, when Christ came to be our Savior, and in the future, when "he will come again to judge the living and the dead" (Apostles' Creed). But there is a third coming of Jesus, a present one. Through the Spirit, Jesus comes right now to live in his friends—whom he defines as those who love him and keep his commands.

So as we prepare to celebrate Jesus' incarnation and birth, and as we wait and watch for his return at the end of this age, we can also welcome him now—provided we meet his definition of "friends."

PRAYER: Lord Jesus, I call myself your friend.
Make me a better one today.

Series: *Waiting, Watching, Welcoming*

READ: John 1:1-9

The True Light

The light shines in the darkness, and the darkness has not overcome it. (John 1:5)

If you live where I do, the weather in December can be pretty depressing. The days are short. It's usually cloudy. We sometimes go for weeks without ever seeing the sun. It seems appropriate that we should celebrate the coming of the Light into the world during the darkest time of the year (at least in North America). There's a reason we light candles to mark the weeks of Advent!

Light and darkness are universal symbols. They can stand for good and evil, for truth and falsehood, for wisdom and ignorance. Later in John's gospel Jesus will declare himself to be "the light of the world" (John 8:12). The darkness may seem strong, stronger even than the light, but never fear. Jesus is the Light. Darkness did not overcome him, though it tried mighty hard. And it won't win in the end.

Here in his prologue, John also reminds us of a truth we might tend to overlook during this season: the light has always been here. "The true light, which gives light to everyone, was coming into the world" (v. 9). God did not enter the darkness of our fallen world for the first time at Christmas. He's always been coming here, and not just here, but everywhere; not just with us, but with everyone. Christians call this light of God's presence "common grace," as in "common to all." Because of that, everything that is good or true or beautiful, wherever in the world it is found, comes from him. Whatever light there is, shines from the gracious presence of the Lord.

PRAYER: Jesus, draw me to your light, wherever it is shining.

Series: *Waiting, Watching, Welcoming*

READ: Isaiah 40:1-8

Comfort My People

Comfort ye, comfort ye my people, saith your God. (Isaiah 40:1 KJV)

Whenever I read this verse, I hear it as music in my head—the first words of Handel's *Messiah*. For most of us that word "comfort" suggests relaxation or pleasure. We're happy when we can put on comfortable clothes; we turn to comfort food to cheer us up. Or we may think of comfort as soothing, as when a mother kisses her child's "owie."

But when God speaks comfort to his people, he doesn't just change how they feel; he changes where they are. Biblical comfort isn't an emotional boost; it's a promise of deliverance from exile. It's no accident that the word "comfort" has "fort" in it. Comfort is all about strength, the strength we draw from the hope of the salvation proclaimed by God.

God's comfort is just as much for us today, because whatever bondage sin—whether our own or others'—may have landed us in, whatever wilderness we may be wandering through, the Lord has promised to free us and see us safely home. "For the LORD comforts Zion; he comforts all her waste places and makes her wilderness like Eden, her desert like the garden of the LORD; joy and gladness will be found in her, thanksgiving and the voice of song" (Isa. 51:3).

Isn't all this just a happy dream, that there's a loving heavenly Father out there who someday will make everything right? How do we know it's true? The reason is because "the mouth of the LORD has spoken" (Isa. 40:5). In a world where all is passing away, one thing endures: the Word of God.

PRAYER: Lord, I believe your word.
Help me to hold fast to your promises.

Series: *Waiting, Watching, Welcoming*

READ: John 1:6-8, 15

Bearing Witness

He came . . . to bear witness about the light, that all might believe through him. (John 1:7)

We all know and love the familiar characters of the Christmas story; we set them up each season in our Nativity scenes: Mary and Joseph, the shepherds, angels, and wise men, and, of course, the baby in the manger. But what about the characters of Advent? Are there any? There's at least one—John the Baptist. John appears near the beginning of all four gospels. Matthew, Mark, and Luke all connect him to the great prophecy of Isaiah 40. John was the voice crying in the wilderness, "Prepare the way of the LORD" (v. 3). John's preaching was so powerful that some were wondering if he might be the Messiah, so they asked him. "Not me," replied John, "I'm not worthy to untie his shoes." In other words, don't look at me, look at Jesus.

John the evangelist says this about John the forerunner: "He was not the light, but came to bear witness about the light" (John 1:8). John the Baptist wasn't the light himself; he was just a witness to the light. Later, Jesus would say that John *was* a light. "He was a burning and shining lamp, and you were willing to rejoice for a while in his light" (John 5:35). John was a light, but he wasn't the sun. He was more of a moon. He didn't produce the light, he reflected it, by pointing others to Jesus.

Might this be what Jesus meant when he said that *we* are the light of the world (Matt. 5:14)?

PRAYER: Lord, I want my life to reflect your light.
May those who see me be drawn to you.

Series: *Waiting, Watching, Welcoming*

READ: Psalm 27

Wait for the Lord

Wait for the LORD, be strong, and let your heart take courage; wait for the LORD! (Psalm 27:14)

The Bible places a great premium upon the act of waiting. John Calvin, the great Reformed theologian, once said this: "It is contrary to the nature of faith to insist on the adverb *now*." We cry out to God to fix our problems, to relieve our suffering, to rescue us from the mess we're in (whether personal or global). We would like him to act immediately. But he rarely does, and so we wait.

Waiting could almost be a synonym for faith. A good part of what it means to be a believer is to hold on to the conviction that a loving God is ruling the world and caring for us even when it seems like he's absent, or you might even think he isn't real.

People who don't believe in God have a difficult time making sense of suffering. If you no longer trust that God is in control of your life and that his plans for you are good, then suffering has no meaning. There's no reason to wait, no one to wait for.

But for believers even the most awful things can have some meaning or purpose because God can and will use them to bring about our final salvation, as one of the Bible's boldest claims states (Rom. 8:28). Moreover, we know that he is with us, even in the darkest valley. So we wait for the Lord, and our hearts take courage.

PRAYER: Lord, show me your beauty today, so that I may be satisfied with you as I wait for your salvation (see Psalm 27:4).

Series: *Waiting, Watching, Welcoming*

READ: Isaiah 30:18-26

Blessed Are Those Who Wait

For the LORD is a God of justice; blessed
are all those who wait for him. (Isaiah 30:18)

Legalized euthanasia is a sinister trend creeping into western societies. Some governments have concluded that it's easier (and cheaper) to allow doctors to kill people with terminal illnesses or disabilities—or even those who are just depressed—rather than to treat them. Whatever else might be said about this chilling movement, it certainly represents a loss of faith in God.

To the world waiting seems like a waste of time at best; at worst, an unbearable prolonging of suffering. But God's Word says it is blessed. Waiting in the Bible sense means refusing to give up on God. Waiting is what people do who wonder why God hasn't answered their cries for help but who continue to pray nevertheless. Those waiting for the Lord include the young man in a wheelchair who believes he will be healed— one day. And the widow who wakes up each morning and remembers she's alone, but knows she's not alone. Waiting is the oppressed who long to be free, the hungry who long to be filled, the sick who long to be whole, the victimized who long to see justice—and who say with the psalmist, "I believe that I shall look upon the goodness of the Lord in the land of the living" (Ps. 27:13).

Why is waiting blessed? Because those who wait continue to trust in God no matter what. Blessed are those who know that the Lord will surely be gracious, that one day they will dwell in Zion and weep no more, and who wait in faith for that day to come.

PRAYER: Lord, give me strength today to keep waiting.

Series: *Waiting, Watching, Welcoming*

READ: Psalm 130

I Wait for the Lord

I wait for the LORD, my soul waits,
and in his word I hope. (Psalm 130:5)

What are you *waiting* for? That question is usually asked with impatience or exasperation. What we really mean is, "Hurry up, will you? Get a move on!" But there is another way to ask this question. Advent is all about waiting. So what are we waiting *for*? The short answer is that we're waiting for the Lord.

Waiting for the Lord is an act of faith. We believe that God can and will deliver us when we cry out to him from the depths. But waiting is also an exercise in hope. To have hope you need a future. "Where there's life, there's hope," goes the old saying. But when there is no longer life, there's no hope either. King David stopped praying when his child died. Maybe you have shared his experience of hopelessness after a terrible loss. But maybe you know this truth from something much less serious—like the way you stop cheering when your team is behind by 20 points.

I once worked as a part-time night watchman, and I can attest to the truth that nobody looks more eagerly for the dawn than someone who's been up all night on guard. The Lord will come, as surely as the sun will rise in the east; our waiting will not be in vain. But what are we waiting for? What do we hope Jesus will do when he comes again? The answer lies in why he came in the first place.

PRAYER: I praise you, God, for the hope of your word.

Series: *Waiting, Watching, Welcoming*

READ: John 6:25-40

He Came to Do the Father's Will

I have come down from heaven. (John 6:38)

When we first meet someone we often ask, "Where are you from?" If you asked me that I would say I'm from Grand Rapids, Michigan. If you had asked Jesus you might have expected him to say, "Well, I was born in Bethlehem and grew up in Nazareth, but I'm now living in Capernaum."

Listen to what Jesus actually says about where he's from: "I have come down from heaven" (v. 38). Who in the world would talk like that? Well, God would. Jesus, the divine Word, has existed with God and as God from all eternity (John 1:1). Jesus' coming into the world was the result of a deliberate choice he made, along with the Father, to give up his divine position and prerogatives and become one of us (Phil. 2:5-11).

You and I didn't choose to be born. We had no say in the matter; our coming was the decision of others—who didn't even know they were choosing us! But Jesus chose himself to come into the world. And in choosing to come, he also chose to leave.

> *Thou didst leave Thy throne and Thy kingly crown,*
> *When Thou camest to earth for me.*
> ### (Thou Didst Leave Thy Throne)

Why? Jesus came to do the will of the one who sent him (v. 38). And what is the Father's will? That we should never be lost, but have eternal life through faith in Jesus. "I am the bread of life," says Jesus. "That life-saving manna your ancestors ate in the wilderness—that was me. I am the one who gives life to all who receive me."

PRAYER: Thank you, Jesus, for choosing to come,
and all that this meant.

Series: *Waiting, Watching, Welcoming*

READ: John 4:7-15

He Came to Give Life

I came that they may have life and have it abundantly. (John 10:10)

"Get a life!" It's what we say to people who obsess over trivial matters, like chronic nitpickers. It could also be the subtitle of the fourth gospel: *(How to) Get a Life!* John states this explicitly when he gives his reason for writing near the end of his book: "but these are written so that you may believe that Jesus is the Christ, the Son of God, and that by believing you may have life in his name" (John 20:31).

The word "life" occurs 43 times in John's gospel, and it's always connected to Jesus. "I am the bread of life" (6:35). "I am the resurrection and the life" (11:25). "I am the way, and the truth, and the life" (14:6). "I came that they may have life and have it abundantly" (10:10).

The life Jesus came to give goes by a special name. It's not *bios*, physical life; it's *zoe*. *Zoe* is often modified by the adjective *aioniou*, which literally means "of the ages," but is usually translated "eternal." Eternal life isn't just everlasting life, the thing we get when we go to heaven. Eternal life is abundant life, life that is infinite in quality, not just quantity. It's real life, satisfying life, the life everyone wants, and it comes from receiving Jesus.

Jesus put it this way: "whoever drinks of the water that I will give him will never be thirsty again" (John 4:14). What he said literally was, "he will never be thirsty forever." The life Jesus gives is like a spring of water inside, "gushing up to eternal life."

PRAYER: Thank you, Lord, for the life you give.

Series: *Waiting, Watching, Welcoming*

READ: 1 John 3:1-9

He Came to Destroy the Works of the Devil

The reason the Son of God appeared was to destroy the works of the devil. (1 John 3:8)

This statement in John's letter bothers me: "No one who abides in him keeps on sinning; no one who keeps on sinning has either seen him or known him" (v. 6). The reason is obvious: I keep on sinning. Does that mean I don't know the Lord?

If continuing to sin disqualifies us from salvation, then no one can be saved, because all of us sin. So what does John mean here? He's talking about two different kinds of people. One kind pursues righteousness. They love God and seek to follow his Law. They hate the sin that still dogs them, and when they fall into it, they repent and turn back to the Lord. The other kind of people live without regard to God and without concern about sin. In fact, they often see nothing in themselves to confess. So it's not sinning that separates one from Christ; it's sinning without repentance.

"You will recognize them by their fruits," said Jesus (Matt. 7:20). Sin is the devil's fruit. But Jesus came to destroy the works of the devil. One of the best reasons I have for looking forward to Jesus' return is that then I will finally be rid of all the devil's fruit in my life, and be made completely Christlike. "Beloved, we are God's children now, and what we will be has not yet appeared; but we know that when he appears we shall be like him" (v. 2). What a promise!

PRAYER: Lord Jesus, I repent of my sins, both large and small, old and new, and I renounce the devil and all his works.

Series: *Waiting, Watching, Welcoming*

READ: Hebrews 9:11-28

He Came to Save

Christ Jesus came into the world to save sinners. (1 Timothy 1:15)

G. K. Chesterton converted from atheism to Roman Catholic Christianity as a young man. When people asked him why, he replied, "To get rid of my sins" (*The Autobiography of G. K. Chesterton*).

Christ's advent brought many wonderful things into the world, but it's important not to forget the most basic and important one for each of us: personal salvation. Jesus came to save sinners, to deliver us from the guilt and penalty of sin, and finally from sin's very presence. To do that, he went to the cross and offered himself as the sacrifice for our sin. The book of Hebrews makes much of the fact that forgiveness has always required the shedding of sacrificial blood. Hebrews says flatly that without that blood there is no forgiveness (Heb. 9:22). We may wonder why, but we cannot doubt that it's true—unless we think we know more about God than the Bible does.

Hebrews also insists that with Jesus' death the true sacrifice for sin has been offered, once for all. Jesus has done what all those animal sacrifices could never finally accomplish. He has "put away sin" (v. 26), wiped out sin's guilt and broken sin's power, for all who believe in him. Nothing more ever needs to be offered by anyone in payment for the sin of the world. Jesus will come again, not to deal with sin—he's already done that—but to set us and the whole creation free from sin's presence forever (v. 28).

PRAYER: Thank you, Lord, for the gift of forgiveness and salvation.

Series: *Waiting, Watching, Welcoming*

READ: 1 Corinthians 4:1-5

Jumping to Conclusions

Therefore do not pronounce judgment before the time, before the Lord comes. (1 Corinthians 4:5)

People who are prone to jumping to conclusions tend to be quick to criticize or judge others. The Corinthians were doing that with Paul. We might ask, so what? Paul says. "With me it is a very small thing that I should be judged by you" (v. 3). I love that verse. Every leader should have it memorized, against the inevitable day when unjust criticism comes his or her way.

Some people are prone to judging God as well. You say God is great and God is good? OK, explain children's cancer or the Holocaust to me. Those are tough questions, to be sure. The fact that our loving, all-powerful heavenly Father allows evil and suffering to continue is terribly troubling. But the apostle offers one very helpful—we might say, timely—reminder. Don't judge too quickly. Don't jump to premature conclusions, especially about God's goodness, power, and justice.

Paul can take human criticism in stride because, whether it is justified or not, this is not the judgment that really matters. The judgment that matters will happen on *the* Day, the day when Christ returns in glory. Then the hidden things will be brought to light. Motives will be revealed, secrets will be laid bare, truth will be known, questions will be answered.

The problem with passing judgment, whether on people or on God, is that we don't know enough now to make an informed decision. But one day, we will.

PRAYER: God, give me the grace to withhold premature judgment—of others and of you.

Series: *Waiting, Watching, Welcoming*

READ: 2 Peter 3:1-13

The Lord Isn't Slow

The Lord is not slow to fulfill his promise. (2 Peter 3:9)

Have you heard about the "Slow Food" movement? It's a trend popularized by some chefs and cooks that encourages a nation of fast-food addicts to slow down and rediscover the joys of a home-cooked meal. But what is fast, and what is slow? It's all relative, isn't it? When you're an active seven-year-old, a year seems like forever. When you're an active seventy-year-old, the years rush past like a bullet train.

We've been waiting a long time for the Lord to come back and fulfill his promises. If people were already mocking the idea of the end of the world in Peter's day, imagine what they're saying now. But what is a long time? Peter reminds us that God doesn't work on our clock. The Lord is patient, "not wishing that any should perish, but that all should reach repentance" (v. 9). Paul adds this: "Do you not realize that God's kindness is meant to lead you to repentance?" (Rom. 2:4 NRSV).

The Lord has a trend of his own; call it the "Slow Salvation" movement. Today there is still time for repentance. Maybe you and I are impatient for his return, but there are still many who need to hear the gospel, turn from their sins, believe in Christ, and be saved. The Lord isn't slow, he's waiting. He is extending the day of salvation. That's why he hasn't returned yet.

But one day, suddenly, he will.

PRAYER: Lord, I remember before you those who still need to hear or respond to the gospel.

Series: *Waiting, Watching, Welcoming*

Stay Awake, Keep Watching

Now when these things begin to take place . . . raise your heads, because your redemption is drawing near. (Luke 21:28)

While most people are oblivious to Christ's return, some seem obsessed with it. They are constantly on the lookout for signs of the second coming—heavenly portents, convulsions in nature, wars on earth, persecutions for the church—and predicting dates for the end. Is that what Jesus meant when he told his disciples to stay awake and watch for his coming?

The first three gospels all record Jesus' apocalyptic discourse, delivered in the temple just before his crucifixion. It's hard to understand because Jesus interwove teaching about his return with warnings about the fall of Jerusalem, which happened a generation later in AD 70.

But the important point is clear. Watching for his return doesn't mean standing around looking up at the sky, or panicking at every sign of doomsday. The signs are always present. And no matter how hard people try to predict it, the end will still come "suddenly like a trap" (v. 34). So what does it mean to watch? It means avoiding the heart-numbing worldliness that thinks only about earthly pleasures. It means living by faith, so that you're ready at all times to stand before him. It means patiently doing what Jesus told us to do, which is to seek his kingdom and righteousness. Above all, it means lifting your head in hope, because your redemption is drawing near.

PRAYER: Lord, I give thanks that "salvation is nearer to us now than when we first believed" (Romans 13:11). Help me to be filled with hope, and to serve you as I wait for you.

Series: *Waiting, Watching, Welcoming*

READ: 1 Corinthians 1:1-9

We've Got Everything We Need

You are not lacking in any gift, as you wait for the revealing of our Lord Jesus Christ. (1 Corinthians 1:7)

"Have you got everything you need?" We once asked our daughter that the day before she was leaving for a study semester abroad, only to discover she had lost her passport.

It's an important question when you prepare for a long trip—or a long wait. The Corinthians are embarked on the pilgrimage of faith. Do they have everything they need as they walk in faith and wait for the Lord's return? Yes they do, says the apostle. "You are not lacking in any [spiritual] gift."

What resources do we have to help us wait in the time between the times of Christ's advent and return? There's prayer, and God's Word, and the church. But first and foremost we have the presence and power of the Spirit. "And it is God who . . . has . . . given us his Spirit in our hearts as a guarantee" (2 Cor. 1:21-22). That word "guarantee" is *arrabon*, meaning *down payment*; it's the earnest money offered to seal the deal. The gift of the Holy Spirit is proof that God is in earnest about saving us.

So we lack no gifts while we wait for "the revealing of our Lord Jesus Christ." Notice how Paul describes Christ's return: the "revealing." Now Jesus can only be seen with the eyes of faith by the power of the Spirit. But when he comes again every eye will see him. The wait will be over.

PRAYER: Thank you, Jesus, for your Spirit's presence and power in my life.

Series: *Waiting, Watching, Welcoming*

READ: Isaiah 35:1-7

The River of Life

Then the angel showed me the river of the water of life . . .
flowing from the throne of God. (Revelation 22:1)

A satellite image of the Sahara Desert shows a vast expanse of brown, a sea of sand that looks completely dry and dead. Except for way over on the right-hand edge, where a ribbon of green traces the course of the Nile. Wherever in the desert the waters of the river can reach, there is life.

Isaiah sings of the miracle of life blossoming in dry and barren places. When God comes to his people, it's as though flower gardens will suddenly spring up in a wasteland. It will be like mountain forests and alpine meadows planting themselves smack in the middle of the desert. You can't explain how it happens, but it does. God brings life to our dry and thirsty souls. He makes the desert places in our lives bloom with flowers. He heals our brokenness and infirmities.

When John the Baptist was arrested, he sent his disciples to ask Jesus a question. "Are you the one . . . or shall we look for another?" (Matt. 11:3). You can understand John's discouragement. He thought Jesus was the one to finally bring in God's kingdom, but there John was in jail, and life with all its misery and injustice just kept going. Go tell John what you see, Jesus replied—how the lame walk and the deaf hear, the blind see, and the lepers are cleansed. The kingdom has come. The kingdom will come. Jesus is the one.

PRAYER: Lord Jesus, keep me focused on you today.
Refresh my soul with the water of life.

Series: *Waiting, Watching, Welcoming*

READ: Revelation 19:1-10

The Marriage Supper of the Lamb

Let us rejoice . . . for the marriage of the Lamb has come, and his Bride has made herself ready. (Revelation 19:7)

The Bible often describes life in the world to come as a wonderful feast. Here is Isaiah: "On this mountain the LORD of hosts will make for all peoples a feast of rich food, a feast of well-aged wine . . . He will swallow up death forever; and the Lord GOD will wipe away tears from all faces (Isa. 25:6, 8). Then there is the beatitude given to John in his vision of the end: "Blessed are those who are invited to the marriage supper of the Lamb" (Rev. 19:9).

So it's not just any party; it's a wedding banquet. Does that image do it for you? Maybe you've been a guest at a wedding where you didn't know anybody very well, and the dinner was a bit of a drag. If you're the parents of the couple, it might be hard to relax and enjoy the evening; so much to worry about, including how much everything is costing! But imagine you are the bride, seated at the head table with your husband, celebrating the night with the one you love.

That's what it will be like for us when Jesus returns. We are the Bride. The church, the whole people of God throughout the ages, is the Jerusalem that is above, coming down from heaven adorned like a beautiful young woman coming down the aisle to join her beloved (Rev. 21:2).

PRAYER: Jesus, you are the One I love. I long for your coming.

Series: *Waiting, Watching, Welcoming*

READ: Isaiah 62

What's in a Name?

For Jerusalem's sake I will not be quiet, until her righteousness goes forth as brightness. (Isaiah 62:1)

"What's in a name?" asked Juliet. Why should it matter that she and her boyfriend Romeo came from feuding families with different names? If you recall what happened to them, you know it actually did matter. Names matter a lot.

Isaiah 62 has a bunch of names. They are in the footnotes of your Bible: *Azubah, Shemamah, Hephzibah, Beulah.* In the exile, Israel thought of herself as "Forsaken" and "Desolate." But then came the salvation described in the new names the Lord gave to his people: "My Delight Is in Her," and "Married."

It hasn't fully happened yet. All too often we still feel desolate and forsaken. Isaiah offers some remarkable advice: "You who put the LORD in remembrance, take no rest, and give him no rest until he establishes Jerusalem and makes it a praise in the earth" (vv. 6-7). Wait, did he just say we should remind God of his promises, and hound him until he fulfills them all? Is prayer like that permitted? The psalmist thought so. "Why do you hold back your hand, your right hand? Take it from the fold of your garment" (Ps. 74:11). Have you ever urgently prayed that God would take his hands out of his pockets and finish the job?

A wise teacher once remarked passionately to me, "I no longer ask God *why*; I ask him *when*. When are you gonna come and fix things?"

PRAYER: Lord Jesus, so often I'm filled with anger and impatience as I look at all that's wrong in the world—and in me! Please come soon and make it right.

Series: *Waiting, Watching, Welcoming*

READ: Isaiah 9:1-7

To Us a Child Is Born

For to us a child is born, to us a son is given. (Isaiah 9:6)

Human kings proclaim their pride and cruelty in the titles by which they are known—"Ivan the Terrible," "William the Conqueror," "Alexander the Great." But the child whose birth Isaiah foretells would be a very different sort of ruler. Just how different is shown by his titles: *Wonderful Counselor, Mighty God, Everlasting Father, Prince of Peace.*

The Messiah, the true King, would have no need of counselors or advisers because he would possess in himself all the wisdom he needed. Unlike leaders whose great plans can be frustrated by the lack of the wherewithal to carry them out, the Messiah's plan of salvation would be powered by the omnipotence of God himself. His love and care would be those of the everlasting Father. Best of all, he would reign as the Prince of Peace. His kingdom would not be built on the foundation of war and conquest, like the kingdoms of the world. It would come to be established through invincible love. He would conquer his enemies not by killing them but by dying for them.

Human rulers come and go, the good and bad alike. Human nations rise and fall, even the mightiest of them. The Messiah's reign will bring peace, worldwide *shalom*—that wonderful state where everything has been put to rights and everyone is flourishing. And of the increase of his government and of peace there will be no end.

PRAYER: Prince of Peace, bring shalom to my life, family, community, and to the world.

Series: *Waiting, Watching, Welcoming*

READ: Galatians 4:4-7

Born Under the Law

. . . born under the law, to redeem those who were under the law. (Galatians 4:4-5)

What is it like to be "born under the law?" It's hell, to put it bluntly. The law proclaimed a curse upon all who failed to live according to its commands. The law declared that the wages of sin is death. The law pronounced that the law-breaker's body should be suspended between heaven and earth, for "cursed is everyone who is hanged on a tree" (Gal. 3:13).

Jesus was born under the law in order to redeem those who were under the law's curse. A price had to be paid to get us out of prison, so to speak. He alone was both willing and able to pay the full price of redemption. That is why he was born. That's why the shadow of Golgotha already falls across the Christmas story.

An ancient legend says that the cross on which Jesus was crucified was made of beams from the stable of Bethlehem. As history that's highly doubtful, but as theology it's spot-on. Jesus' whole life, from his birth onwards, was a preparation for his redeeming death. In one of his sermons John Donne put it this way: "His birth and his death were but one continual act, and his Christmas Day and his Good Friday are but the evening and the morning of one and the same day."

Christmas Eve, Good Friday afternoon, Easter morning; his birth, his death, his resurrection—one and the same day, and all for our salvation.

PRAYER: "Glory to God in the highest!" (Luke 2:14)

Series: *Waiting, Watching, Welcoming*

READ: 1 Peter 1:1-12

The Fullness of Time

*But when the fullness of time had come,
God sent forth his Son. (Galatians 4:4)*

The apostle Paul says that Jesus was born in "the fullness of time," that is, at just the right time, when everything was perfectly ready for his advent into the world. Preachers often ask what made this the right time. Answers tend to include things like Roman law and power, which unified the Mediterranean world, or the Roman road network, which made travel easier for the early missionaries, or the widespread use of the Greek language, which enabled the apostles to preach and teach everywhere and facilitated the writing of the New Testament.

But thinking along those lines just raises more questions. Like, why didn't he come sooner, when there were only a few people in the world, all living together and speaking just one language? Or if he was going to wait, why didn't he wait until the 16th century when the invention of the printing press made Bibles more plentiful? Or what about the 20th century? If he had come then, Jesus could have gone on television!

The fullness of time doesn't refer to our time or to any factors we might identify that would make it seem just right for the incarnation. Paul is talking about God's time. It was when the time was ripe for God's purposes that Caesar Augustus decided he needed a census of his empire, and unwittingly set that whole plan in motion.

We can't understand the when of it. We can only rejoice at the wonder of his coming, and adore.

PRAYER: Thank you, Lord, not just for coming into the world but for coming into my life.

Series: *Waiting, Watching, Welcoming*

READ: Revelation 12

How Long?

*How long before you will judge
and avenge our blood? (Revelation 6:10)*

If you ask where the Christmas story is told in the Bible, you might not immediately think of Revelation 12. But it's there in the opening verses—a retelling of the Jesus story for our right brain, rather than our left; for our imagination rather than our rationality.

Revelation 12 also tells our story, the story of the church. What's the message for us? It's this: We are living in the wilderness. We are under attack. We have a fearful enemy who pursues and seeks to destroy us. But the enemy has been defeated, cast down from heaven. The reason the devil attacks so fiercely is because he knows his time is short.

The question is, how long is that time? John tells us: we'll be in the wilderness for 1,260 days, or three and a half years. In Revelation, seven is the number of fullness or completion. So if you ask how long three and a half years is, the answer is "Not forever." When will the battle be over? Soon enough, in God's time.

So our challenge is to stay faithful. On earth Satan rages, but in heaven the triune God reigns. The message of the cross is that Christ's victory is not won by worldly weapons but by the power of sacrificial love. As Christians we believe that the truth is not worth killing for, but it is worth dying for. "Be faithful unto death, and I will give you the crown of life" (Rev. 2:10).

PRAYER: God, please give me the strength to remain
faithful to Jesus unto death.

Series: *Hearing Jesus*

READ: Revelation 1:7; Acts 1:6-11

He Is Coming Again

This Jesus . . . will come in the same way as you saw him go into heaven. (Acts 1:11)

A lot of ink has been spilled over Jesus' second coming. Will there be a millennium, a literal thousand-year reign of Christ on the earth? Will the church be snatched away in a miraculous rapture? Is the end just around the corner?

I have to confess that I'm not terribly interested in debate over the details of the Lord's return, or in combing the often-puzzling images of Revelation for clues. I am interested, though, in holding up what the Bible says about it. Here's what all faithful Christians believe about what the apostle Paul called "our blessed hope, the appearing of the glory of our great God and Savior Jesus Christ" (Titus 2:13).

First, Jesus' return will be personal, visible, and physical. "Behold, he is coming with the clouds, and every eye will see him, even those who pierced him, and all tribes of the earth will wail on account of him" (Rev. 1:7). This is not some kind of secret, spiritual event. It's as public as a parade. "For the Lord himself will descend from heaven with a cry of command, with the voice of an archangel, and with the sound of the trumpet of God" (1 Thess. 4:16).

Second, Jesus' return will be glorious and triumphant: "they will see the Son of Man coming on the clouds of heaven with power and great glory" (Matt. 24:30). He came once in humility, to die on a cross. Next time, it's going to be very different.

PRAYER: Even so, come, Lord Jesus! (Revelation 22:20)

Series: *Hearing Jesus*

READ: Isaiah 65:17-25

The New Creation

And he who was seated on the throne said,
"Behold, I am making all things new. (Revelation 21:5)

In Isaiah 65, the life of the world to come is described as life on earth, but with all the tragedies and sorrows removed once and for all. Much of what we're told about the new creation is what is *not* there: no stillborn infants, no premature deaths, no sounds of weeping. The new creation means life without pain, misery, frustration, or loss.

In the world to come, suffering will be replaced with glory. In fact, the Bible says that whatever suffering we experience now isn't worth comparing with the glory that will be then (2 Cor. 4:17). Suffering is temporary, but glory is forever. In the coming world, futility will give way to freedom. The creation itself is going to be "set free from its bondage to corruption" (Rom. 8:21). The new creation will mean the end of all the things that frustrate us and spoil our happiness here and now. There will be no loss. There will be no more goodbyes.

But how can we even begin to imagine this new universe, where wolves and lambs graze peacefully together, and lions feast *with* cattle instead of upon them? That would seem to require some pretty radical reengineering of nature. The Bible suggests there will be great changes in the world to come. God does say he will make all things new. But it will still be our world, and—more importantly—his.

PRAYER: Lord, you make all things new. Please do that with me.

Series: *Waiting, Watching, Welcoming*

READ: Revelation 21:1-4

No More Tears

*You have sorrow now, but I will see you again,
and your hearts will rejoice. (John 16:22)*

Do you remember the old ad for Johnson & Johnson baby shampoo? "No more tears," went the slogan. No one can escape tears. When the final and most awful plague, the death of the firstborn, struck Egypt, "there was a great cry in Egypt, for there was not a house where someone was not dead" (Exod. 12:30). No exceptions; from Pharaoh in his palace to the captive in the dungeon, death visited every family. It's true in our lives too. No one is immune from sorrow.

Grief is our natural reaction to the pain of loss, and life here is an inevitable journey into loss. Our bodies—weak and frail, aging, prone to accident and sickness, still given to sin—are subject finally to death. But one day they will be transformed and glorified. There will be no more loss, ever. No more tears. Death will be no more.

I sometimes try to picture how it's going to be when the Lord returns and we are raised in the world to come: beauty that never fades, strength that never diminishes, blooms that never wither, bodies that never die. But I'm at a loss. In a sense, we are only half-saved. We still live in what older generations called the "vale of tears." Full and final salvation is something to look forward to and wait for patiently, until the day when God makes all things new. But don't forget to hope, especially if you are grieving now. The day is coming. "No more tears."

PRAYER: Father, I can't even imagine what lies ahead for us who are in Christ. Give me that hope when the days are hard.

Series: *Waiting, Watching, Welcoming*

READ: Isaiah 35:8-10

The Way of Holiness

And a highway shall be there, and it shall be called
the Way of Holiness. (Isaiah 35:8)

Interstate highways all look pretty much the same. Just pick the right number—I-75, I-80—and take it where you want to go. But there was a time, when there weren't so many of them, that highways were special. Sometimes they had names, and the names were magical: The Dixie Highway, Chicago Drive, Route 66. Isaiah's highway has a name too.

The highway God promises to build will be called the Holy Way, because those who travel on it will be redeemed and sanctified. It will be plain to see and impossible to lose. Even careless travelers won't go astray, once they have been brought into the way. So good that nothing evil will enter it, so clear that no one who is the Lord's can miss it, so safe that nothing can hurt those who travel it—this is the Lord's highway through the wilderness of this world. Travelers on this road sing songs of rejoicing, because they know that the way they are on is leading them to Zion; in other words, it's taking them home.

So when will it happen? The lame leaping, blind eyes opened, deaf ears unstopped, sorrow and sighing forever banished; when will we see that? The answer is: when our God comes to save us. Until then, "Be strong; fear not! Behold, your God . . . will come and save you" (Isa. 35:4).

PRAYER: Lord, as you came once to save us,
please come again soon and finish the job.

Series: *Waiting, Watching, Welcoming*

READ: Luke 18:1-8

When He Comes

*Nevertheless, when the Son of Man comes,
will he find faith on earth? (Luke 18:8)*

At first glance this parable seems to be a lesson in persistent prayer. If at first you don't succeed in getting what you're asking for, try, try again. But the widow is praying for something very specific. She's not asking for a new house or a better job or good health. She is crying for justice, for vindication, for deliverance from the adversary. She represents the church as it waits and watches for the Lord to come again at last, as it cries out for the final victory, as it prays the prayer Christ taught: "Deliver us from evil."

Sometimes it seems as if we're losing; have you noticed that? The church I grew up in, where I first heard the gospel and came to faith, has been turned into an apartment building. Wherever you look you see evidence that Christian belief and practice and even influence are on the wane. You get the feeling that many people would like to see it disappear altogether. So we come to Jesus' poignant question. "When the Son of Man comes, will he find faith on earth?" Or will the last flicker of love for Christ and longing for his return have died out?

Not to worry. He is coming. Notice, he said "when," not "if." And when he does, he will find faith on earth. King Jesus will always have subjects. But here's a question to ask yourself as you near the beginning of another year: When Jesus comes will he find faith in *me*?

PRAYER: Come, Lord Jesus!

Series: *Waiting, Watching, Welcoming*

READ: Luke 2:8-20

What Child Is This?

*For unto you is born this day in the city of David a Savior,
who is Christ the Lord. (Luke 2:11)*

Though the citizens of Bethlehem—including, apparently, Joseph's relatives—didn't think enough of Jesus to do him honor at his birth or even to give the family a decent place to stay, there were those who acknowledged his true worth. Some knew right from the start who he really was. In ancient society shepherds were outcasts, but God chose to send heavenly messengers to lowly shepherds in the hills outside Bethlehem with the astounding news of the Lord's birth. Maybe he knew that they just might be unsophisticated enough to believe it.

Who is Jesus Christ? "He is the Savior, Christ the Lord!" proclaims the angel. The shepherds decided to head into Bethlehem and check out this rather fantastic story. But when they came to town, they saw that it was just as they had been told, sign and all. And so, naturally, they glorified God and told everyone within earshot the incredible news of the Savior's birth. What else could they have done?

Who is Jesus Christ? He is the Word made flesh, who dwelt among us, the Bible declares. He is God of God, Light of light, very God of very God, the church confesses. He is Lord of all.

PRAYER: "O come, let us adore him." (*O Come, All Ye Faithful*)

Series: *Christmas*

READ: John 1:1-14

The Word Became Flesh

The Word became flesh and dwelt among us. (John 1:14)

"The Word became flesh and dwelt among us." What e=mc² is to physics, this sentence is to human history. It's one of those simple statements whose implications are so radical it changes everything that comes afterward.

St. Augustine once introduced a Christmas sermon this way: "Listen to what you know, reflect on what you have heard, love what you believe, and preach what you love. Just as we celebrate the yearly coming of this day, so you may expect the sermon that is this day's due."

What is the message that is this day's due? Is it "peace on earth, goodwill toward men"? That's part of it, sure. Is it Immanuel, "God with us"? Certainly! But it's deeper and stranger than that. God isn't just with us invisibly, in a spiritual sense—a lot of people believe that. Christians believe God came in the flesh. We believe that the eternal, omnipotent Creator and Ruler of the universe became a little baby, who cried and was fed, who needed to be changed, who was put to bed in a manger—all without ceasing to be God. Try to get your head around that!

It is impossible to accept what John writes in its full meaning and not become a worshiper of Jesus Christ. You can't believe what John says and also believe that Jesus was merely someone with special spiritual powers. You can't believe what John says and also believe that Jesus was only a good man, or a prophet with a highly developed understanding of God. You can't believe what John says and be anything other than an orthodox Christian. In the words of St. Bernard of Clairvaux, "It is rashness to search too far into this truth. It is piety to believe it. It is eternal life to know it."

PRAYER: Glory to God in the highest, and peace to all on this day of days.

Series: *Waiting, Watching, Welcoming*

READ: Matthew 1:1; Romans 1:1-7

The Son of David

. . . Jesus Christ, the son of David . . . (Matthew 1:1)

At the outset of his gospel Matthew draws special attention to Jesus' descent from King David, just as the apostle Paul does at the beginning of his letter to the Romans (Rom. 1:3). King Herod was very sensitive about the fact that he was not from the house of David. How enraged he would have been to see Jesus' royal family tree!

If, as Matthew records, Jesus Christ is the son of David, the son of Abraham, then he is the fulfillment of the greatest of all God's promises. When God called Abraham, he promised: "I will make of you a great nation, and I will bless you . . . and in you all the families of the earth shall be blessed" (Gen. 12:1-3). As time went on that promise was focused upon David and his line. "There shall come forth a shoot from the stump of Jesse, and a branch shall grow out of his roots" (Isa. 11:1). And the fulfillment of the promise came at last with the birth of great David's greater son, Jesus.

God always keeps his word. We may forget his promises or lose hope in them, but God never forgets; if he says something, it will come to pass. "Christians should remember this . . . Their Father in heaven will be true to all his engagements" (J. C. Ryle).

PRAYER: God, we praise you as the great Promise Keeper.

Series: *Christmas*

READ: Matthew 1:1-17

A Mixed Bag

. . . and Jacob [was] the father of Joseph the husband of Mary, of whom Jesus was born, who is called the Christ. (Matthew 1:16)

Reading Matthew's genealogy is like reading a page in the telephone directory: there may be some nice people in there, but most of them don't mean anything to us. This is surely the least read part of the Christmas story. Children don't recite it in the Sunday school Christmas program; it's never sung in any carols. A biblical genealogy is like your appendix—there's no denying it's there, but it's hard to say what it's good for.

But here's something this genealogy is good for. Look at it more closely and note who is there. It's a mixed bag: wicked and godly people, men and women, Jews and gentiles. There is no racial purity or moral superiority in God's family tree. Wherever people may have gotten their desire to keep their families or communities "uncontaminated" by those who are different, they didn't get it from God.

Most of the names are of unknowns and nobodies. Who were Hezron, Nahshon, or Salmon? Azor, Achim, or Eliud? God doesn't use just famous people to accomplish his purpose. Whoever you are, if you are willing, God will accept you. God will make something out of your life. After all, isn't that why Jesus came into our world?

PRAYER: Lord, you use all kinds. Use me too.

Series: *Christmas*

READ: Matthew 1:18-23

Immanuel

They shall call his name Immanuel
(which means, God with us). (Matthew 1:23)

China was the scene of one of the most intensive missionary efforts in history. And then with the victory of Mao and the communists in 1949, all the Christian missionaries were expelled. The small Chinese church became the object of intense repression: many Christians were killed or imprisoned, some went underground, some fell away. But those who were left had been tried by fire, and their faith was purified. They weren't just playing at following Jesus; they really meant it. And in the coming years their witness would produce unprecedented growth for the church in China.

During the time of harshest persecution, a letter was received by some Christians in the West from representatives of the Chinese church. Reading it, you could understand why the Communist authorities had allowed it to be sent. It went something like this:

> We are good Communists here. We don't need your western religion. We don't agree with your Christianity anymore. Please leave us alone.

But below the signature was a P.S., just a single word the censors obviously didn't understand: Immanuel. And that one word changed everything.

One word does change everything. Because in Jesus, God is truly with us.

PRAYER: "Pleased as man with us to dwell, Jesus, our Immanuel;
Hark! the herald angels sing, Glory to the newborn King!"
(Hark! The Herald Angels Sing)

Series: *Christmas*

READ: Matthew 1:21; Acts 4:1-12

Call His Name Jesus

You shall call his name Jesus, for he will save his people from their sins. (Matthew 1:21)

Jesus is the Greek form of the Hebrew name Joshua, meaning "The Lord [Yahweh] saves." Jesus is the Savior. That is why he came—not just to be an example, or to teach; not to show God's love in merely a general way, but to save.

Jesus is the only Savior. In the ancient world most people believed that the heavens were populated by a whole host of spirits that barred the way to salvation. The only way to get past them was to acquire the secret knowledge of their names, and the passwords that could open the countless gates those spiritual forces guarded. Imagine how it must have felt to hear the news that there was only one name you needed to know in order to be saved—Jesus (Acts 4:12). That really was gospel, "good news"!

Today the challenge is different. Most people don't believe there are many roadblocks on the way to heaven—they tend to think there aren't any at all. People assume that everybody will be saved by calling on any name they choose, or even without calling at all. We need to proclaim the truth that Jesus is the only Savior, and the only way to be saved is to believe in him.

His name says it all.

PRAYER: Jesus, Savior, I trust in you.

Series: *Christmas*

READ: Luke 1:26-38

Ave Maria

. . . let it be to me according to your word. (Luke 1:38)

The modern prejudice is that people in earlier times accepted stories of angels and supernatural births because they didn't know about science, but we moderns understand that such things must be legendary. Well, listen to Mary's response when Gabriel says she will bear a child: "How will this be, since I am a virgin?" Just because Mary didn't know about Einstein's theory of relativity doesn't mean she didn't know the facts of life.

The key thing, though, is what Mary says next. "I am the Lord's servant. Let it be to me according to your word." Did Mary know what that submission would cost her? She could not have foreseen all the honors that would come to her eventually. But she could very well imagine a difficult interview with Joseph. How could she possibly explain to him? Then there was the shame and even the threat of death for someone suspected of adultery in a conservative place like Nazareth. God wasn't asking much of her; just to risk her marriage and her life. And for what? Who knows?

But Mary said yes to God, come what may. Mary's obedience would cost her, but she was willing to pay the price. That's what real faith is like. Faith stakes everything on the word of God, and accepts the consequences.

PRAYER: Thank you, Lord, for Mary, a hero of faith.

Series: *Christmas*

READ: Luke 2:1-7

Away in a Manger

And she gave birth to her firstborn son and . . . laid him in a manger, because there was no place for them in the inn. (Luke 2:7)

We read a lot about the retail economy during the Christmas season. We also hear a lot of complaints about all the commercialism. Isn't Christmas really about love and peace and goodwill?

Appealing as such things undoubtedly are, the gospel of Luke doesn't start with them when it tells the Christmas story. It starts with the headlines of the day: "A decree went out from Caesar Augustus." Caesar decided he needed to update the empire's tax rolls in order to deal with that perennial government problem, the budget deficit. Who could have imagined that all this effort was being superintended by God just to bring Mary to Bethlehem for the birth of her baby? And of all the millions of souls numbered in Caesar's great census, surely none was as insignificant as this poor Jewish child.

Augustus in the imperial purple in Rome and Jesus wrapped in swaddling clothes lying in a manger are worlds apart. Yet today Augustus is only a name in a history book, while Jesus lives and reigns in the hearts of hundreds of millions—and on the throne of the universe as well!

PRAYER: "Be near me, Lord Jesus; I ask Thee to stay close by me forever, and love me, I pray." (*Away in a Manger*)

Series: *Christmas*

READ: Matthew 2:12, 16-18

The Dark Side of Christmas

*A voice was heard in Ramah, weeping
and loud lamentation. (Matthew 2:18)*

The holidays can be tough on people. A season where everything is supposed to be merry and bright is too much for some hurting folks to bear. But the idea of Christmas as nothing but jollity is bogus. The Bible doesn't tell that kind of story. In the Bible Christmas has a dark side. The air around Bethlehem is filled one moment with the sound of angels' singing and the next with mothers' weeping. The magi have scarcely left the scene before they are replaced by Herod's blood-stained stormtroopers. It's all there on the pages of the gospel: murderous rage, genocide, refugees fleeing for their lives.

The dark side of Christmas reminds us that the world into which the Savior was born was—and is—not a very nice place, which is why he had to enter it in the first place. Christmas has always been a story of conflict and contrast: good and evil, light and darkness, joy and grief, hope and despair.

The message of Christmas is not that there's no reason to weep; there are plenty of reasons for weeping, as we all know. No, the message of Christmas is that because God has come into the world as one of us, now there is reason for comfort and joy as well.

PRAYER: O, tidings of comfort and joy—give thanks!

Series: *Christmas*

READ: 1 John 4:7-14

God So Loved the World

*The Father has sent his Son to be
the Savior of the world.* (1 John 4:14)

The incarnation didn't mean Jesus was running away from home. It was part of a divine plan agreed upon by the Father and the Son: "The Father has sent his Son to be the Savior of the world."

"God is love," says John famously (v. 8). This is not an abstract statement about the divine nature. God is love in action. God manifested his love by sending his Son into the world so that we might be saved through him. Jesus came to offer the atoning sacrifice for our sin (v. 10). "But God shows his own love for us in that while we were still sinners, Christ died for us" (Rom. 5:8).

The most important word in the most famous verse in the Bible is the shortest one—"so". "God *so* loved the world that he gave . . ." John 3:16 isn't just about God loving the world; it's about how much God loves the world. The true measure of love is what it will give for the sake of the beloved. God gave the world his one and only Son so that whoever believes in him should not perish but have eternal life. Such a gift, offering so much to so many! All for those who will just believe.

We should also note how John uses that same little word in his epistle. "Beloved, if God *so* loved us, we also ought to love one another" (1 John 4:11).

PRAYER: Fill me with your love and help me share it with others.

Series: *Christmas*

READ: Matthew 11:20-30

Come to Me

*He came to his own, and his own people
did not receive him. (John 1:11)*

The majestic prologue that opens the gospel of John announces the incarnation of the divine Word. God became human in order to make humans his children, "born, not of blood . . . but of God" (John 1:13). But in the middle of John's prologue comes a sad truth. Jesus was rejected by most of the people he came to save. One reason for this rejection is that he didn't meet their expectations of what the Messiah should be.

> *They all were looking for a king*
> *To slay their foes and lift them high;*
> *Thou cam'st, a little baby thing*
> *That made a woman cry.*
> *(George MacDonald)*

Jesus still comes to his own, for in his humanity Jesus is one with all of us. And his own still do not receive him, mostly because they are looking for a different kind of savior or another type of life than the one he offers. The greatest tragedy in the world is as John Stott memorably put it, that people who were made by God, like God, and for God are nevertheless living without God. So they seek rest for their souls in other things or experiences or relationships, rather than in the only One in whom it can be found.

Jesus comes to us. But we also must come to him. "But to all who did receive him, who believed in his name, he gave the right to become children of God" (John 1:12).

PRAYER: Thank you, God, for the new birth that makes me your child.

Series: *Waiting, Watching, Welcoming*

READ: John 1:14-18

Grace upon Grace

From his fullness we have all received, grace upon grace. (John 1:16)

There are two witnesses named John in the opening chapter of the fourth gospel. The first is John the Baptist, who came to bear witness about the Light "that all might believe through him" (John 1:7). The other is John the evangelist, who testifies concerning the Word made flesh that "we have seen his glory, glory as of the only Son from the Father, full of grace and truth" (v. 14). Here John is referring to himself and his fellow disciples. They were the ones who beheld Jesus' glory firsthand—on the Mount of Transfiguration (Luke 9:28-36), for example, and in the Upper Room on Easter evening (24:36-49).

But Jesus' glory wasn't just the radiance of his glorified body. His true glory was his grace. We saw it up close and personal, writes John in effect, we knew him, lived with him, and our testimony is that Jesus was all about grace. And truth, he adds, because sometimes gracious people can downplay truth, and sometimes those who love the truth aren't very gracious. Jesus was both: not just sort of gracious or mostly truthful, but "full of grace and truth."

In verse 16, John adds another word of testimony: "From his fullness we have all received, grace upon grace." Who is John describing here? Who's the "*we*"? Not just himself, not just himself and the other apostolic eyewitnesses, but himself and every Christian believer. We *all* have received grace from Jesus' fullness. We've been saved by grace. But we live by grace as well. In fact, it's all grace all the way, "grace upon grace." In the end we will discover that every day, everything that has happened in our lives will turn out to be grace.

PRAYER: Thank you for your grace and truth.

READ: 1 Timothy 1:12-17

A Trustworthy Saying

*The saying is sure . . . that Christ Jesus came into the world
to save sinners . . . (1 Timothy 1:15)*

As we come to the end of Christmastide, it is worth reflecting once more on the purpose of the Incarnation. A medieval English Christmas meditation went like this: "Who he is, and from whom he came, and at what price he redeemed thee . . . do thou consider."

Why did Jesus enter our world? Why did God become a man? Was it to show how much he cared for us? Yes. Was it to teach us most clearly what he is really like, by putting a human face on God? Yes again. Was it to set us an example of what he meant a human life to be? That too. But most of all, he came to save us.

An example can't save us. It can only show us how far we fall short. A teacher can't save us; he can only point us toward the truth. Only a Savior can save us. It's often been said that the gospel is not good advice, but good news. The good news is that Christ came to save sinners who cannot save themselves. For God to take human nature upon himself just to inspire us or set us a good example simply doesn't make sense. That's like using a Ferrari on an Amazon delivery route; it's too much car for the job. The world has plenty of religious teachers and moral examples to learn from and imitate. We don't need Jesus to be just another one of those. We need him to be a Savior.

That's why he came, you can be sure.

PRAYER: Lord, thank you for coming to save sinners, including me.

Series: *Trustworthy Sayings*

Epiphany

Epiphany

Epiphany is the second season in the Christian year. Taken from a Greek word meaning "manifestation" or "appearing," Epiphany is a season for focusing on the events of Jesus' earthly ministry—his work of preaching, teaching, and healing.

The first day of Epiphany, January 6, is also known as "Three Kings Day"—the day associated with the visit of the Magi who came to worship the child in Bethlehem. It's appropriate that this season celebrating Jesus' appearance in the world begins by remembering the Magi, who themselves appear out of nowhere in chapter two of Matthew's gospel. Matthew wants us to understand right from the outset that Jesus is not just the king of the Jews, he's the king of the Gentiles too. And what a king he is! We see the glory and beauty of Jesus' character revealed in his words and actions.

Depending on the Christian tradition you follow, the season of Epiphany lasts from January 6 until either February 2 (Candlemas), or until Ash Wednesday and the beginning of Lent. Because the date of Ash Wednesday is determined by the date of Easter, it varies widely, which means Epiphany can be longer or shorter in any given year.

The devotionals this season are drawn from six series.

* *The Good Life: Sermon on the Mount*, published in February 1998, takes us through the Sermon on the Mount, Jesus' famous sermon found in Matthew.

* *Christmas,* published in December 2008, shares the Christmas story as told in all four gospels.

* *What It Means to be Human,* published in January 2017, explores the way Jesus serves as the model for how humans ought to live.

* *Beatitudes: The Complete Christian Life,* published in April-May 2017, is a study of the Beatitudes and the way they describe a complete Christian life.

* *Jesus' Public Ministry,* published in November 2021, looks at the three years of Jesus' public ministry shared in the gospels, a beautiful example for all Christian ministry.

READ: Matthew 2:1-11

Wise Men Still Seek Him

And going into the house they saw the child . . . and they fell down and worshiped him. (Matthew 2:11)

"We three kings of Orient are . . ." Three claims about the wise men in that old carol, only one of which we know for sure: they were from the Orient, the east. But they weren't kings, they were magi, astrologers. And though Matthew mentions three gifts, that doesn't necessarily mean there were three magi.

The really important thing about them isn't how many they were but who they were. They were gentiles—astrologers to boot!—who were drawn to worship Jesus as king. The magi are a preview of all the different nations who come in faith to Christ the Lord.

Think of it. No Bible, no temple, just a hint from the heavens, and off they went, pressing onward through the weeks and across the miles. The magi want to honor Christ, even when Herod and the leaders of his own people show no interest in doing so. They believe in Christ, even when the King turns out to be a little baby on a poor mother's lap in a humble village house. But still "they fell down and worshiped him" and presented him with gifts, gold and incense and myrrh.

The real gift of the magi wasn't carried in any box. They themselves were the gift. If the magi, with so little to go on, could worship him with heart and treasure, how about us?

PRAYER: Lord, I give you my heart.

Series: *Christmas*

READ: Hebrews 2:5-18

What It Means to Be Human

. . . made like his brothers in every respect. (Hebrews 2:17)

The ancient world was full of stories about the gods coming down to earth and taking on a human disguise. They would adopt a body briefly, as actors might put on a costume to play a role, usually to take advantage of some unsuspecting mortal. But Jesus wasn't like these mythological gods. His body was no disguise. No one ever came up to Jesus and said, "Say, you aren't really human, are you?" He appeared to be one of us because he was one of us. He was like us in every way, says Hebrews, except for sin (see 4:15).

Jesus was not only a real human being, he was *the* human being. He was, as Martin Luther called him, *der rechte Mann*, "the proper human." After a wonderful dinner you might push back your chair, heave a satisfied sigh, and exclaim, "Now, that was a proper meal!" What you mean is that it was ideal, dinner as dinner was meant to be, the sort of meal all meals would be like in a perfect world. That is just the kind of person Jesus was. Jesus is humanity's ideal. Jesus doesn't just show us what God is like; he shows us what *we* should be like. And if we're Christians, one day we will be.

Jesus of Nazareth: the proper man. His was *the* life among all human lives ever lived. He is the model of what it means to be human.

PRAYER: Lord, help me to be more human,
to be more like you in every way.

Series: *What It Means to be Human*

READ: Luke 18:35-41

Pity

Jesus, Son of David, have mercy on me. (Luke 18:38)

The stoics were ancient philosophers who had developed a way of dealing with human suffering by practicing *apatheia*, which literally means "not-feeling." The Stoics' response to the misery of human existence was to cultivate apathy. How do you handle disappointment, pain, and loss? "This too shall pass," said the Stoics. So, just try not to care that much.

Jesus of Nazareth was not a stoic. His example makes one thing very clear: the ideal life is not one with an attitude of detachment and indifference toward people. No, a life well lived is marked by pity for our fellow sufferers.

"Jesus, Son of David, have mercy on me!" cried the blind man, in an appeal to Jesus' pity. We tend to think of pity as a feeling—feeling sorry for someone. But Jesus did more than just feel pity for sufferers. He also took pity on them. Jesus gave the blind man his sight. Because he was more than simply a tenderhearted man, Jesus' pity brought health and wholeness to those who turned to him for help.

Jesus' pity—it is our future hope. Because he feels for us, he will heal us all, if not today, then when he awakens us from our last sleep. But his pity is also our present guide. Look around you. Do you see someone who is in pain? Let your heart go out to them. And do whatever you can to bring hope and healing to them right now.

PRAYER: We bless you, Lord, that you feel for us.

Series: *What It Means to be Human*

READ: Mark 12:28-34

Obedience

Although he was a son, he learned obedience through what he suffered. (Hebrews 5:8)

Many people think that personal freedom is the goal of life—the freedom to do whatever they want to. For Jesus, obeying God was the most important thing, more important even than life itself. Once when his disciples urged Jesus to have something to eat, he replied that he had his own private source of food. What's this, they wondered, has someone been secretly feeding Jesus? No, he said, you misunderstand me. "My food is to do the will of him who sent me" (John 4:34). If Jesus is the best model of what it means to be human, then the secret of a life well-lived is obedience to the will of God.

Contrary to popular opinion, the key to being authentically human is not having the freedom to "follow your dreams." Our ultimate identity can only be discovered in a relationship with the God who made us. Our true humanity is found in knowing and doing God's will. Here's one of life's paradoxes. You rarely find happiness by pursuing it as your goal. Happiness usually comes as a by-product of living for something more important than yourself. Similarly, if you decide to make up your own rules and obey only your own feelings, you become less free, not more. We only find real freedom by submitting to the will of God. And what is that? Simple, says Jesus. Love God with all you have, and love your neighbor, too.

PRAYER: Lord, your service is perfect freedom.

Series: *What It Means to be Human*

READ: Philippians 2:1-11

Humility

I am gentle and lowly in heart. (Matthew 11:29)

Nobody likes an egotist. Yet Jesus made some of the most egotistical-sounding claims ever. According to Jesus, no one anywhere can know God except those to whom he makes him known. God has entrusted everything to him (Matt. 11:27). And then in the next breath, Jesus says that he is the lowliest and humblest of men. Why doesn't that strike us as bizarre? What is it about Jesus that makes both the claim to supremacy and the claim to humility ring true?

Mostly it's understanding what humility actually is. Humility means lowering yourself; the word comes from the Latin *humus*, "earth." But it doesn't mean denying your gifts or value as a person. Rather, humility is the willingness to put others' needs ahead of your own. Nowhere is Jesus' greatness and humility better illustrated than in the great hymn of Philippians 2.

Here's the thing, though. In order to think like Jesus we have to become humble ourselves. If you are bound and determined to have it your own way, to make your own rules, to run your life without interference from God or anybody else, then you will just have to go on carrying your burdens all alone. If you are familiar with the Bible, you will know this: the way up is down. In order to be exalted you first have to humble yourself and become a servant to others. Just like Jesus did.

PRAYER: Lord, help me to think with the mind of Christ.

Series: *What It Means to be Human*

READ: Matthew 9:35-38

Compassion

When he saw the crowds, he had compassion
for them. (Matthew 9:36)

Prometheus was a minor Greek deity who decided to help the starving human race by bringing them fire. When the other gods found out, they chained Prometheus to a rock, where his liver was torn out and eaten by an eagle every day—for eternity. The ancients didn't think much of compassion. They saw it not as a virtue but a weakness.

Not so Jesus. Of all his qualities, none is more attractive—or more often displayed—than his compassion. The term *compassion*, like *sympathy*, means to "suffer with." The Gospel writers frequently mention Jesus' feelings for the sick or sorrowing. "Moved with pity, he stretched out his hand and touched him" (a leper; Mark 1:41). "Jesus in pity touched their eyes" (two blind men; Matt. 20:34). "He had compassion on [the crowds] . . . and he healed their sick" (Matt. 14:14). "When Jesus saw her, his heart broke" (a widow whose only son had died; Luke 7:13 MSG).

But Jesus also had compassion for spiritual suffering. His heart went out to the crowds who were "harassed and helpless, like sheep without a shepherd" (Matt. 9:36). God's first reaction toward us isn't anger but pity. What he feels for folks like you and me, who stumble along through life and suffer because of bad decisions and moral weakness, is compassion.

Our feeling of compassion for others is what makes us human. God's feeling it for us is what gives us hope.

PRAYER: Thank you, compassionate Lord, for saving this lost sheep.

Series: *What It Means to be Human*

READ: Mark 10:13-16

Openness

Let the children come to me; do not hinder them. (Mark 10:14)

One of the qualities of Abraham Lincoln that most deeply impressed his contemporaries was his tenderheartedness. One of Lincoln's associates said of him, "No man clothed with such vast power ever wielded it more tenderly and forbearingly." That description fits someone else I can think of even better than Abraham Lincoln.

When parents were bringing their little ones to Jesus for his blessing, Jesus' disciples tried to stop them. But Jesus rebuked the disciples and welcomed the children. His heart, always tender toward the lowly or despised, went out to them. I learned that in Sunday school. "They are precious in his sight; Jesus loves the little children of the world."

In the ancient world, children were without status or importance, which is exactly why the disciples were turning them away. In thinking that Jesus had time only for important people, his disciples were following human reasoning, not God's. In the world, only "somebodies" have the chance to spend time with the high and mighty. But that's not how it is in God's kingdom. Jesus is open to welcoming and receiving everyone. There is this one thing, though. He said that in order to enter the kingdom we all must become like a little child.

To enter the kingdom we have to receive it the way a baby receives everything, not as a reward or a prize, not as a result of our own efforts, but simply as a gift of God's love. "To receive the kingdom as a little child is to allow oneself to be given it" (C. E. B. Cranfield).

PRAYER: "Nothing in my hand I bring,
simply to thy cross I cling." (*Rock of Ages*)

Series: *What It Means to be Human*

READ: Matthew 11:11-19

Friendship

. . . a friend of tax collectors and sinners. (Matthew 11:19)

Of all the biblical titles of Jesus, one of my favorites is this one: he is "the friend of sinners." Jesus is a friend to people who aren't successful, people who have tried life and failed at it, people who have used up all their chances, people who can't make it on their own, people who don't deserve God's favor, and know it. In short, people who are sinners. I don't know about you, but if that's the basic requirement for friendship with Jesus, I certainly qualify.

Jesus' friendship is a gift. It is offered to all, but only received by those who acknowledge their need for it. If we go on clutching our money, stuff, status, and shreds of self-righteousness, if we derive our sense of worth and importance from such things, then Jesus' friendship will mean little to us. God looks with favor upon the lowly; the proud he sends away empty. As long as you go on thinking you are Somebody Special, and that you're doing God a favor by believing in him, you'll never be a friend of Jesus. Martin Luther wrote these wise words to a friend: "Beware of aspiring to such purity that you will not wish to be looked upon as a sinner, or to be one. For Christ dwells only in sinners."

One other thing: if Jesus could be a friend of sinners, can't we? Don't reserve your friendship only for those who deserve it, or can repay it.

PRAYER: What a Friend we have in Jesus. Indeed!

Series: *What It Means to be Human*

READ: John 11:17-37

Grief

Jesus wept. (John 11:35)

As every Sunday school child knows, it's the shortest verse in the Bible: "Jesus wept." But it's also one of the more puzzling. Why should Jesus be crying when he's about to raise Lazarus from the dead? The most obvious explanation is the one mentioned in the story itself. Jesus cried because he was grief-stricken. "See how he loved him!" commented the onlookers (v. 36).

Jesus wasn't one of those carefree folks who joke their way through life and who never seem to be deeply touched by anything. He knew what it was like to have a broken heart. The Bible never says Jesus laughed, although I'm sure he did. But it does say that he wept. And it shows him doing so more than once.

Jesus Christ, the perfect human, knew tears and grief. Suffering is a mystery to me. I don't understand why and when it strikes. Some people seem to be spared most of the pain that life can offer. For them the sun is usually shining. It's always springtime, never bleak midwinter. But Jesus was one of the many whose souls are rubbed raw with suffering. When the prophet described him centuries before, he called him "a man of sorrows" (Isa. 53:3).

Whenever sorrow comes to any of us, Jesus both cares and understands. He knows exactly how such pain feels. What is more, he can and will do something about it (John 11:25-26).

PRAYER: Jesus, Man of Sorrows, Resurrection and Life,
my comfort and hope are in you.

Series: *What It Means to be Human*

READ: John 16:31-33

Loneliness

You . . . will leave me alone. (John 16:31)

Frontiersman Daniel Boone said that if he could see the smoke from a neighbor's chimney on the horizon, it was time to move further west. American tradition honors the rugged individualist, the man who can go it alone. But the Bible paints a different picture of what it means to be human. It says we were made for community and so we need one another. As God said of Adam, "it is not good that . . . man should be alone" (Gen. 2:18).

But the second Adam, Jesus, was left alone on his last night on earth. He knew the pain of loneliness. Jesus looked for support from his closest friends and they let him down. The disciples all scoffed at the suggestion that they wouldn't be there for Jesus. But when Jesus asked them to watch with him in the garden, they all fell asleep. "Could you not watch with me one hour?" (Matt. 26:40). And when the soldiers came to arrest Jesus, the disciples did run, every last one of them.

No one should have to be alone. Family, friends, church—these should produce people to be there for us. But even if others fail us, there is still the Lord. "You . . . will leave me alone," said Jesus. "Yet I am not alone, for the Father is with me." And for us, there is Jesus himself. "I will never leave you or forsake you" (Heb. 13:5). "Behold, I am with you always, to the end of the age" (Matt. 28:20).

PRAYER: Lord, may I never fail or forsake you.
Thank you that you will never fail or forsake me.

Series: *What It Means to be Human*

READ: Mark 6:1-6

Wisdom

Where did this man get these things? (Mark 6:2)

When Jesus talked about the kingdom of God, he regularly blew people's minds. At the end of the Sermon on the Mount, Matthew says the people were "astonished at his teaching" (Matt. 7:28). Astonished because Jesus spoke with such authority. And astonished because Jesus' wisdom seemed like foolishness, with its topsy-turvy system of values.

Søren Kierkegaard, the 19th-century Christian philosopher, offered a parable to describe Jesus' teaching about the kingdom. Someone breaks into a store one night, but instead of stealing anything he just rearranges all the price tags. The next day customers arrive to find diamond necklaces on sale for pennies and junk with price tags in the thousands. Jesus' wisdom is like that. It overturns our values. What we think important he dismisses as trivial. What we despise he prizes. What we hold precious he counts worthless. What we call failure he judges to be success. Those we admire he condemns, those we scorn he honors. Everything is turned upside down when we substitute Jesus' wisdom for worldly wisdom.

So the question remains. Where did Jesus get all this? Jesus' first hearers thought they had him pegged. "Isn't this the carpenter's son?" But what if he really did know what he was talking about? What if his wisdom came from his real Father?

Our response to Jesus' wisdom reveals just how wise we are.

PRAYER: Jesus, give me wisdom to value what you do.

Series: *What It Means to be Human*

READ: Matthew 18:21-35

Forgiveness

Father, forgive them . . . (Luke 23:34)

In Shakespeare's *The Merchant of Venice*, Shylock, a Jewish moneylender, has been shamefully treated all his life thanks to the prejudice of his fellow merchants—so-called Christians. When one of these, Antonio, asks him for a loan, Shylock demands as collateral a pound of Antonio's flesh. The loan comes due, Antonio cannot pay, and Shylock insists on collecting: "'tis mine and I will have it . . . I stand for judgment . . ." We can understand how Shylock feels; I'd want my pound of flesh, too. Wouldn't you?

But Jesus taught us the duty of forgiveness—in fact, the necessity of forgiving as many times as need be, without keeping score. And he practiced what he preached. No one was more shamefully and abusively treated than Jesus of Nazareth. Yet as he died he prayed, "Father, forgive them, for they know not what they do."

Ignorance may explain, but it cannot justify what they did to Jesus. It's really no excuse; ignorance is not the same as innocence. Just because people may not realize the wrong they are doing does not mean they deserve to be forgiven for it. In fact, no one ever *deserves* to be forgiven. That's not how it works. Forgiveness is grace, a free gift to those who neither deserve it nor earn it. To forgive is one of the most beautiful of human acts, and also one of the most necessary. Forgiveness is not only what it means to be human; it's what it takes to be human.

PRAYER: Lord, as you forgave, help me to forgive.

Series: *What It Means to be Human*

READ: John 8:1-11

Mercy

Let him who is without sin . . . be the first to throw a stone. (John 8:7)

One day, as Jesus was teaching at the temple, the religious authorities approached him for the usual reason—to try to discredit him. But they came with an unusual case, a woman "caught in adultery" (v. 3). Here is where my questions start. Why is this the story of "The Woman Taken in Adultery"? Why not "The Couple Taken in Adultery"? Is this another example of society's notorious double standard, where the woman is charged and the man let off? It seemed like Jesus was facing an inescapable dilemma. He would either have to forfeit his reputation for mercy or seem to contradict the law's sentence. What would Jesus say?

At first he didn't say anything, he simply scratched words in the dirt (the secret sins of those Pharisees? Bible texts about God's mercy? Wouldn't we like to know!). Then he spoke the words that made them all slink away. "Let him who is without sin cast the first stone." But what about Jesus himself? After all, he *was* without sin. Jesus could have thrown that stone. But he didn't.

"Let him who is without sin cast the first stone." As the noted preacher G. Campbell Morgan commented, "That one sentence put me out of the stone-throwing business for good." "Neither do I condemn you." *That* one sentence gives me hope.

PRAYER: Thank you, Lord, for being gracious and merciful, slow to anger, and abounding in steadfast love.

Series: *What It Means to be Human*

READ: Mark 10:35-45

Servanthood

Whoever would be great among you
must be your servant. (Mark 10:43)

You can always tell who the most important people are. They're all celebrities—politicians, athletes, movie stars, wealthy business leaders. It's easy to spot them by the jobs they have, the clothes they wear, the cars they drive, the places they live, the people they hang out with. They're usually surrounded by bodyguards, personal assistants, press agents, various groupies. So if you want to know who the greatest people are, just look for the ones with the most money, power, and fame, and those with the biggest posse.

Once again Jesus turns the world's ideas upside down and inside out. On the way to Jerusalem the disciples were squabbling about who would get the money, power, and fame in Jesus' soon-to-come kingdom. Jesus stops them short. In the world—among "the rulers of the Gentiles," as he put it—greatness is defined by position and power (v. 42). The higher you climb, the more you can "lord it" over others, the greater you are.

But Jesus says that things are different in God's kingdom. In his kingdom, the way up is down. Greatness there is determined by how low you can go, not how high you might climb. It is achieved through lowly, modest, unpretentious service to others. Whoever wants to be great must become a servant. And, as always, Jesus himself is the perfect model of this. "For even the Son of Man came not to be served but to serve, and to give his life as a ransom for many" (v. 45).

PRAYER: Lord, help me to achieve true greatness.

Series: *What It Means to be Human*

READ: John 15:1-14

Love

Love one another as I have loved you. (John 15:12)

When people puzzle over the mysteries of life, one of the deepest is the question of why anything exists at all. Why is there something rather than nothing? The Bible's one-word answer to that question is "love." God's love is the power that called the universe into being. God's love is the reason you and I were created, and why we're still alive to draw breath at this very moment. Love is the very nature of God, and he wants it to be the nature of people as well. Love is the supreme mark of an authentic human life.

The words Jesus spoke to his disciples in the upper room on the last night of his life constitute a sort of last will and testament for the family of his followers. His central instruction was short and simple: "Love one another as I have loved you."

One of the things the Bible makes perfectly clear is that Christlike love is the only true measure of a successful life. All other gifts and abilities are negated, every other form of success is rendered null and void, where love is lacking. As the great theologian Karl Barth observed, all of your life's accomplishments, without love, are like a string of zeroes without a positive number in front: however long the list, it still adds up to nothing.

So what does real love look like? It looks like Jesus, of course.

PRAYER: Lord Jesus, may each day of my life
find me looking a little more like you.

Series: *What It Means to be Human*

READ: Matthew 4:23-25

Jesus' Public Ministry

And he went throughout all Galilee . . . (Matthew 4:23)

Matthew 4 and Matthew 9 contain two almost identical passages (compare 4:23-25 and 9:35). Between these bookends is a series of snapshots illustrating the three major elements in Jesus' public ministry.

First, he preached. He "went throughout all Galilee . . . proclaiming the gospel of the kingdom" (v. 23). That is, Jesus announced publicly the good news that God's rule had come personally into the world. Second, Jesus taught people how they should live as his disciples. Matthew 5-7 records the heart of the ethical and religious teaching of Jesus in the Sermon on the Mount. Finally, because God's reign ultimately means an end to all evil and suffering, the stories in Matthew 8 and 9 show Jesus healing the sick, delivering the demon-oppressed, and even taming the unruly forces of nature as signs of the already but not yet kingdom of God.

What stands out here about Jesus' ministry is its comprehensiveness. Jesus had an all-inclusive approach to meeting physical and spiritual need. And he did it everywhere. Matthew says that Jesus went through all the towns and even the villages teaching, preaching, and healing. He didn't calculate how big the crowd would be when he preached, or whether his ministry would be adequately publicized. He simply went where there was physical and spiritual need—as should we.

PRAYER: Thanks, Jesus, for coming to my town,
to my home, to my heart.

Series: *Jesus' Public Ministry*

READ: Matthew 4:12-17

The Message of Jesus

Repent, for the kingdom of heaven is at hand. (Matthew 4:17)

This might surprise you, but Jesus wasn't a Christian. A Christian is someone who has been saved by grace through faith in Christ. Jesus wasn't justified by faith; he was justified by his own righteous works. Christians have been reconciled to God by Christ's atoning death. Jesus wasn't reconciled to God at all, because his relationship with the Father was never broken—apart from those three terrible hours on the cross.

Here's a second surprise. Jesus didn't preach the gospel—at least in the sense the New Testament defines it. The gospel is the story of salvation—"the mighty works of God," as those who first heard it preached exclaimed (Acts 2:11). The gospel, in the apostle Paul's elevator speech version, is "that Christ died for our sins in accordance with the Scriptures, that he was buried, that he was raised on the third day in accordance with the Scriptures" (1 Cor. 15:3-4). What Jesus preached was the "gospel"—the "good news"—of God's kingdom come: "Repent, for the kingdom of heaven is at hand."

His message was this: God's kingdom has arrived, so reorient your life toward it. When the president boards Air Force One, it becomes the center of government for the United States. When he's not on board, it's just an airplane. His presence is what makes the difference. It's the same with the kingdom. The kingdom of God has come because Jesus, the King, has come. So, reorient your life toward him.

PRAYER: Help me to seek your kingdom first (Matthew 6:33), and may your kingdom come (Matthew 6:10).

Series: *Jesus' Public Ministry*

READ: Luke 10:25-37

The Good Samaritan

Which of these three . . . proved to be a neighbor? (Luke 10:36)

Jesus loved to use parables—little stories of everyday life—to illustrate his teaching. And one of the most famous of all the parables is this one, the parable of the good Samaritan. The story hinges on a series of questions. First is the question the lawyer (i.e., the expert in Torah; in our terms, the theologian) asked about how to inherit eternal life (v. 25). "Well," replied Jesus, "you're a lawyer. What does the Law say?" "Love God and my neighbor," said the theologian. Bingo! Go do it!

Jesus has thrown this guy on the defensive, so he asks another question, "desiring to justify himself" (v. 29). He tries to redirect the conversation by making it theoretical again. Let's talk about the concept of "the neighbor." In response to that, Jesus tells his famous story featuring a Samaritan as the good guy.

Jesus' final question to the lawyer is the key to understanding the point of the parable. It's clear that the man in the road is my neighbor. My neighbor is anyone I see in need, whatever the need, whoever the person. But Jesus' question is slightly different: "Which of these three, do you think, proved to be a neighbor to the man who fell among the robbers?" (v. 36). "The one who [most unexpectedly] showed him mercy." Now comes the punchline: "You go, and do likewise" (v. 37). The issue is not so much "Who is my neighbor?"; it's "Am I being a neighbor?" Jesus' concern is not that we can *identify* our neighbors; it's that we *help* them. He expects action from us.

PRAYER: Lord, give me eyes to see need,
and strength to help those I see.

READ: Luke 15:11-32

The Prodigal Son

This my son . . . your brother . . . was lost, and is found. (Luke 15:24, 32)

The prodigal son's story turns on a phrase in verse 17: "he came to himself." Something happened that caused the scales to fall from his eyes. The Bible says that one reason people don't believe the gospel is because the devil has convinced folks that they're happy living in the pig pen (2 Cor. 4:4). Conversion begins when we realize we don't belong there, when we recognize that the Father's house is our real home.

Of course the prodigal would never have gotten back into the house if he had been treated with strict justice. "You've made your choice," the father could have said, "Now live with it." Many fathers have said exactly that. But not the one in Jesus' story. He is, in preacher-theologian Helmut Thielicke's phrase, "The Waiting Father." More than that, he is the Seeking Father, who runs out to embrace his son even before the boy can stammer his apologies.

And then there's the other son. Luke opens chapter 15 this way: "Now the tax collectors and sinners were all drawing near to hear him. And the Pharisees and the scribes grumbled" (vv. 1-2). If there is so much joy in heaven when sinners repent, why is there so much grumbling about it on earth? Jesus wants us to read this story as if we are looking in the mirror. You may never have been a prodigal. Maybe you've stayed close to the Father's house all your life. But are we also like the elder brother in other ways? Do we resent grace when it's given to those who don't deserve it? Do we think they should have to prove themselves before being welcomed home? Are we outwardly religious, but inwardly cold-hearted and joyless? If so, like the older brother, we might be the ones who are lost.

PRAYER: Father, help me to rejoice in your grace.

READ: Matthew 5:1-2

The Good Life

And he opened his mouth and taught them . . . (Matthew 5:2)

What sort of pictures come to your mind when you hear the words "the good life"? For most of us the pictures would include beautiful houses with manicured gardens, tennis (or maybe pickleball!) courts and swimming pools . . . fancy new vehicles . . . lavish feasts of rich food and drink . . . expensive clothes . . . frequent trips to places like Hawaii or the Caribbean.

But I'm thinking of the good life in an entirely different sense. Not good as in rich or enjoyable or pleasurable, but good as in moral, virtuous, righteous. As we consider Jesus' teaching ministry it's appropriate to reflect on Jesus' Sermon on the Mount, the supreme guide to the good life.

Jesus' words in Matthew 5-7 are addressed to his disciples, to those who already know him and are seeking to obey him. The Sermon on the Mount is not the plan of salvation. Jesus' main concern here is not to explain to people how they can be saved; rather, it is to teach them how to live once they have been saved.

In the Sermon on the Mount, Jesus shows us what the truly good life actually looks like. His words attract and inspire us with their beautiful picture of life as God intended it to be. And if they leave us feeling frustrated because of our failure to live up to them, well, there is one Person we can turn to for help to turn our moral defeats into victories.

PRAYER: Lord, I want to live "the good life." Please help me.

Series: *The Good Life: Sermon on the Mount*

READ: Matthew 5:1-12

The Complete Christian

When he sat down, his disciples came to him. (Matthew 5:2)

In Matthew 5-7, Jesus addressed his famous Sermon on the Mount to his disciples. But this is not salvation by good works. Jesus' point is not that we can qualify for heaven by keeping this new law he gives us. He's not explaining how we can earn a relationship with him; he's explaining how a relationship with him ought to be lived out in daily life.

Jesus begins his sermon by pronouncing eight blessings, known collectively as "The Beatitudes." When he says, "Blessed are . . ." eight times over, what Jesus means is: "These are the attitudes and actions of the person who is pleasing to God, who is completely the person God means us to be."

It's important to understand that the Beatitudes don't describe eight different traits, each of which can earn God's approval. They are comprehensive; eight facets of a Christian character. Each of us should exhibit all of them. You can't pick and choose, thinking, "Well, I'm not very meek, and as for peacemaking, let's leave that for the pacifists. Maybe I'll try to get God's blessing by mourning."

I once was watching my wife make a dress for one of our young daughters. First, she cut out the pattern pieces, which she then stitched together. The Beatitudes are something like that dress pattern. Each piece is useful by itself. But they all need to be stitched together into a single life to show what the complete Christian looks like.

PRAYER: Help my life match your complete pattern.

Series: *Beatitudes: The Complete Christian Life*

READ: Luke 18:9-14

Blessed Poverty

Blessed are the poor in spirit, for theirs
is the kingdom of heaven. (Matthew 5:3)

We don't generally include "poor" under the column of things labeled "blessed." For us poor is bad. We link it with failure. When we apply it to people, it's usually a term of sympathy: "Poor old Joe." "Oh, that poor woman!" We're much more likely to associate blessedness with being wealthy.

But Jesus says blessedness begins with poverty. He's not saying that it's good to be poor in a literal sense. (No one who's ever been really poor would recommend the experience!) Notice, it is spiritual poverty Jesus speaks about here. "Blessed are the poor *in spirit*."

Poverty of spirit grows only in a humble heart. The "kingdom of heaven"—gospel shorthand for the blessing of God's presence and rule over our lives—can be experienced only if we have learned to see ourselves honestly, as God sees us. We need to recognize that we have nothing to offer God except our desperate need of him. "Nothing in my hands I bring," goes the old hymn, "simply to thy cross I cling."

Do you know how to sing that tune? The only way to receive God is to humble yourself, to empty your hands of the qualities and accomplishments (including the religious ones) that make you feel deserving of God's favor, and then turn to him and ask for mercy. Sort of like the tax collector we read about.

PRAYER: "Rock of Ages, cleft for me, let me hide
myself in thee." (*Rock of Ages*)

Series: *Beatitudes: The Complete Christian Life*

READ: 2 Corinthians 7:9-10

Happy Sorrow

Blessed are those who mourn, for they
shall be comforted. (Matthew 5:4)

What kind of sorrow is "happy sorrow"? Jesus does not narrow it down to one particular type of grief. He says simply, "Blessed are those who mourn." There is something wonderful about the fact that God's blessing rests upon people who are sad or bereaved. God's comfort is promised to the broken-hearted, not the carefree.

But the Beatitudes are primarily concerned with our spiritual condition rather than our emotional state. Just as the poverty that Jesus spoke about in the first beatitude referred to the humility of the poor in spirit, so the mourning of which he speaks here is primarily spiritual grief. It is sorrow for sin—for our own sins and shortcomings, but also for the tragic brokenness of a sin-ravaged world.

It's not so much the sorrow that is blessed, in and of itself. The blessedness of mourning lies more in what our sorrow can lead to. The apostle wrote about "godly grief," which is the kind of sorrow for sin that leads to repentance and ultimately to salvation (2 Cor. 7:9-10). The premier expression of this kind of grief in Scripture is in the penitential psalms, where David reminds us that the most acceptable sacrifice we can offer to God is a broken and contrite heart (Ps. 51:17).

Jesus' disciples will always seek to cultivate the sorrow that produces repentance—until the day when the Lord wipes away all our tears, and sorrow and sighing flee away.

PRAYER: Lord, may your comfort be with all who mourn.

Series: *Beatitudes: The Complete Christian Life*

READ: 1 Peter 5:1-7

Who Gets What?

Blessed are the meek, for they shall inherit the earth. (Matthew 5:5)

What sort of person comes to mind when you hear the adjective *meek*? I think of Winston Churchill's description of one of his political opponents as "a sheep in sheep's clothing" and "a modest little man with much to be modest about."

Jesus pronounces a blessing on the meek. If you want to enjoy God's favor, then meekness is one of the qualities you want. But meekness isn't what you might think. To be meek does not mean to be weak or wimpy. It doesn't turn you into a sheep—or a chicken! To be meek is to be humble and non-self-assertive. It is to be like Jesus himself, "gentle and lowly in heart" (Matt. 11:29).

In this beatitude Jesus is letting us in on God's little joke, or perhaps I should say, God's big joke. The joke is on all the greedy and ambitious people, who believe that they can carve out personal empires for themselves, who think that in this world you have to grab for what you want and fight your way to the top. God's joke is that it's actually the meek who will inherit the earth. The first will be last, and the last will be first. The fast track to success ends up heading nowhere, because God owns the earth, and he's planning to give it to his Son's friends. Humble faith in the Lord is the key to everything. So follow Peter's advice: Humble yourselves under the mighty hand of God.

PRAYER: We look forward to the day, Lord, when you will put down the proud and exalt the humble.

Series: *Beatitudes: The Complete Christian Life*

READ: Philippians 4:8-9

The Hunger That Will Be Satisfied

Blessed are those who hunger and thirst for righteousness,
for they shall be satisfied. (Matthew 5:6)

"You are what you eat." That statement was originally made by a German philosopher, and it's even more clever in the original, because it makes a pun: *Man ist was er isst.*

What's true for our bodies is also true for our spirits. Our souls take on the characteristics of what we feed them. If you consume only a steady diet of spiritual junk food—reality TV shows, video clip viewing, Facebook posts and Twitter feeds— your soul will shrink and you will become a shallower person.

But if you are hungry for the good, the true, and the beautiful; if you think about the things that are honorable, just, pure, lovely, commendable, excellent, and praiseworthy; if you feed on God's Word and seek first God's kingdom and his righteousness, then you will grow and flourish. You will become a better, deeper, healthier, and more truly human man or woman. You are what you eat.

Jesus promises that the desire for God and his righteousness is the one kind of hunger that will always be satisfied. Everyone who longs for holiness of life and for justice among people and nations will be filled to overflowing, finally and forever. In the meantime, we can devote ourselves to feeding on good things, the things that make for health and wholeness, both personally and socially.

PRAYER: Father, help me feed on good things.

Series: *Beatitudes: The Complete Christian Life*

READ: Luke 6:32-38

Measure for Measure

Blessed are the merciful, for they shall receive mercy. (Matthew 5:7)

When I was visiting one of the ancient cathedrals of England, I noticed a very interesting feature in the choir, the area where in medieval times the monks gathered for prayers. They used to pray around the clock, with seven different services during every 24-hour period, and the monks were required to stand throughout each service. But in the choir stalls where they stood there are little carved wooden benches that they could lean against for some relief. Those half-seats were called *misericords*, from the Latin word for "mercy."

That's a good illustration of what mercy is. Mercy means giving people a break. Mercy is offering help to the weak and the weary, and forgiveness to those who have stumbled.

I wonder if we realize how high a value God places on mercy. One of Jesus' favorite Bible verses was Hosea 6:6: "I desire mercy, not sacrifice" (NIV). God wants us to be merciful. He expects us to show mercy to others, especially if we want to receive mercy from him! Jesus reminds us in this beatitude of a basic rule in God's kingdom: what we give is what we will get—measure for measure. If you never need any mercy for yourself, then I guess you don't have to worry about extending it to anyone else. But if you're like me, you will want to receive a whole lapful of mercy. So we had better be giving a lot of it to others.

PRAYER: Lord, help me to show mercy to others
as much as I want it for myself.

Series: *Beatitudes: The Complete Christian Life*

READ: Colossians 1:15-20

How to See God

Blessed are the pure in heart,
for they shall see God. (Matthew 5:8)

How can we see someone who can't be seen? That is what the Bible says about God—that he can't be seen. God "dwells in unapproachable light, whom no one has ever seen or can see" (1 Tim. 6:16). But the Bible also says that this invisible God has made himself visible by becoming a real, flesh-and-blood human being, Jesus, in whom "all the fullness of God was pleased to dwell" (Col. 1:19). So Jesus could tell his disciples, "Whoever has seen me has seen the Father" (John 14:9).

Why is it then that so many can look at Jesus and not see God? All they see is a human teacher or prophet, or even a fictitious character. Maybe the problem is with us, not him. It's not that God is not there to be seen in Jesus; it's that we fail to recognize him because our hearts are not pure. If we want to see God in the face of Jesus Christ, and to live in the very presence of the triune God someday, we need to change and become pure within.

In one sense this change is easy. All you have to do is believe in Christ. But that's only the beginning. Your heart must then be purified by the power of God's Spirit, and more often than not the way of refining is by the fire of suffering. But in the end, it's worth it. We will see God. And what you see is also what you get!

PRAYER: "Create in me a clean heart, O God." (Psalm 51:10)

Series: *Beatitudes: The Complete Christian Life*

READ: Ephesians 2:11-22

Peacemaking

Blessed are the peacemakers, for they will
be called children of God. (Matthew 5:9 NRSV)

When he uttered this famous beatitude, Jesus certainly touched upon a glaring need. Whether it is an attempt at negotiations in the Middle East or an effort to mediate the warring parties in South Sudan or even just a wise and mature adult to referee between two squabbling children, our world has a pressing need for peacemakers.

Why is life so filled with conflict? The problem is that there's something wrong with us, inside in our very nature. The Bible calls it sin. Before we can have peace with each other, we need to be reconciled with God, a work only God can do. The good news of the gospel is that he *has* done it in the person of Jesus Christ. "Through him God was pleased to reconcile to himself all things, whether on earth or in heaven, by making peace through the blood of his cross" (Col. 1:20 NRSV).

Peace with God is just the beginning. What Jesus is talking about in this beatitude has more to do with person-to-person peace. He's concerned with the need for healing in human society and relationships. He wants his followers to become a fellowship of peacemakers, bringing people back together, as he has done by creating "in himself one new humanity in place of the two, thus making peace" (Eph. 2:15 NRSV).

Jesus is a peacemaker. He calls us to be the same. It's how you know you are a child of God.

PRAYER: Lord, help me be an agent of peace.

Series: *Beatitudes: The Complete Christian Life*

READ: Matthew 5:10-12

Upside-Down Blessings

Blessed are those who are persecuted for righteousness' sake,
for theirs is the kingdom of heaven. (Matthew 5:10)

Do you know what an oxymoron is? An oxymoron is a figure of speech in which the words seem to contradict each other, like a restaurant menu offering "Jumbo Shrimp." Or how about this one, straight from the Beatitudes: "blessed persecution"?

Jesus' ideas about blessedness are the exact opposite of most peoples'. According to humanity's collective wisdom, the happiest place is at the top, not the bottom. The good life means being free of troubles and cares, being comfortable and popular, going with the flow of majority opinion.

The world values wealth, power, security, health, and self-sufficiency. Jesus says the truly blessed are his defenseless disciples, who voluntarily accept suffering rather than compromise the truth. Does this make sense? Only if there is a God and only if heaven is real, because heaven is exactly what the Lord promises to those who are persecuted for his sake. One day their suffering will be more than made up to them.

We don't think enough about how greatly God's outlook and values differ from ours. What people laugh at, God blesses and honors. What the world persecutes, God rewards. The kingdom of heaven doesn't belong to the proud, the high, and the mighty; it belongs to faithful followers of Jesus Christ who remain loyal to him no matter what the cost. In the end, they get the biggest blessing.

PRAYER: Father, bless all who suffer for the sake of Christ.

Series: *Beatitudes: The Complete Christian Life*

READ: Jeremiah 29:1-7

Salt of the Earth

You are the salt of the earth. (Matthew 5:13)

"He's the salt of the earth" we might say about a friendly, humble, easy-to-get-along-with guy. But Jesus is calling us to be more than just good guys (or gals). Salt was a crucial commodity in his world. Because of its purifying qualities, salt was used as an antiseptic. Salt is also a food preservative—very important in an age with no refrigeration. On the other hand, salt that isn't salty is nothing but white sand.

What's the most useless thing you can think of? Snow skis in the desert? A flat spare tire? A hairbrush for a man whose head looks like a cue ball? That's what "saltless" Christians are like—good for nothing. Christ's salt metaphor points to the whole range of positive roles we are meant to play in the world, things that preserve communities from decay or add zest to life. Jesus wants his followers to be a powerful force for good. Just as it doesn't take a lot of salt to flavor a dish, so even a few salty Christians in a town, neighborhood, office, or school should make it both a better and a happier place. Even if we are living as exiles in the world we must seek the good of the earthly cities where the Lord has put us.

Years ago our church's youth group went on a short-term mission trip to Trinidad. The leader of the ministry they worked with there taught our kids a simple slogan that guided them throughout their time of service: *Name Christian? Live Christian!* That pretty much says it all.

PRAYER: Help me to be salt today
in a world where much is decaying.

Series: *Beatitudes: The Complete Christian Life*

READ: Matthew 5:14-16

The Light of the World

You are the light of the world. (Matthew 5:14)

There are many ways the image of light and darkness is used in the Bible. Here are at least three. One, light suggests truth, as opposed to the darkness of ignorance or error. *Dominus illuminatio mea* is the motto of Oxford University; that's Psalm 27:1: "The LORD is my light." Two, light stands for good, darkness for evil. "And this is the judgment: the light has come into the world, and people loved the darkness rather than the light because their works were evil" (John 3:19). Three, light represents life, and darkness death. "For you have delivered my soul from death, yes, my feet from falling, that I may walk before God in the light of life" (Ps. 56:13).

Jesus said that he was the light of the world, and that whoever followed him would never walk in darkness but would have the light of life (John 8:12). He also said *we* are the light of the world. Here's the great, obvious thing about light: it's visible. Even a little light carries a long way on a pitch-black night. Darkness can never conquer light. "The light shines in the darkness, and the darkness has not overcome it" (John 1:5). Darkness can't extinguish our lights, but we can, if we choose to hide them.

The world can no longer see Jesus and his light physically, but it can see us. *Hmm.* Do you suppose he meant for the light of his truth, goodness, and life to continue shining through our good works?

PRAYER: "This little light of mine,
I'm gonna let it shine!" (*This Little Light of Mine*)

Series: *Beatitudes: The Complete Christian Life*

READ: Matthew 5:17-20

Jesus Talks about the Bible

I have not come to abolish them but to fulfill them. (Matthew 5:17)

The phrase "the Law and the Prophets" was the usual way a Jew of Jesus' time referred to the Hebrew Scriptures. So in these verses Jesus is talking about the Bible as it was then constituted—what we call the Old Testament.

Jesus *loved* the Bible. He had the greatest regard and esteem for it. That comes through every word he speaks about it. Jesus *lived* by the Bible. "Man does not live on bread alone," Jesus recited, "but on every word that comes from the mouth of the LORD" (Deut. 8:3 NIV; see Matt. 4:4). That is exactly how Jesus himself lived. Jesus *fulfilled* the Bible. That is what he said he came to do—to fulfill, not just in the sense of obeying all the commands of God's Law (which he did) but to fulfill in the sense of completing the Scriptures. Jesus is the one to whom the whole Old Testament points. He's the climax and point of the entire story.

Evangelical Christians are sometimes criticized for practicing bibliolatry, the worship of a book. That's a false accusation. We don't worship a book; we worship Jesus. But because we do that, we also reverence the Word of God just as he did. Authentic Christianity is always *biblical* Christianity, a faith marked by love for the Bible and commitment to the authority of the Bible.

PRAYER: Thank you, Lord, for your Word.
Help me to live by it faithfully.

Series: *Beatitudes: The Complete Christian Life*

READ: Matthew 5:21-26

Jesus Talks about Anger

Everyone who is angry with his brother will be liable to judgment
. . . and whoever says, "You fool!" will be liable to the hell of fire.
(Matthew 5:22)

I can still remember hearing this verse in church when I was a boy and feeling nervous. I was pretty sure I had never said, "You fool!" to my brother Tom, but I thought it was lucky for me that Jesus hadn't said, "Whoever says to his brother 'You jerk!' will be in danger of hell!" But of course, that is exactly what he meant. It's not the particular words we choose. It is talking this way at all that is wrong. And it is in entertaining the feelings that give birth to the words that we actually begin to break the sixth commandment.

Jesus expands the Law's commandments in two ways. First, he internalizes them. According to Jesus, God is interested in the attitudes lying behind our actions. These are what lead up to them or actually trigger them. "Listen," he says, "when the law forbids murder, it's also condemning the ways we can kill people in our thoughts or with our words, even if we never lay a hand on them."

The other thing Jesus does is to point toward the positive steps the commandment requires us to take. God's law isn't just negative. Every commandment implies its opposite. Here in the command against verbal killing and inward hating, the positive duty Jesus talks about is taking the initiative to restore a broken relationship (v. 24).

PRAYER: Lord, help me be a healer not a hater.

Series: *Beatitudes: The Complete Christian Life*

READ: Matthew 5:27-30

Jesus Talks about Lust

Everyone who looks . . . with lustful intent
has already committed adultery. (Matthew 5:28)

The seventh commandment deals with sexual sin. Just in case I might be thinking that if I have avoided being physically unfaithful to my spouse I'm in the clear with respect to this commandment, Jesus goes deeper once again. "You may think you can avoid adultery by defining it narrowly," he says, "but I'm telling you that you commit a kind of adultery every time you look lustfully."

So what are we to do? Here is yet another commandment we discover ourselves breaking all the time. We can cry out for mercy, certainly. But Jesus shows us a practical response as well. His commands about tearing out eyes and cutting off hands are dramatic figures of speech, deliberately exaggerated. Jesus is not recommending that we mutilate our thoughts. What he means here is that we must fight physically to control ourselves, and we have to be utterly ruthless about it.

The principle here is that just as the roots of sin are internal, rising from our fantasies and desires, so the roots of self-control must be as well. We must discipline our eyes, ears, hands, and feet—the things we look at and view (nowadays especially online), the places we go, the people or objects we lust over. Our struggles with sin will not be ended all at once, but with God's help they can end increasingly in victory.

PRAYER: Lord Jesus, help me to be pure, both within and without.

Series: *Beatitudes: The Complete Christian Life*

READ: Matthew 5:31-32

Jesus Talks about Divorce

*Whoever marries a divorced woman
commits adultery.* (Matthew 5:32)

It's one thing to listen to Jesus' teaching about marriage and divorce. It's quite another to apply it to the lives of frail, struggling, imperfect sinners like ourselves. I agree with one commentator who said that explaining Jesus' teaching on divorce is unpleasant work because it often hurts and puts down people who perhaps have been hurt and put down enough already.

Nevertheless, there it is. Jesus was strongly for marriage and against divorce, except in the case of unfaithfulness (v. 32). It helps to know that Jesus spoke these words to a culture of male dominance, where women had few rights and a man could divorce his wife for even trivial offenses. Rejected wives often had no recourse but to turn to prostitution for survival. So Jesus' strong teaching served to protect defenseless women.

Still it's hard for us today, in an age where people drift apart and marriages crumble. But remember this: the Lord who hates divorce still loves divorced *people*. The same Jesus who says "no" to sin also says "yes" to sinners—and we are all sinners. Remember the woman who was brought to Jesus having been taken in the act of adultery (see John 8:1-11)? "Let whoever is without sin cast the first stone at her," he said. When he looked up a few moments later, the crowd had melted away and only the woman was left. "Where are your accusers?" he asked her. "They've all gone," she said. "Then neither do I condemn you, go and sin no more."

PRAYER: Lord, have mercy on me, a sinner.

Series: *Beatitudes: The Complete Christian Life*

READ: Matthew 5:33-37

Jesus Talks about Lying

Let what you say be simply "Yes" or "No." (Matthew 5:37)

When I was a boy I used to watch a television program called *Truth or Consequences*. It was a little game where contestants had to answer a question truthfully or suffer a consequence. What would it be like if real life were that way? Imagine a world where everyone had to pay an immediate penalty whenever they said anything false or misleading. There wouldn't be any more television commercials. Sales staff would all need extensive job retraining. Politicians would say things like, "You know, my opponent is actually the better candidate."

But it's not "truth or consequences" in real life. People don't tell the truth. They twist it, distort, or disguise it in a hundred ways. They slander, gossip, create false impressions, exaggerate, utter outright lies—and pay no immediate penalty. Oftentimes it even seems to benefit them.

When Jesus tells his followers not to swear an oath, he's not saying we can't do things like recite the Pledge of Allegiance or swear to tell the truth in a court of law. Rather, he means that for Christians, truthfulness should not be reserved for special occasions only, when we are bound by an oath. When he tells us to let our "yes" mean "yes," he means we should speak plainly and without misleading or evasive statements. The first stereos were known as "hi-fis," short for "high fidelity." Christians ought to be high-fidelity people, whose word can be trusted.

PRAYER: "Let the words of my mouth . . . be acceptable in your sight, O Lord." (Psalm 19:14)

Series: *Beatitudes: The Complete Christian Life*

READ: Matthew 5:38-48

The Ethics of Jesus

Love your enemies. (Matthew 5:44)

Do you wish Jesus hadn't said all this? Turning the other cheek, going the second mile, loving our enemies—does he actually expect us to do that? Well, yes.

This behavior directly contradicts the way the world operates. It goes against every ordinary human instinct. Our natural rule is "tit for tat," an eye for an eye. Give what you get. Don't get mad, get even. But Jesus tells us to do good to others, even when they deserve the opposite, and to help people even when they won't help us back. Those are the ethics of Jesus.

Jesus gives two reasons for living this way. One is that Christians *should* behave better than people of the world. "Look," he says, in effect, "even Nazis can be good to their friends and kind to their children. What's so great about that? I expect much more from you." If we know Jesus it ought to make our actions so different that unbelievers sit up and take notice. When a prominent Turkish Christian journalist was assassinated by anti-Christian extremists, his widow said on television, "I forgive them." The secular reporter interviewing her blurted out, "That was Jesus Christ speaking." Exactly.

Second, we must act this way because this is how God behaves. We need to repay hostility with love and show mercy to the undeserving because this is exactly what our heavenly Father does. If we really are God's children, shouldn't we bear a family resemblance?

PRAYER: "O God, command what you will, and give what you command." (St. Augustine)

Series: *Beatitudes: The Complete Christian Life*

READ: Matthew 6:1-8, 16-18

How to Be Religious

And your Father who sees in secret
will reward you. (Matthew 6:4, 6, 18)

I once saw a book with the intriguing title *How to Be a Christian Without Being Religious*. It wasn't really arguing against being religious. It was arguing against being religious in the wrong way. That's what Jesus is doing in today's passage which could be called, *How to Be Religious While Being a Christian*.

Jesus' point is simple. He says that religious acts must be done for God alone. "Beware of practicing your piety before others in order to be seen by them" (v. 1). Jesus reminds us that there is only one proper audience for all our good works, and *he* doesn't have to be told who has done what. Religion isn't something we do before other people in order to enhance our reputation for spirituality. It's something we do for God, to honor him and express our love and thanks to him.

Here's a practical test: Do you feel the need to blow your own horn (v. 2)? Do you feel upset if your good works aren't acknowledged? Then ask yourself why you did them. If it was to stroke your own ego, then of course you should make sure you get the credit, and once you have it, you also have your reward—the only reward you'll ever get (vv. 2, 5, 16). But if you give and pray and do good out of love for God, then you'll want to keep these things secret, so that they can be just between you and your Father.

PRAYER: Heavenly Father, you see what is done in secret.
Receive my secret prayers today.

Series: *The Good Life: Sermon on the Mount*

READ: Matthew 6:9-15; Matthew 7:7

How to Pray, Part 1

*When you pray, go into your room and shut the door
and pray to your Father who is in secret. (Matthew 6:6)*

Christians pray; it's as simple as that. We may pray badly, we may pray
infrequently, but we pray. The great Christian teacher of the 19th century,
Bishop J. C. Ryle, put the matter succinctly: "God has no [mute] children."

The question then becomes how to pray. We might well echo the
disciples' request, "Lord, teach us to pray" (Luke 11:1). Jesus offers us some
pointers here in his sermon, both in the explicit instructions he gives and
in the model prayer he offers, the Lord's Prayer. Here are four suggestions
for how we should pray, spread over two days of devotional time.

First, pray confidently. Jesus teaches us to address God as "Father,"
using the very name he himself did. We don't gain access to God through
prayer. We pray because we have access to him through Jesus. If by faith
in Christ you are God's child, you need never hesitate to come to him.
Jesus urges us to approach God in prayer with confidence by using one
of his favorite arguments, the "how much more" argument: "If you then,
who are evil, know how to give good gifts to your children, how much
more will your Father in heaven give good things to those who ask him!"

Second, pray simply, from the heart. "When you are praying, do
not heap up empty phrases as the Gentiles do." Prayer is not a matter
of learning the right technique, or repeating the correct formulas. You
don't score more prayer points for reciting more words.

Tomorrow, we'll consider the final two suggestions.

PRAYER: Thank you, Father, that we can come
so freely to you in prayer through your son Jesus.

Series: *The Good Life: Sermon on the Mount*

READ: Matthew 6:9-15; Matthew 7:7

How to Pray, Part 2

Ask, and it will be given to you. (Matthew 7:7)

Let's keep going with Jesus' next two points about prayer.

Third, pray comprehensively. In his model prayer Jesus teaches us to pray not just for our own concerns but for God's as well. In fact, we are to begin with God's concerns: his name, his kingdom, his will. Then we turn to our own needs, both physical and spiritual. The pronoun Jesus uses is also important. In the Lord's Prayer he teaches us to use the plural: not just me and mine but our and us. "*Our* Father . . . Give *us* . . . Forgive *us* . . . Lead *us*." Whatever we ask for ourselves we really must be asking for others too.

Fourth, pray earnestly. We can and should ask for needs when we pray; we have strong encouragement to do so. And we don't have to be shy; we must ask with earnestness and conviction. Jesus says that we should "Ask, seek, knock"; his repetition is meant to stimulate our efforts.

We must decide once and for all that prayer is a priority. We always seem to find time for the things that are most important to us. So, make a plan for daily praying, and then get on with it. Prayer is an exercise. We develop our spiritual muscles the same way we improve our physical ones. Discipline is hard for us. But when the doctor says it's diet and exercise or die, we somehow find time to walk each day. We need to realize that the same thing is true for the life of our souls. It's pray or die!

PRAYER: "Lord, teach us to pray." (Luke 11:1)

Series: *The Good Life: Sermon on the Mount*

READ: Matthew 6:12, 14, 15

Praying for Forgiveness

If you forgive others their trespasses, your heavenly Father will also forgive you. (Matthew 6:14)

In the Lord's Prayer Jesus teaches us to ask for forgiveness. At the end of the prayer, he tells us to offer forgiveness to others. In both places, he connects our receiving forgiveness with our readiness to extend it to those who have wronged us.

It is easy to ask God for forgiveness. It is very hard to give it to others. Yet give it we must. Jesus knew that I can never truly experience the mercy of God for myself unless I am also merciful toward others. You can no more get forgiveness without giving it than you can breathe in without breathing out!

Corrie Ten Boom, imprisoned by the Nazis for hiding Jews, was approached by a man after the war. She immediately recognized him as one of the cruel guards from her concentration camp. He said, "I am a Christian now. I ask you to forgive me." Then he extended his hand. Forgive him? The man who had tormented her and had helped to kill her sister! For a moment Corrie froze. Then she prayed, "Lord, I can't forgive this man, but I know I must. Help me!" At that instant she felt a power begin to move her arm toward the man, and when their hands clasped, Corrie knew that God had worked a miracle in her.

If God could help Corrie Ten Boom to forgive, couldn't he do the same for you and me?

PRAYER: Forgive us our sins, as we forgive those who sin against us.

Series: *The Good Life: Sermon on the Mount*

READ: Matthew 6:19-24

Split Loyalties, Divided Hearts

*For where your treasure is there your heart
will be also. (Matthew 6:21)*

One day a man came to Jesus with a question. "Teacher, what's the most important commandment in the law?" Jesus replied, "Love God with all your heart; that's the greatest commandment."

I wish I could say that I love God with all my heart all the time, but I don't. I love so many different things. I love God, but I also love money and the things it buys. I love God, but I also love success and importance. When our hearts are divided, our lives send out contradictory messages, like the car I once noticed with two bumper stickers. On the left side one said, "I love Jesus," and on the right was another stating, "Capricorns are sexy." So which is it?

Jesus makes a blanket statement about divided hearts and loyalties: "No one can serve two masters. You cannot serve both God and Money." Notice, this is not a request—"Please don't try to serve both God and money." It isn't an opinion—"I think you shouldn't try to live for both the world and God at the same time." No, this is just a fact.

The conclusion to draw here isn't, "Okay, I can't have both so I'll choose Money!" What Jesus wants is for us to serve God and store up treasure in heaven by investing our lives and resources in his kingdom. Wherever you put your treasure is the place your heart is, and wherever your heart is, that's where you yourself will end up!

PRAYER: God, help me to love you
with all my heart, mind and strength.

Series: *The Good Life: Sermon on the Mount*

READ: Matthew 6:25-34

Is Anxiety Eating You Up?

*Therefore I tell you, do not be anxious
about your life. (Matthew 6:25)*

All of us have times when we worry. We worry about how to pay the bills, whether our health will hold up, how our children will turn out, where our career is going. But if anxiety is eating us up, we should recognize this sort of anxiety for what it is. It's a form of practical atheism. When Christians are over-anxious about our lives we're living like unbelievers. We're acting just like people who don't know God (v. 32). Anxiety spoils our usefulness for God, since we cannot put his kingdom first if we are obsessed with our personal needs. Most of all, anxiety is unnecessary. If we could only really believe what Jesus says to us here, we would never be anxious again.

Please don't think I'm saying that anxiety is easy to overcome or that I never worry about anything. Jesus mentions worry over what we eat, drink and wear. Food and clothing aren't luxuries; they're necessities. So what he says here is not just for good times, but for when the cupboard is bare and the bank account is empty, and we're not sure how we're going to make it to next week's paycheck.

The main thing to remember is that anxiety is a form of fear. The opposite of fear is faith. This means that the cure for anxiety is to learn to trust in the God who feeds the birds of the air and clothes the flowers of the field, but who loves and cares for us even more.

PRAYER: Lord, help me not to worry about tomorrow,
but to trust you to take care of me.

Series: *The Good Life: Sermon on the Mount*

READ: Matthew 6:33

The Great Priority

But seek first the kingdom of God
and his righteousness. (Matthew 6:33)

What exactly is the kingdom of God? Well, it's not like the kingdom of England or Spain. It's not a geographical realm. You can't point to it on a map. God's kingdom is his reign over human persons, institutions, and cultures. God already rules everything and everyone in the sense of being in control of the final outcome of all things. God's *kingdom* is his active, conscious rule in individuals, churches, and societies that acknowledge the authority of Jesus Christ.

You may have heard of the Great Commandment and the Great Commission. Well, here is the Great Priority: "...more than anything else, put God's work first and do what he wants" (v. 33 CEV). God's business should be the Christian's primary concern; seek *first* the kingdom. Most of us do just the opposite. We seek first all these other things. (We call it "making a living.") Then we may give some leftover time or money to God. We worry more about putting away a little extra for ourselves than we do about advancing Christ's cause.

Jesus says, "I want you to be most concerned about kingdom business, not your own business, and trust God to take care of you." Look at your checkbook and your daily calendar and ask yourself, "Am I living my life like a believer or an unbeliever?"

PRAYER: Father, take the leadership now,
beginning in my life and world.

Series: *The Good Life: Sermon on the Mount*

READ: Matthew 7:1-6

Judging vs. Being Judgmental

Judge not, that you be not judged. (Matthew 7:1)

Judging is both a wonderful and a necessary thing. One of the most respected professions in any land is that of a judge. Judging is also important for us in our everyday lives. It's a high compliment to say that someone has good judgment.

Why then does Jesus tell us we must not judge? Obviously Jesus must be using the word in a different sense here. To judge can mean to recognize the truth and make appropriate decisions in the light of it. In that sense we should all be judging constantly.

But to judge can also mean to condemn and reject people, to criticize harshly, to be faultfinding, to tear others down. That is the kind of behavior Jesus forbids in those who want to be his followers. And he tells us why. One reason is that judgment has a way of boomeranging: "Do not judge, *or you too will be judged.*" In this, as in other things, God's rule is that you get what you give. Another reason is that we are neither good enough nor wise enough to judge others. That's the meaning behind Jesus' sarcastic saying about the speck and the plank. (Just try to picture it and you'll get the joke.) We are usually not qualified to pass judgment on others because our own faults may be just as bad or even worse.

PRAYER: Lord, give me good judgment
and keep me from being judgmental.

Series: *The Good Life: Sermon on the Mount*

READ: Luke 6:27-31

The Golden Rule

Whatever you wish that others would do to you, do also to them, for this is the Law and the Prophets. (Matthew 7:12)

The writer Thomas Carlyle had very little respect for the Christianity of his native Scotland. Once, when he was speaking with his mother, he expressed scorn for all the preaching that went on week after week. "It's all such a waste of time!" Carlyle exclaimed. "Why, if I were a preacher, I would simply say to the people, 'You know what you should do; now go and do it!'" "Aye, Thomas," his mother responded, "but would you tell them *how*?"

We all know what we ought to do. The Golden Rule ("golden" because it is so valuable) says it all: "Do unto others as you would have them do unto you." Even cultures far removed from the Bible know the Golden Rule. For example, the Chinese philosopher Confucius offered this admonition: "Do not do to others what you would not wish done to yourself."

Many teachers can tell us what we ought to do. But only Jesus can also tell us *how*—because Jesus isn't just a teacher; he's a Savior. Jesus gives us the power to overcome our self-centeredness so that we can not only love God but also love our neighbor as ourselves. And that, says Jesus, is "the Law and the Prophets"—the whole of biblical ethics in a nutshell.

PRAYER: Lord Jesus, I thank you that you are so much more than just a teacher. Give me the strength to love others rightly.

Series: *The Good Life: Sermon on the Mount*

READ: Matthew 7:13-23

The Way to Heaven

The gate is narrow and the way is hard
that leads to life. (Matthew 7:14)

In the interest of health and safety, the government requires warnings to be attached to dangerous products. No one can force us to heed them, but even if we ignore them, they still serve a purpose. Warnings leave people without excuse. Jesus also issues some serious warnings. One is about choosing the narrow gate and the difficult road. Jesus is talking here about the decision first to *believe* in him (he is the gate), and then to *follow* him (on the hard way of discipleship).

Isn't this terribly intolerant? Isn't it much kinder, much more respectful, to say that people can choose whatever way they want? Shouldn't they have the right to follow their own beliefs, their own pathway? Doesn't life contain many different roads to God? Isn't it arrogant of Christians to insist that ours is the only true way?

But remember, *we* aren't saying this. *Jesus*, the Son of God, is! According to him, all religions don't lead to the same place. Going to heaven isn't like going to Rome ("All roads lead to Rome"). Only one way leads to God. It is the way of faith in Christ. The others may look very promising and be thronged with devoted followers, but they turn out to be dead-ends!

PRAYER: Lord Jesus, you are the Way, the Truth, and the Life.
Help me to walk the difficult path of discipleship.

Series: *The Good Life: Sermon on the Mount*

READ: Matthew 7:24-29

A Tale of Two Houses

Everyone then who hears these words of mine and does them will be like a wise man who built his house on the rock. (Matthew 7:24)

Like all good teachers, Jesus ends his lessons on the good life with a memorable application. He tells a story which is really a call to action. The two houses in the story represent two different ways of living. But how are they different? Not in their outward appearance or environment. They were built with the same plans. The same storms struck both. The same forces battered them.

The difference between the two houses was in their foundations. What separates these two lives is where they are built. One house was built on the rock and the other on sand. Every life is based on some foundation. The question is: What sort of foundation? The smart person is the one "who hears these words of mine *and puts them into practice.*" The fool is one "who hears these words of mine *and does not put them into practice*" (vv. 24, 26). What makes people wise or foolish, saved or lost, is not just whether they hear Jesus, but whether they *obey* him.

PRAYER: "Almighty God, give us grace to be not only hearers, but doers of your holy word; not only to admire, but to obey your teaching; not only to profess, but to practice your religion; not only to love, but to live your gospel. So grant that what we learn of your glory we may receive into our hearts, and show forth in our lives: through Jesus Christ our Lord. Amen." (*Prayer composed for the Lambeth Conference of Anglican Bishops of 1948*)

Series: *The Good Life: Sermon on the Mount*

READ: Matthew 7:28-29

The Authority of Jesus

And when Jesus finished these sayings, the crowds were astonished at his teaching, for he was teaching them as one who had authority, and not as their scribes. (Matthew 7:28-29)

Most theology books are based on works by other theologians—you can read about them in the footnotes and bibliographies at the back of the volume. This was the method of the scribes. They taught by citing authorities. Not Jesus. He didn't teach from authorities, he taught *with* authority—and his listeners had never heard anything like it.

Running throughout Jesus' teaching is a refrain that went like this: "You have heard that it was said of old, but I say to you . . ." Jesus is saying, in effect, "The law and its various commentators said this, but now I am telling you *this*. This is what you actually have to do." It's not that he denies or contradicts the law, it's more like he personally claims the authority to explain the law's deepest meaning. Jesus talks like somebody who is "above the law," not in the bad sense of the scofflaw who thinks it doesn't apply to him, but in the good sense of the lawgiver who knows that the law itself derives its authority from him. When we listen to Jesus' teaching about right and wrong, and good and evil, we are listening to the very source of all goodness and morality.

And he insists that we do more than just listen. "If you know these things, blessed are you if you do them" (John 13:17).

PRAYER: Lord, give me the strength to be a doer as well as a hearer of your Word.

Series: *Jesus' Public Ministry*

READ: Matthew 8:1-4

Jesus' First Miracle

And Jesus stretched out his hand . . . (Matthew 8:3)

The man who approached Jesus after his Sermon on the Mount was a hopeless case. Leprosy, with its hideous symptoms, was incurable. Those who suffered from it were unclean—literally untouchable—and were forced to warn off passersby lest they also become infected. In Scripture, leprosy is a symbol of the ultimate defilement, sin. So there was a real point to this man's hesitant statement, "Lord, if you will, you can make me clean" (v. 2). This man had no doubt about Jesus' ability to heal. The only question in his mind was whether Jesus was willing.

Jesus' response was immediate. He "stretched out his hand and touched him, saying, 'I will; be clean.'" Jesus didn't have to touch people to make them well. So why did he do that to this particular man? Isn't it obvious? The leper had wondered whether Jesus would be willing to heal him, to have contact with him, to get involved in his messy life and its gross problems. The touch was the answer. Jesus touched the man to show him that not only was he willing, but that no one was too off-putting for him to care.

In his comment on this story, John Calvin observes that in the incarnation Jesus did far more than just reach out and touch us. He climbed into our flesh so that he could cleanse us from all defilement and pour his holiness over us. None of us is untouchable to him.

PRAYER: Lord Jesus, thank you that your love touches me and your blood cleanses me.

Series: *Jesus' Public Ministry*

READ: Matthew 8:5-13

A Man under Authority

I too am a man under authority. (Matthew 8:9)

It wasn't easy to surprise Jesus. Only twice are we told in the Gospels that something astonished him. One was the lack of faith among his hometown friends and neighbors—"he marveled because of their unbelief" (Mark 6:6). The other was the faith of this Roman centurion. When Jesus heard what the man said, "he marveled," exclaiming, "with no one in Israel have I found such faith" (Matt. 8:10). This is the first time the word "faith" appears in the New Testament. Isn't it interesting that it's used not of a disciple but of this foreigner?

What was so amazing about the centurion's faith was its combination of self-effacing humility and boundless confidence in Jesus' power. Just as he was willing to touch a leper, so Jesus also offered to go to this gentile's house to heal his servant. "Lord," he objected, "I am not worthy to have you come under my roof, but only say the word, and my servant will be healed. For I too am a man under authority" (vv. 8-9). A lifetime in the army had taught him all there was to know about both taking orders and giving them. He knew authority when he saw it. "So just give the order, Lord, and sickness and suffering and even death itself will have to obey you."

I identify with this guy. As a Christian, I too am a man under authority. A key question is whether we acknowledge the authority of God's Word or choose to define for ourselves what's true or false and right or wrong.

PRAYER: Gladly and willingly I acknowledge
your authority over me, Lord.

Series: *Jesus' Public Ministry*

READ: Matthew 8:14-17

He Takes Our Illnesses

He touched her hand, and the fever left her. (Matthew 8:15)

In Jesus' culture, women were second-class citizens. They were not allowed to enter the inner courtyard of the temple. They literally didn't count in the synagogue; thirteen men were required in order to organize a congregation. Outside of marriage, men and women were not allowed any physical contact.

But Jesus' first three healing miracles of a leper, a gentile, and a woman show him ignoring taboos and smashing prejudices. New Testament scholar Frederick Dale Bruner notes that the structure of the temple reflected the exclusions that characterized Old Testament worship. The outermost courtyard was the Court of the Gentiles. Next came the Court of the Women, then the Court of Men, then the Holy Place, and finally the Holy of Holies, where only the high priest was allowed to enter once a year with the blood of atonement. But Jesus broke down all of these walls that kept people apart from one another and distant from God. At the climactic moment of Jesus' death, even the curtain that veiled the Holy of Holies was torn in two, "from top to bottom" (Matt. 27:51). Bruner comments, "Jesus is the great Wallbreaker. A leper, a centurion, and a woman; one physically excluded, one racially excluded, and one sexually excluded from the innermost worship of the community—these Jesus heals *first*" (*Matthew*, rev. ed., 1:386).

What message do you think this action of Jesus might have for his church today?

PRAYER: Thank you, Jesus, for breaking all the barriers.

Series: *Jesus' Public Ministry*

READ: Matthew 8:18-20

Would-Be Followers

I will follow you wherever you go. (Matthew 8:19)

During his public ministry, Jesus attracted large crowds but few followers. So when a man came up to him and declared boldly, "Teacher, I will follow you wherever you go," you might think Jesus would accept such an eager volunteer gladly and be grateful for his commitment.

This man was a scribe, a professional Bible teacher. Maybe he had just heard the Sermon on the Mount and was impressed by Jesus' authority. He approached him as one rabbi to another. Maybe he had a collegial relationship in mind. But Jesus doesn't need colleagues, he wants disciples. He's not interested in people who simply call him, "Teacher." He's looking for people who call him, "Lord."

Jesus put the Bible teacher off with a warning about what life with him is like: "Foxes have holes, and birds of the air have nests, but the Son of Man has nowhere to lay his head" (v. 20). That's a word for us comfortable Christians to meditate on. If you offer to follow him anywhere, you may end up with nowhere.

The scribe was clueless about discipleship. In his commentary on verse 19, John Calvin says about him: "He wishes indeed to follow Christ, but dreams of an easy and agreeable life, and of dwellings filled with every convenience; whereas the disciples of Christ must walk among thorns, and march to the cross." If you think that following Jesus is a free ticket to the good life, you haven't looked at where Jesus himself was going. He was headed to the cross.

PRAYER: Jesus, give me the strength to take up
the cross and follow you today.

Series: *Jesus' Public Ministry*

READ: Matthew 8:23-27

Stilling the Storm

*Then he . . . rebuked the winds and the sea,
and there was a great calm.* (Matthew 8:26)

With the disciples panicking and screaming for him to save them, Jesus
calmly rebuked them for their lack of faith. After that he proceeded to
rebuke—that's Matthew's word—the storm on the lake. Jesus stood up in
that boat in the middle of a howling gale, with the wind roaring around
him and water pouring over the gunwales and his crew of professional
sailors working desperately to keep from capsizing, and he proceeded to
speak to the elements like a parent addressing unruly children. And they
instantly obeyed.

Wow. "What sort of man is this," indeed! The power and authority
Jesus flashed for a brief instant in that boat did not come from anywhere
in this world. It opened the disciples' eyes to his true identity, and it
made them tremble.

One of the beautiful ways in which the early church used this story
was by seeing that little boat as a symbol for the church. "The boat is
the present Church," wrote the Venerable Bede in the 8th century, "in
which Christ passes over the sea of this world with His own, and stills
the waves of persecution." Here are the disciples, gathered together
inside the boat, with Jesus in their midst. The church is the community
of all who are living in fellowship with the Lord and with one another.
Around us the perils and storms of life are swirling, but as long as Jesus
is with us, all will be well.

PRAYER: I thank you, Lord, that you are with me in the storm.

Series: *Jesus' Public Ministry*

The In-breaking Kingdom

What have you to do with us, O Son of God? (Matthew 8:29)

C. S. Lewis described our world as enemy-occupied territory. This story in Matthew 8 offers a clear sign of what happens when the kingdom of God invades it. In the person of Jesus, God's rule has arrived in the world, and when God's kingdom comes into conflict with Satan's, evil is vanquished. Jesus the Great Deliverer overthrows the power of Satan, the Great Usurper.

The Devil is no match for the Lord; the contest between good and evil is not a struggle between equals. When Jesus deals with these oppressed men the outcome is never in doubt. The demons cringe and cower at the sight of the Son of God. They realize who he is and what their end will be. In the day of judgment they will be cast into the abyss (see Luke 8:31). And here and now they cannot hurt even a bunch of hogs without Jesus' permission.

But did you notice the reaction of the locals? "All the city came out . . . and . . . they begged him to leave their region" (Matt. 8:34). Here is this tremendous demonstration of the power of Jesus to deliver, and all these folks can think about is the loss of their pigs. Jesus was simply too disruptive for them. The values of God's kingdom come into conflict with the economics of their society, and money wins. In their own way, these people were just as much in bondage to the Devil as the two demon-possessed men. They just didn't realize it.

PRAYER: Heavenly Father, deliver us from evil—of every kind.

Series: *Jesus' Public Ministry*

READ: Matthew 9:1-8

The Forgiveness of Sins

Take heart . . . your sins are forgiven. (Matthew 9:2)

Every time we recite the Apostles' Creed we say, "I believe in . . . the forgiveness of sins." But do we? Really? Most everyone thinks there are some sins that couldn't and shouldn't be forgiven (Human trafficking? Sexual abuse of children?). The idea that all sins can be forgiven is actually scandalous.

The scribes who witnessed Jesus' healing of the paralytic were certainly scandalized. When Jesus told the man his sins were forgiven, they thought, "This is blasphemous! Only God can forgive sins." And they were absolutely right. If you told me that you had committed some sin against your neighbor, and I said to you, "I forgive you," the proper response would be, "Huh? Who do you think you are?" It looks here like Jesus thinks he's God.

He asks a question: "Which is easier, to say, 'Your sins are forgiven,' or to say, 'Rise and walk'?" (v. 5). It's easier to say "You're forgiven" because there's no way of proving whether or not it's true. But which of those things would be harder to do? In fact, it's much easier to heal paralysis than it is to forgive sin. Jesus could heal the man just by telling him to get up. But to be able to forgive his sins Jesus would have to die on a cross.

Jesus really does have the authority to forgive, an authority he earned by paying sin's penalty. The crippled man in Capernaum received a miraculous gift that day. He also got back the use of his legs.

PRAYER: Jesus, all authority belongs to you.
Thank you for forgiving my sins.

Series: *Jesus' Public Ministry*

READ: Matthew 9:9-13

Follow Me

*As Jesus passed on from there . . . he saw a man
called Matthew sitting at the tax booth. (Matthew 9:9)*

The only thing Matthew tells us about himself is his occupation, but that says it all. Matthew was a tax collector. The Romans farmed out the tax collection to locals who would bid for the privilege of raising money from a particular district. What the Romans cared about was receiving their cut. How much the local tax collectors actually raked in and what methods they employed to collect it were of little concern to them. You can imagine the results. Tax collectors were a combination of mob extortionist and Nazi collaborator.

Jesus must have known Matthew well, since his place of business was just outside Capernaum (Matt. 9:1). Jesus would have passed by that tax booth often in the years that he lived there. If so, Matthew had regularly put the squeeze on Jesus—and his widowed mother and family—to extract money they could not well afford to pay.

But now Jesus invites Matthew to become one of his disciples. "Follow me," he says. It's exactly the way Jesus had called Peter, James, and John as they sat mending their nets. No matter who or what or where we are, Jesus' call to us is the same. It is at once an invitation and a command. Being a notorious sinner like Matthew does not disqualify us from receiving the invitation; being a respectable businessman like Peter, James, or John does not excuse us from obeying the command. To each and every one of us Jesus says, "Follow me."

PRAYER: Lord Jesus, I choose to follow you this day.

Series: *Jesus' Public Ministry*

READ: Matthew 9:18-26; Mark 5:21-43

A Dead Girl and a Sick Woman

Little girl . . . arise. (Mark 5:41)

This section of Matthew recounts two intertwined miracles. In both cases Jesus is not contaminated by contact with the unclean (a bleeding woman and a corpse), but instead is the source of healing and life.

Mark describes the scene at Jairus's home in exquisite detail. Jesus approached the dead girl, took her by the hand and said, "*Talitha cumi*," that is, "Little girl . . . arise!" (5:41). Jesus spoke in Aramaic, the people's heart language. When he summoned this child back to life, Jesus called out to her heart. These words must have made a great impression upon the disciples who witnessed them because decades later when Peter came to tell Mark the story, he repeated them verbatim.

But this is more than just a wonderful story. It is a sign pointing to the nature of God's kingdom. It's just not right that we live in a world where children die. Things like sickness and hunger and war and death don't belong here. These horrible things come to us in the wake of humanity's sin, but they cannot finally remain where God is. They were not part of God's original creation; and they won't be part of his kingdom when it comes in its fullness.

So kingdom miracles offer us a glimpse of the shalom of heaven and the world to come. And these signs serve as a preview of coming attractions. Because one day the Lord will take you by the hand, and say, "Child, get up." And you will!

PRAYER: I thank you Lord, for the promise of resurrection and eternal life when you make all things new.

Series: *Jesus' Public Ministry*

READ: Matthew 9:27-34

Two Last Miracles

Never was anything like this seen in Israel. (Matthew 9:33)

Opening the eyes of the two blind men and loosening the tongue of the deaf-mute are the ninth and tenth healing miracles that Matthew records in chapters 8 and 9. Jesus cleansed the lepers, healed the sick, delivered the storm-tossed and the demon-oppressed, restored the paralyzed, made pure the bleeding, raised the dead, and gave sight to the blind and voice to the mute. You would think all this would be cause for rejoicing, and it was. The crowds marveled and said, "Never was anything like this seen in Israel."

But not everyone was happy with Jesus. His enemies, the Pharisees, witnessing the very same things, said this: "He casts out demons by the prince of demons" (v. 34). The contrast could not be sharper: blind eyes recognized him and mute tongues spoke of him, but the religious establishment rejected him as a demon.

Jesus was—and still is—a polarizing figure. When brought face to face with his power, some responded with faith-filled awe. Others rejected Jesus with a sneer, blaspheming rather than believing. The same sort of thing is happening today. There are those who look at Jesus and dismiss him, judging it all to be a fraud. And then there are those who, looking at Jesus, prize him above all else and are willing to give up everything to follow him. The question is, which sort of reaction to Jesus do you have?

PRAYER: Lord, open my eyes to your beauty
and my lips for your praise.

Series: *Jesus' Public Ministry*

READ: Matthew 9:35-38

Therefore, Pray

Therefore pray . . . (Matthew 9:38)

"The harvest is plentiful," said Jesus. There's a tremendous opportunity. But there's also a serious problem: "the laborers are few." So what are we to do? "Therefore *pray*."

I have often wished Jesus had said, "Therefore *give* (especially to Words of Hope!)" I wonder why he didn't say, "Therefore *go*" (though later he would send them out to the ends of the earth). But Jesus started with prayer. What makes prayer so important for accomplishing the mission of God?

First, because prayer reminds us that it actually is his mission, not ours. We can't bring in the harvest, only God can; and only workers called and sent by God will be effective.

Second, because whenever we pray (and mean it) we are also offering ourselves as an answer to our prayers. A 19th-century minister named Bennett Tyler wrote these powerful words on prayer: "When you pray for the poor around you, that they may be warmed and filled, in what way do you expect God will answer your prayers? Will he convert the stones into bread for their sustenance . . . while you . . . have enough and to spare? And in what way do you expect that your prayers for the conversion of the heathen will be answered? Will God rain down Bibles from heaven, and commission his angels to preach to them the gospel? No; but he will put into your hearts to do what lies in your power to send them the gospel."

PRAYER: God, don't help me in my mission, use me for yours.

Series: *Jesus' Public Ministry*

Lent

Lent

The season of Lent is a time for personal reflection and preparation, prior to the celebration of the resurrection of Jesus. The forty days from Ash Wednesday to Easter (Sundays aren't counted as part of Lent) reflect both the forty years when Israel wandered through the wilderness and the forty days Jesus spent there in fasting, praying, and facing temptation.

The tradition of "giving something up for Lent" may be helpful, but the real purpose of fasting is to place priority on our spiritual needs over our physical wants—a reminder that "man does not live by bread alone" (Deut. 8:3, see Matt. 4:4). Lent is also a time to join Jesus on his journey toward the cross. It reaches its climax in Jesus' saving acts: his suffering, death, and resurrection. We will focus on the gospel accounts of Jesus' passion, beginning with what some call the fifth gospel—the gospel according to Isaiah. As we draw closer to the end of Lent, we will focus on the story of Jesus' final day, from Thursday evening in the Upper Room to Friday evening in the garden tomb.

The devotionals this season include many new devotionals written for this book, as well as devotionals drawn from eight series.

* *Faith's Hall of Fame*, published in May 1990, looks at the heroes of faith listed in Hebrews 11.

* *What to Believe*, published in December 1999, defines the robust theological words that capture the vital basic meanings

of Christian faith.

* *Trustworthy Sayings*, published in January 2008, shares "trustworthy sayings" from Paul, things that we can be especially sure of as we face an unknown future.

* *Jesus' Last Day on Earth*, published in April 2009, recounts the events leading up to and culminating in Jesus' death and resurrection.

* *Walking in the Fear of the Lord*, published in April 2011, studies the great Biblical theme of the fear of the Lord, and the healthy balance between grace and judgment, love and fear.

* *Easter*, published in April 2015, looks at the items associated with Jesus' death.

* *What It Means to be Human*, published in January 2017, looks to Jesus as the model for how humans ought to live.

* *Walking in the Way of Wisdom*, published in July 2022, studies Proverbs and the practical teaching it provides in helping us live day-to-day as God intended.

READ: Joel 2:12-13

Return to Me

Return to me with all your heart, with fasting, with weeping, and with mourning. (Joel 2:12)

Lent begins on Ash Wednesday, the day many Christian churches observe with a special service that includes the marking of worshipers with ashes as a symbol of humility and repentance.

The people of Israel were looking forward to what they called "the day of the LORD." They couldn't wait for it to arrive because they believed that it would bring judgment on their enemies. Not so fast, says the prophet Joel. "Alas for the day! For the day of the LORD is near, and as destruction from the Almighty it comes" (Joel 1:15). When God comes it means judgment for *everyone*.

But while making this clear, Joel also highlights God's alternative. The God of the Israelites is a God of mercy. If there is terror and destruction for the wicked when he comes, there can also be peace and security for those who repent and turn to him. "'Yet even now,' says the LORD" (2:12)—those words are an invitation. They remind us that it is still not too late to repent, to turn back to God. Biblical repentance means changing our minds about what's true, changing our hearts about the things we value, changing our actions to please God. The great message of the Bible is not inescapable doom; it's about how to be saved.

There's another great verse in the book of Joel: "Everyone who calls on the name of the LORD shall be saved" (Joel 2:32). The apostle Paul quoted that verse in Romans 10:13 to explain how the gospel works. The name of the Lord revealed in the Gospels is "Jesus," and he really does save everyone who calls upon him in faith.

PRAYER: Lord, I return to you in repentance and faith.

READ: Luke 4:1-13

Temptation

Jesus . . . was led by the Spirit in the wilderness for forty days, being tempted by the devil. (Luke 4:1-2)

Temptation—what does the word suggest to you? Does it call to mind the pangs you feel when a box of chocolates is passed around? Does it describe your struggle with spending too much on your favorite shopping website? Those are everyday temptations, but the serious kind is far more dangerous. When Satan tempts, he's not trying to spoil your diet or throw off your budget; he's playing for keeps—for *you*.

Nowhere is this more evident than in the gospel account of Jesus' temptation in the wilderness. The devil's aim was to separate Jesus from his Father and destroy the gospel before it even got started. To do that Satan employed the three most basic weapons in his arsenal: appetite, ambition, and approval. He suggested that Jesus use his power to satisfy his own hunger. Then he promised Jesus the world, literally. In fact, the day would come when Jesus would be able to say, "All authority in heaven and on earth has been given to me" (Matt. 28:18). But Satan suggested that Jesus take these things right away, the easy way. No suffering, no cross, no death—essentially, "just worship me and I'll give it all to you." It's a lie, of course. But sadly, many don't realize that until it's too late. The final temptation is to make God come through for you. How can you be sure that God is caring for you, or that he's even real? Don't take it on faith; ask for—no, demand—a miracle.

Unlike the first Adam, the last Adam saw through the lies and defeated the tempter. Not for the last time.

PRAYER: I praise you, Jesus, for your perfect obedience.

Series: *What It Means to be Human*

READ: Matthew 4:1-11

The Mouth of God

Man shall not live by bread alone, but by every word that comes from the mouth of God. (Matthew 4:4)

It's often been observed that the way Jesus defeated Satan's temptations was by means of Scripture. Three times the devil tempted him to doubt God's word and take what he wanted for himself. Unlike Adam and Eve, Jesus didn't do that, he didn't fail the test. Instead, he quoted that word—three texts from the book of Deuteronomy—back at his tempter. Satan was stymied, and left Jesus alone. For a while (see Luke 4:13).

But here's something you might not have noticed. Did you catch what Jesus said here about the Bible? He called it "the mouth of God." "Every word" comes from the mouth of God. When Old Testament prophets (and later New Testament apostles) produced the writings which eventually became our Bible, they were not just jotting down their own ideas. They were recording God's word in written form. "Prophecy never had its origin in the human will, but prophets, though human, spoke from God as they were carried along by the Holy Spirit" (2 Peter 1:21 NIV). Though as humans what they wrote, naturally, was human words, nevertheless supernaturally they were speaking "from God."

The words of Scripture come from the mouth of God. Do you remember what little Samuel said when he heard a voice addressing him in the night? "Speak, Lord, for your servant hears" (1 Sam. 3:9). There's no question God is speaking to us today. The question is, am I listening?

PRAYER: Lord, when you speak to me in your Word today, help me to listen.

Series: *Faith's Hall of Fame*

READ: Matthew 4:12-17, Luke 15:11-24

Repentance

Repent, for the kingdom of heaven is at hand. (Matthew 4:17)

Jesus' public ministry began where John the Baptist's left off: with a call for people to repent. The Greek word for repentance is *metanoia*, which literally means to change your mind. Repentance is closely linked with conversion, which literally means to turn around. So Jesus begins by urging us to stop and think. Are my values in line with the kingdom's? Is God first in my life? Maybe I need to rethink some of my basic assumptions about God and myself. Lent is a good time to do that.

It's also the season when we should check our spiritual compass. Which way am I headed? Am I facing towards God, aiming my life in his direction, or moving away from him? Do I need to turn around? The classic story of conversion in the Bible is Jesus' parable of the prodigal son. You remember him, don't you? He's the guy who dissed his father, grabbed his share of the family fortune, and went off to live it up. But one day he woke up in misery and knew he needed to at least try to head back home.

Here's the thing, though: this is not a one-time deal. If you are at all like me, you need to be converted again and again. Because the prodigal in us doesn't go away. We're constantly wandering off into a "far country" (v. 13), places that are a long way away from our heavenly Father. And he is constantly waiting for us to come to our senses and return: "He is patient with you, not wanting anyone to perish, but everyone to come to repentance" (2 Peter 3:9 NIV).

PRAYER: Father, when I wander, prompt me to return.

READ: 1 Timothy 4:6-10

In Training

Train yourself for godliness. (1 Timothy 4:7)

Kids like to imitate superstar athletes, the way they dress, how they talk, the moves they make on the court or the field. That's why the superstars get paid so much for endorsing shoes.

But that's really missing the point. What kids should imitate, if they want to compete well at their level, is the discipline of elite athletes. It's their commitment to training for strength and skill development that ought to be copied. We stand in awe of the grace and power of a Michael Jordan or Tiger Woods. But what we don't see is the years of hard work—endlessly repeated drills, countless shots, unrelenting sessions of tough conditioning. We don't see the discipline, the drive, the determination to be the very best.

That's exactly the approach Paul tells us to take to our spiritual lives. The spiritual disciplines are neither complicated nor glamorous: fasting and prayer, Bible study, and worship; plus, giving, service, and obedience. Yet these are the exercises we must continually practice, day in and day out, until we achieve the goal of spiritual fitness—of a godly life.

And here's why, says the apostle. All our physical training can only postpone the inevitable: the decline of our strength and death of our bodies. But godliness is good for us not just in this life, but in the next as well. Spiritual training has benefits that are literally out of this world. Like diet and exercise, the spiritual disciplines ought to be our daily practice. Lent is a good time to begin if you haven't already.

PRAYER: Lord, help me to train for godliness.

Series: *Trustworthy Sayings*

READ: Philippians 2:12-13

Working Out Our Salvation

Be holy, because I am holy. (1 Peter 1:16 NIV)

Martin Luther described the dynamics of the Christian life this way: "This life is not health but healing; not being but becoming; not rest but exercise. We are not yet what we shall be, but we are growing towards it . . . This is not the end, but it is the road." The 18th-century writer John Newton put that idea more memorably: "I'm not what I ought to be, I'm not what I'm going to be, but thank God I'm not what I used to be!"

Christians have been saved in the sense that our sins are forgiven because Christ has paid their penalty. Being credited with Christ's righteousness is what makes us acceptable to God. The theological word for this is *justification*. But that's not the end of the Christian life, it's just the beginning. God does not intend simply to credit Christ's righteousness to us. He wants us to actually become righteous, to do right in our thoughts, words, and actions; in other words, to become more like Jesus. The word for this is *sanctification*.

Sanctification involves moral effort on our part: fighting against sin, practicing obedience to God's Law. It means work! Paul urges us to "work out" our salvation (v. 12), to begin to grow into the new life we have received through God's gracious mercy. Sanctification takes patience. We will never be completely free of sin until we die and experience the fulness of salvation in heaven. In the meantime, though we often falter and fail, God is constantly at work within us, helping us to both want and do his will (v. 13).

PRAYER: Father, help me to become more and more like Jesus every day.

Series: *What to Believe*

READ: Romans 6:1-11

Dying with Christ, Living with Christ

If we have died with him, we will also live with him; if we endure, we will also reign with him. (2 Timothy 2:11-12)

If you are a Christian, then you will be familiar with talk about Jesus' death on the cross. Christ died for us, for our sins. But there is another way to think about Christ's death. It's also true that we died with him. "I have been crucified with Christ" (Gal. 2:20). "You have died, and your life is hidden with Christ in God" (Col. 3:3). This is a dramatic way of describing the difference between life before Christ and after Christ. It's like dying and being buried, and then being raised from the dead into new life.

Two things follow from this. The first is that we must live into the new life, not the old one. "So you also must consider yourselves dead to sin and alive to God in Christ Jesus" (Rom. 6:11). The second is that this new life is forever. Death is not the end for those who have put their faith in Jesus, it's just the beginning.

Paul tells Timothy this saying is trustworthy. You can take it to the bank. However, it is also conditional: *if* we have died with Christ, we will live with him; and *if* we endure, we will also reign with him. To die with Christ means to identify with him in his death and resurrection and to mortify—put to death—the sin that remains in us. To endure means to keep doing that to the very end. The promise of life isn't to those who start the Christian race, but to those who finish it.

PRAYER: Lord, help me finish the race of faith.

Series: *Trustworthy Sayings*

READ: Job 28

Where Is Wisdom Found?

Behold, the fear of the Lord, that is wisdom. (Job 28:28)

Job 28 offers a wonderful glimpse of ancient technology. You can almost see and hear the miners as they dig shafts and carve out tunnels with primitive picks and shovels in their quest for gold and gems. But where does wisdom come from, the writer asks (v. 20)? People still search desperately for wealth today; wisdom, not so much.

"God understands the way to it" (v. 23), and he tells us. Wisdom is found in "the fear of the Lord" (v. 28). To fear God is to put yourself in the posture that is appropriate for a sinful, finite creature with respect to the infinitely holy Creator.

Ours is a therapeutic age. We place a high value on feelings, especially personal feelings of comfort, happiness, and peace. We're not so keen on fear. Of course, it's natural to prefer being happy to being afraid. But sometimes fear is healthy—when you're hiking in the woods and meet a bear, for example. The fear of the Lord is another type of healthy fear. "The fear of the LORD is the beginning of wisdom" (Prov. 9:10). If you're setting off on a search for true wisdom, this is where to start.

Adopting the right attitude toward the Creator is a smart thing to do. It means you are living "with the grain" of ultimate reality. Disrespecting God is like running your hand the wrong way across a piece of rough lumber; it doesn't hurt him, but it will hurt you. As Jesus said to Saul on the Damascus Road, "It is hard for you to kick against the goads" (Acts 9:5 NKJV).

Hard, and also not smart.

PRAYER: God, help me find true wisdom.

Series: *Walking in the Fear of the Lord, Walking in the Way of Wisdom*

READ: Proverbs 1:1-7

Walking in the Fear of the Lord

Walking in the fear of the Lord and in the comfort
of the Holy Spirit, [the church] multiplied. (Acts 9:31)

The Bible says a lot about the fear of the Lord, but what exactly does that mean? Preachers usually explain it as feeling awe for God, adding that it doesn't mean we should be afraid of him. Really? Aren't you just a little bit afraid of God? I know I am (see Heb. 12:18-29).

Bible scholar Alec Motyer defined the fear of the Lord as "a filial dread of offending God" (*The Message of Philippians*). Our fear is *filial*, it's the attitude of a son or daughter. It rests on the confidence that we are God's beloved children. The fear of the Lord is not the fear of a slave cringing before a terrible master or a child shrinking from a raging adult. But it's also "dread of offending." The last thing we should ever do is treat God casually or presume upon his grace. "With you there is forgiveness, that you may be feared," said the psalmist (Ps. 130:4).

Acts 9:31 describes a balanced season in the early church that led to growth. In Lent we're reminded that the Christian life is a journey. To walk you need to balance between two steps: left, right, left, right. Or in Acts' terms: fear, love, fear, love—the fear of the Lord and the comfort of the Holy Spirit. John Henry Newman put it like this: "No one can love God aright without fearing him. Fear is allayed by the love of him, and our love sobered by the fear of him. Fear and love must go together; always fear, always love, to your dying day."

PRAYER: Lord, give me the right balance of fear and love.

Series: *Walking in the Way of Wisdom*

READ: Genesis 20

Men Have Forgotten God

By the fear of the LORD one turns away from evil. (Proverbs 16:6)

We've been thinking about what the fear of the Lord is. Now let's consider what it does: what it does for us, in us, and to us.

The first thing the fear of the Lord does is make us wise, as the Bible repeatedly says (Prov. 9:10). It's the foundation upon which all true wisdom is built. Fear puts us in right relationship with the Creator and therefore in tune with the universe.

A second thing it does is protect everyone from the worst evils that fallen humans are capable of. When Abimelech remonstrated with Abraham for lying about his relationship with Sarah, Abraham replied, "I did it because I thought, 'There is no fear of God at all in this place, and they will kill me because of my wife'" (v. 11). The fear of God (and of the laws he has given us) is what makes human society possible. It is the thing that restrains individuals—or governments—from lying, stealing, or killing; the only thing standing between us and the law of the jungle.

In his acceptance speech for the Templeton Prize, Aleksandr Solzhenitsyn quoted words he had heard spoken by old people in Russia more than 50 years earlier: "Men have forgotten God; that's why all this has happened." The great writer then added, "If I were asked today . . . the main cause of the ruinous Revolution that swallowed up some 60 million of our people, I could not put it more accurately than to repeat: 'Men have forgotten God; that's why all this has happened.'"

Makes you wonder what might happen to us today, doesn't it?

PRAYER: Lord God, have mercy on our land.

Series: *Walking in the Fear of the Lord*

READ: Genesis 22:1-14

The Faith of a Son

*Now I know that you fear God, seeing you have
not withheld your son . . . from me. (Genesis 22:12)*

Genesis 22 offers a story about Abraham that is both more familiar to us and more flattering to the patriarch than the one in Genesis 20. We know, and Abraham did too, that God does not want literal human sacrifice. We also know, as Abraham did not, that God himself would provide his own Son as the ultimate sacrifice, and in just about the same place where Abraham found that ram caught in a thicket. (The mountain where Abraham built his altar was later the site of the Temple in Jerusalem.)

For Abraham, the trial consisted in responding to a clear command from the Lord that seemed to contradict the equally clear promise of the Lord to bless him through Isaac. Yet Abraham obeyed, because he trusted God to provide a way. His obedience also proved another thing: "Now I know that you fear God, seeing you have not withheld your son . . . from me."

Fear prompts us to obey God, not so much because we are afraid he will punish us if we don't but because we take his commandments seriously. Obedience is the basis of our relationship with the Father we love and who loves us. "What does the LORD your God require of you, but to fear the LORD your God, to walk in all his ways, to love him . . . and to keep the commandments . . . of the LORD" (Deut. 10:12-13).

PRAYER: Lord, help me to do what's required.

Series: *Walking in the Fear of the Lord*

READ: John 19:1-11

Fear God, Honor the Emperor

Do not fear those who kill the body but cannot kill the soul. Rather fear him who can destroy both soul and body in hell. (Matthew 10:28)

The Roman governor was incredulous. As he interrogated the prisoner brought before him on a charge of treasonous activity, he could get no response to his questions. Finally, an exasperated Pilate said to Jesus of Nazareth, "Don't you realize I have power either to free you or to crucify you?" (John 19:10 NIV). Jesus calmly responded, "You would have no power over me if it were not given to you from above" (John 19:11 NIV). Jesus could stand fearless in the face of a terrible death because he had complete trust that his heavenly Father was in actual control of the whole situation.

The apostle Peter expressed our Christian duties succinctly: "Fear God. Honor the emperor" (1 Peter 2:17). That is to say, offer appropriate respect to the powers that be, but save your fear for the One who is truly sovereign. Many times, we reverse those commands. We honor God, at least to some extent. But what we truly fear is the emperor: the government or the boss or the trendsetters and opinion makers.

The fear of God liberates us from the fear of man. Jesus stands before Pilate, but who is the prisoner, and who is the free man? He bids his followers to act the same way when our time of trial comes. Don't fear—whatever person or power there may be, they can do no more than kill your body. Fear God!

Augustine got it straight: "Let us fear therefore, that we may not fear."

PRAYER: Father, deliver me from all lesser fears.

Series: *Walking in the Fear of the Lord*

READ: Psalm 34

Fear the Lord, You His Saints

Those who fear him have no lack. (Psalm 34:9)

Some think the fear of the Lord is strictly negative. It just means being careful not to do something to make God angry. But Psalm 34 says that the fear of the Lord is the key to happiness. Do you want to have all good things and to lack for nothing? Do you desire a long life? Well then, "Come, O children, listen to me; I will teach you the fear of the LORD" (v. 11). And that's not all. We're also promised spiritual blessings. Listen to Mary: "His mercy is for those who fear him from generation to generation" (Luke 1:50). Listen to the psalmist: "The steadfast love of the LORD is from everlasting to everlasting on those who fear him" (Ps. 103:17).

What more could you ask for? A rich, long, happy life here; eternal life by the mercy of God hereafter. All for those who fear the Lord.

Of course, it's not quite so simple. Psalm 34 also observes that the Lord is "near to the brokenhearted and saves the crushed in spirit" (v. 18). It talks about the many afflictions of the righteous and their cries for help. It points to the suffering of the perfectly righteous Man: "[God] keeps all his bones; not one of them is broken" (v. 20)—words fulfilled for Jesus, the ultimate God-fearer, on the cross.

So it's not necessarily smooth sailing and peaches and cream for all of us, all the way. But somehow we know that it's still true. As we fear the Lord, our lives—all of them, rich or poor, long or short, painful or trouble-free—are blessed beyond measure.

PRAYER: Lord, may we live in your fear and die in your favor.

Series: *Walking in the Fear of the Lord*

READ: Isaiah 52:13-53:2

The Ugliness of Jesus

He had no beauty or majesty to attract us to him, nothing in his appearance that we should desire him. (Isaiah 53:2 NIV)

Isaiah is sometimes called the fifth gospel. Though written centuries before, the portrait of the suffering servant of God—especially in chapter 53—describes in remarkable detail the actual experience of Jesus. It's almost as though in his passion and death, Christ was following a prewritten script, prepared by the Author of history and published by the pen of the prophet Isaiah.

The first thing the prophet talks about is how unattractive the Messiah would be. His appearance would be astonishing, so marred he scarcely looked human (52:14). There would be no majesty about him, nothing to draw people (53:2). When Isaiah writes about the ugliness of Christ, I don't believe he's talking about his physical appearance. Nor do I believe he means that there would be nothing at all desirable about the servant of the Lord. He's talking about the reception the Messiah would receive.

Quite a few years ago (way more than I like to think), when I was a young and somewhat long-haired college student, I was running through an airport to catch a plane. As I rushed up to the door of the jet bridge, two hard-eyed men grabbed me and "invited" me to accompany them to a small room. Afterwards I asked the security agents why they had decided to search me (innocent, harmless, law-abiding little me, I might have added). "Because you fit the profile," one of them growled.

That was the problem with Jesus; he didn't fit the Messiah's profile.

PRAYER: Lord Jesus, I love you. You are truly beautiful to me.

READ: Acts 8:26-39

The Anonymous Messiah

Who is the prophet talking about? (Acts 8:34 NIV)

When the Messiah would come into the world, says Isaiah, he wouldn't "fit the profile." Nothing in his appearance would make people turn their heads when they saw him and think, "There's somebody special." He wouldn't stand head and shoulders above the crowd like King Saul. He wouldn't chase out the Romans and set up the kingdom of Greater Israel. As far as popular opinion was concerned, the Messiah whom Isaiah describes just would not measure up.

Can you think of someone who does fit Isaiah's profile? Someone judged to be undesirable, who went largely unrecognized? Consider Jesus of Nazareth: born poor, a blue-collar guy, briefly popular, dying as an itinerant preacher who didn't even have a bed to call his own.

Because Jesus didn't look like or do what the Messiah was supposed to, most people did not acknowledge him when he came. "He came to his own, and his own people did not receive him" (John 1:11). It's true there were a few who, by the grace of God, did recognize him and receive him. But they were mostly people regarded in their day as unimportant, like fishermen and women. It is also true that the crowd followed him for a time, clamoring for his miracles of healing and feeding. But when he started to say things they didn't like, the crowds melted away (see John 6:66).

Jesus still goes unrecognized among us today. Remember what he said about feeding the hungry or visiting the sick and imprisoned? "Whatever you did for one of the least of these . . . you did for me" (Matt. 25:40 NIV). I wonder how many times I might have seen Jesus and not recognized him.

PRAYER: Lord, draw me closer.

READ: Isaiah 53:3

Rejected

He was despised and rejected by men. (Isaiah 53:3)

Of all the pains life can hold, among the bitterest is the pain and hurt of rejection. Some of us have tasted that and the effects still linger. At school it's called bullying. Online it's "unfriending." At work or on a team it's termed, "going in a different direction." To be told that you're not wanted, that you're not good enough, that you don't measure up, those are terrible things to hear. And that's exactly what God experienced when he became a man.

"He was despised and rejected by men," says Isaiah of the Messiah. Those two things go together. To despise someone means to look down on him. We despise those whom we think are beneath us—physically, socially, racially, morally, economically, intellectually. Those whom we despise we also reject because we don't think they are important enough for us to bother with. And this is just what happened to Jesus. Isn't it astonishing that God, when he became a man, so humbled himself, so lowered himself, that most of those who saw him thought *he* was beneath *them*! And because they despised him, they also rejected him.

People still do that today. Some reject Jesus because he's too familiar. They know all the stories, they've heard it all before. Some reject Jesus because he's too particular. The common assumption is that all religions are more or less true, that they're just different paths leading to the same place. But Jesus said, "I am the way" (John 14:6). Some reject him because Jesus is too demanding. "When Jesus calls a man, he bids him come and die," wrote pastor and theologian Dietrich Bonhoeffer. Jesus demands what we hesitate to surrender, which is *everything*. He offers nothing but himself. But what an offer!

PRAYER: Lord, all I want is you.

LENT

DAY 17

READ: John 11:32-43

A Man of Sorrows

. . . a man of sorrows and acquainted with grief. (Isaiah 53:3)

Some people are spared much of the pain and sorrow of life. For them the sun always seems to be shining. They live and love and work and play and laugh, and are scarcely touched by trouble or loss. But Jesus was not one of those. He was one of the others, one of the many whose souls are rubbed raw with suffering.

When the prophet named him centuries before his birth, he called him "a man of sorrows" (Isa. 53:3). He could have called him a man of eloquence, for no one ever spoke like Jesus did. He could have called him a man of love, for love motivated every deed he ever did, every word he ever uttered. He could have called him a man of holiness, for his life was perfect and pure in every way. But he didn't. He called him a man of sorrows . . . "what a name, for the Son of God, who came," as the hymn says.

The ancient stoics valued one quality more than any other. They called it *apatheia*, which literally means "nonfeeling." Their defense against the pain of life was to cultivate apathy, blocking it out by not caring about anything or anyone. Jesus Christ, the God who is also man, embraced sorrow and suffering for our sakes. What sort of sorrow have you known? The man of sorrows is acquainted with that grief. What a comfort it is to know that this is what God is like. It means that whenever sorrow comes to any of us, God not only cares, he knows how it feels.

PRAYER: Thank you Lord, that you know me and care.

READ: 1 Corinthians 12:1-3

Jesus Is Accursed!

Yet we esteemed him stricken, smitten by God. (Isaiah 53:4)

Imagine that you are part of a gathering for worship at a Jewish synagogue in a typical first-century Greek city—let's say Corinth—in AD 50, give or take a year or two. The preacher, Saul of Tarsus, tells the story of Jesus' death on the cross, followed by the still more incredible news of his resurrection from the dead. Then he drives his whole sermon home with a bold declaration. "Jesus is Lord!"

At this a tumult breaks out in the synagogue. Some signify agreement with Paul's message, but many more are shouting him down. "No," they cry, "Jesus is accursed!" Devout Jews saw the crucifixion as a clear sign that he was cursed by God. The Old Testament law stated plainly: "Anyone hung on a tree is under God's curse" (Deut. 21:23 NRSV). The law required that a criminal guilty of a capital offense be executed by stoning. Then the body was fixed to a stake or hung from a tree until sundown to proclaim in the most vivid possible way that both sin and sinner were under divine judgment.

"Christ redeemed us from the curse of the law by becoming a curse for us," explained the apostle Paul (Gal. 3:13). Those who rejected Jesus thought they had it all figured out. Their logic went like this: Jesus hung from a tree, Jesus was cursed, therefore Jesus was a lawbreaker and not the Messiah. Gospel logic is different. It goes like this: Jesus was cursed (for us), therefore *we are blessed*—if we know him, trust him, believe in him. Instead of God's curse, God's blessing. Instead of God's condemnation, God's favor. Instead of God's rejection, God's friendship and life.

PRAYER: Thank you, Lord Jesus, for taking
my place and bearing my curse.

READ: Isaiah 53:4-5

The Suffering Savior

With his wounds we are healed. (Isaiah 53:5)

The Apostles' Creed, the most ancient summary of Christian belief, describes the entire earthly life of Jesus between his birth and death with just one word: he *suffered*.

When the Creed speaks of the suffering of Christ, it is referring above all to his passion—from *passio*, the Latin word for "suffering"—the final torment Jesus endured when he was condemned, tortured, and crucified by the authorities in Jerusalem. This is the suffering to which Isaiah points in the heart of his 53rd chapter. He speaks of the Servant's wounding and the bruising. He writes of the stripes that will be made on his back by the torturer's lash. In these Old Testament verses, we see most clearly a portrait not just of the life but of the death of Jesus of Nazareth.

In his passion, Jesus suffered both physically and psychologically—the beating, the excruciating pain of crucifixion, the desertion by his friends, the mocking of the crowd. But the most important and profound way he suffered was spiritually: "My God, my God, why have you forsaken me?" (Matt. 27:46; Ps. 22:1). When Jesus spoke those words, he was doing more than just giving vent to his feelings or quoting words from the Bible; he was testifying to something that was actually happening. In some mysterious way beyond our understanding, beyond even our imagining, God *had* forsaken him. Jesus was experiencing hell—the absence of God—as the punishment of sin. But it was our sins he was paying for, not his own: "*He* was wounded for *our* transgressions . . . upon *him* was the punishment that made *us* whole" (Isa. 53:5 NRSV). That's the gospel according to Isaiah.

PRAYER: How can I say thanks?

READ: Luke 15:1-7

What's Wrong?

All we like sheep have gone astray. (Isaiah 53:6)

The prayer of confession for the morning service in the Book of Common Prayer teaches us to pray like this: "Almighty and most merciful Father, we have erred and strayed from thy ways like lost sheep, we have followed too much the devices and desires of our own hearts, we have offended against thy holy laws." Sheep have to be herded, otherwise they wander. Sheep will follow their instincts into all sorts of trouble, from which they cannot extricate themselves. The same is true of us. We prefer to follow the devices and desires of our own hearts instead of God's holy and life-giving laws.

Like the gospel throughout the Bible, the gospel according to Isaiah has bad news for us as well as good news. You can't really understand the good news until you have reckoned with the bad. The bad news in Isaiah 53 is that we have all gone astray. We've become hopelessly entangled in thickets of sin. We've fallen and we can't get up. We're helpless, and we need someone to rescue us. We're lost, and we need a Savior who will go out and search for us until he finds us.

The good news is that he has done exactly that. More than that, he's carrying us back home. We have a shepherd, in fact a Good Shepherd, who lays down his life for the sheep. If we hear his voice and follow him (John 10:14-16), all will be well. And though Isaiah didn't know his name, we do!

PRAYER: Thank you, Lord Jesus, for your seeking, saving love.

Series: *What to Believe*

READ: Isaiah 53:5-8

The Heart of the Gospel

The LORD has laid on him the iniquity of us all. (Isaiah 53:6)

What is the central message of the Christian faith? The apostle Paul summarized his preaching and teaching ministry as "the word of the cross" (1 Cor. 1:18). Later in that same epistle he says the message of the gospel is "that Christ died for our sins in accordance with the Scriptures" (1 Cor. 15:3). Many things are important to the Christian faith, but only one is central—the message of the cross, the purpose and meaning of the death of Jesus Christ.

The Bible offers several reasons for Christ's death. On one level, Jesus' death provides an example of how believers should endure suffering (1 Peter 2:21). It demonstrates the love of God (Rom. 5:8). The death of Christ also reminds us that God himself knows what it's like to suffer and die. "I could never myself believe in God if it were not for the cross," admits pastor John Stott. "In the real world of pain, how could one worship a God who was immune to it?" (*The Cross of Christ*). And the cross is where God defeated the forces of evil (see Col. 2:14-15).

But as with the gospel, so with the cross; many things are important, one is central. "The LORD has laid on him the iniquity of us all" (Isa. 53:6). On the cross, God provided a substitute to take our place and bear our sin. The substitute is Jesus Christ, the sinless one, whose perfect sacrifice satisfies the law's just demand. We have strayed, he has paid.

That's the heart of the gospel. Do you hold it in your heart?

PRAYER: Thank you, Jesus, for doing what I never could.

READ: Mark 14:55-64, Matthew 27:11-14, John 19:10-11

Majestic Silence

*Like a sheep that before its shearers is silent,
so he opened not his mouth. (Isaiah 53:7)*

If you read the account of Jesus' different trials, you see that his silence as he faced his judges was not absolute. He did open his mouth to say some things. When he was sworn under oath to acknowledge whether he was the Christ, the Son of God, he said that he was. When Pilate asked him if he was the king of the Jews, he replied quietly in the affirmative, but added that he was not the sort of king Pilate imagined ("My kingdom is not of this world"; John 18:36). Christ's silence was not that he didn't say anything; it was that he refused to say some things.

First, Jesus would not speak to defend himself. When Pilate saw how things stood, and the crowd was screaming for Jesus' blood, he tried to wash his hands of the whole unjust business. Yet Jesus himself did not protest. He made no reply to his accusers, no self-justifying speech, no appeal for mercy, no complaint against the grossly unfair proceedings. Instead, he maintained a majestic silence. Like a lamb led to the slaughter, he opened not his mouth—except that a lamb is silent because it doesn't know what is coming. Jesus knew very well what was going to happen, and he accepted it as God's will.

Second, Jesus refused to speak against his enemies. Instead of lashing out, he trusted God to vindicate him. And we should do the same, counsels Peter (1 Peter 2:22-23). Our silence in the face of undeserved suffering testifies to our faith in God's goodness and ultimate justice.

PRAYER: Lord, help me to know when to speak,
what to say, and when to keep silent.

READ: Matthew 27:57-60, Isaiah 53:8-9

The End of the Story?

They made his grave with the wicked and with a rich man in his death. (Isaiah 53:9)

The classic depiction of the scene of Jesus' burial is a 14th-century fresco by the Italian artist Giotto. Jesus' body, cold and pale, is being lowered from the cross and wrapped in its shroud. Jesus' mother is looking on, overcome with grief. The other women and John are also observing, their faces etched with anguish at this end of all their hopes and dreams. And the angels above are weeping.

Several things about Jesus' burial are quite unusual. Perhaps most surprising is that it happened at all. Victims of crucifixion were generally not given burial. Once the victim died—that sometimes took several days—the Romans liked to leave the body hanging on its cross a while longer, as a graphic warning to all passersby of what happens to those who defy Roman power. But Jesus died just before the Sabbath of Passover week, so leaving his body would not only have been unsightly; it would have been ceremonially defiling.

Another surprising thing about Jesus' burial is that it was done reverently and lovingly. The two criminals' bodies were undoubtedly thrown into a common and anonymous grave, but with Jesus' body a different disposition was made. It was just as Isaiah had prophesied. Though Jesus would die with the wicked, he would be buried with the rich.

Yes, Jesus really died. He really was buried. But that's not the end of the story.

PRAYER: Lord Jesus, help me consider myself dead to sin and alive to you this day. (Romans 6:3-4)

READ: Isaiah 53:10-12

Satisfaction

After he has suffered, he will see the light of life
and be satisfied. (Isaiah 53:11 NIV)

Of all the amazing details in Isaiah's prophecy about the servant of the Lord, perhaps the most remarkable is this: after his suffering and death, he will "see the light of life". This is what makes the servant more than simply a martyr. A martyr is someone who dies for a cause. But a martyr can take only a momentary satisfaction in the nobility of his act. After that, the martyr is dead and that's the end of it. The Lord's servant is different. He passes from life to death and then to life again.

And then, says the prophet, the servant will be satisfied. What ultimately satisfies Jesus, though, is something more than just being raised to life, more even than being personally vindicated through his resurrection. Jesus finds his ultimate satisfaction in the glory of God, when "every knee should bow . . . and every tongue confess that Jesus Christ is Lord, to the glory of God the Father" (Phil. 2:10-11).

Do you know the only thing that will ultimately satisfy you? It won't be getting everything in life you dream of. It won't even be going to heaven someday, although that's part of it. Because you and I are creatures of God, made by him, like him, and for him, we can be satisfied ourselves only when he is fully satisfied, when God's purposes and plans have at last all been accomplished. Nothing less than the glory of God— witnessing it, contributing to it, enjoying it—can finally satisfy us.

PRAYER: "As for me, I shall behold your face in righteousness; when I awake, I shall be satisfied with your likeness." (Psalm 17:15)

READ: Matthew 20:17-28

Assigned Seats

Jesus answered, "You do not know what
you are asking." (Matthew 20:22)

Be careful what you ask for; you might get it! Jesus' disciples, though, still don't "get it." For the third time Jesus warns them about his impending suffering and death, but they aren't really listening. After all, he's the Messiah, heading toward Jerusalem. What else could Jesus be going there for, except to take his throne?

The mother of James and John, with her sons close behind, approaches Jesus and asks him to promise them the two thrones on either side of his. There is some evidence in the Gospels that this woman was Jesus' aunt, Mary's sister—which perhaps makes her audacity a little more understandable.

Jesus rebuffs the mother and in essence says: "You don't know what you're asking." She doesn't get it. Then he puts a question to the brothers: "Can you drink the cup I'm going to drink?" "Sure," James and John chirp. They *really* don't get it. "Well, you will someday," Jesus says rather grimly, "but those thrones you're asking for are reserved for those whom God has chosen." Notice, Jesus does not deny that he will reign in glory, or that his faithful disciples will reign with him. He simply tells us that heaven's thrones are assigned seats.

Before we worry about which seat is ours, we must drink the cup of suffering for his sake, just as he would drink the cup of wrath for ours. The cross comes before the crown. Do we get that?

PRAYER: Thank you, Lord, that though suffering
is real, heaven is also real.

Series: *Jesus' Last Day on Earth*

READ: Mark 15:21-32, Hebrews 13:10-15

Outside the Camp

Let us go to him outside the camp and bear
the reproach he endured. (Hebrews 13:13)

The events of the last week of Jesus' earthly life occupy 36 percent of Mark's gospel. In a sense, everything else in the story of Jesus has been preparing for and building up to this. The substance of the good news is what took place, not in Bethlehem where Jesus was born or in Galilee where many of his miracles were performed or in the temple courts where he taught, but on Golgotha where he died.

The word is Aramaic for "The Place of the Skull." The Latin Bible translated *Golgotha* as *Calvariae locus*, which is how we got the more familiar term *Calvary* for the hill where Jesus was crucified. Tradition has it that this was a skull-shaped hill just outside the city walls of Jerusalem. The Romans crucified their victims in public places for maximum deterrent effect. The horrible act itself—a fiendishly cruel procedure that managed to combine maximum pain with public shame—is recorded by Mark with dramatic restraint. Just four words in verse 24: "And they crucified him."

Hebrews draws an interesting lesson from Golgotha's location, just outside the city walls. The writer reminds his Jewish-Christian readers of the directions in Leviticus for the disposal of sacrificed animals. Their remains had to be burned outside of the camp. Then he points out that Jesus, the ultimate sacrifice, died outside the city. So let's join him there, he urges, even though it costs us. Let's be willing for Jesus' sake to be "outside the camp." Let's embrace him, even if it costs us exclusion from what C. S. Lewis called "The Inner Ring."

PRAYER: I want to identify with you, Lord, whatever the cost.

READ: Exodus 25:10-22

The Mercy Seat

God put forward [Jesus Christ] as a propitiation
by his blood, to be received by faith. (Romans 3:25)

Exodus 25 describes the elaborate instructions God gave to Moses for the furnishings of the Tabernacle in the wilderness. The central feature of the tabernacle was the inner shrine, the Holy of Holies, and the central object in this most holy place was the ark of the covenant. But the ark itself had a central feature: its cover or lid. On it were the cherubim, above which the very presence of God dwelt.

The Hebrew root word for lid is *kapar*. It means a literal cover, or figuratively it means to atone for or "cover" sin, as on Yom Kippur, the Day of Atonement, when the high priest would enter the Holy of Holies and sprinkle sacrificial blood on the lid of the ark. When the Hebrew Bible was translated into Greek, the word they used for the cover of the ark was *hilastērion*. When Martin Luther translated the Bible into German and came to Exodus 25, he translated *kapar/hilastērion* as *Gnadenstuhl*—"throne of grace." William Tyndale rendered this in his English Bible as *merciseate*, thus coining our beautiful term *mercy seat* for the place where payment for sin meets pardon for sinners.

So why the language lesson? For one reason. In Romans 3:25, Paul says that God put Jesus forward as a "propitiation" (ESV, KJV) or "sacrifice of atonement" (NIV, NRSV) to be received by faith. Translators struggle over how to render the phrase. But what Paul wrote is that God put Jesus forward as a *hilastērion*. That Mercy Seat? It's Jesus!

PRAYER: "Because the sinless Savior died, my sinful soul is counted free; for God the Just is satisfied to look on him and pardon me."
(*Before the Throne of God Above*)

READ: John 19:1-3

The Crown of Thorns

Hail, King of the Jews! (John 19:3)

Pilate's soldiers decided to make fun of Jesus before carrying out his execution. Pleasure before business, you see. So somebody stuck a clump of sharp thorns on his head, as a sort of crown, and to suggest an emperor's royal robe they draped a piece of purple cloth over his bleeding shoulders and back. Then they shouted in mock homage: "Hail, King of the Jews." Very funny.

Apparently these men had gotten wind of the charge against Jesus. They didn't know quite what it was all about—something to do with Jesus claiming to be a king or have a kingdom. The particulars didn't really matter. The soldiers got enough of it to form the basis of their joke. It was, sadly, typical of us: the laughter of a gang against a defenseless victim. Sort of makes you want to pause when you might be tempted to mock or bully someone, doesn't it?

Later, many in the crowd of onlookers at Golgotha joined in the fun, heaping scorn upon the figure on the cross. "Come down from the cross, Mr. Messiah, and we'll believe in you!" Jesus not only endured a hideous death, but people even laughed at him while he died, taking pleasure in what they took to be his comeuppance. But they all spoke truer than they knew. Jesus was the King. He could have come down. But he didn't. Why? Jesus "endured the cross, despising the shame," says the writer to the Hebrews, "for the joy that was set before him" (Heb. 12:2)—the joy that would come from saving us.

Can we ever thank him enough?

PRAYER: Thank you, Lord Jesus, for all you endured for me.

Series: *Easter*

READ: John 19:23-24

Well-Dressed

They have washed their robes . . . in the blood of the Lamb.
(Revelation 7:14)

Crucifixion was nasty work; the members of the execution squad were awarded the possessions of the victim as payment. In the case of Jesus, there wasn't much, only his clothes; so the soldiers parceled them out into four shares. Then they came to the last item. John describes it as a seamless garment, woven in one piece from top to bottom. Not wanting to spoil it, the soldiers decided to toss for it. John says that, like everything else about Jesus' death, this too was done in fulfillment of Scripture—specifically Psalm 22:18.

But those soldiers! The Son of God is dying right over their heads, and all the soldiers do is paw over the goods. Every possible human reaction to Jesus is on display at Golgotha. Some mock him, some worship him, most don't think about him at all. So absorbed in life's business and amusements, they simply don't pay any attention to the cross.

Think about that seamless shirt of Jesus. I wonder what the lucky guy who got it did with it. What if he wore it himself? In spiritual terms, that is exactly what we do when we put our trust in Jesus. Christ's blood covers our sin. His perfect life "clothes" us with righteousness like a bright new garment. The vast host of the redeemed John sees in Revelation 7 differ in most ways—nationality, race, language—but they're all dressed the same, in robes washed white in the blood of the Lamb.

PRAYER: "Jesus, thy blood and righteousness my beauty are,
my glorious dress; 'midst flaming worlds, in these arrayed,
with joy shall I lift up my head." (*Jesus, Thy Blood and Righteousness*)

Series: *Easter*

READ: Matthew 26:36-56

In the Garden

My Father, if it be possible, let this cup
pass from me. (Matthew 26:39)

Luke says that after the temptation of Jesus in the wilderness, the devil left him "until an opportune time" (Luke 4:13). Well, here it is. And just as it was earlier, the temptation is for Jesus to avoid the cross. So he struggles in the garden. (Come to think of it, didn't the very first temptation also happen in a garden?) There's Jesus, praying, sweating, crying out to be delivered from the terrible prospect before him. Jesus was human. When faced with death, he looked for a way out. When the dark hours of suffering descended, he asked his friends to watch with him. And when they failed him, he was disappointed.

But it wasn't just the physical or emotional pain that troubled Jesus. What weighed so upon him was something he called "this cup" (Matthew 26:39), God's holy judgment upon sin. For Jesus, accepting the cup meant experiencing the dreadful curse of separation from his Father.

Jesus neither deserved nor desired that. Humanly, he hoped there could be some other way: "My Father, if it be possible . . ." Don't you think that if he could, God would have granted that prayer? But some things are not possible—even for God. It was not possible for God to forgive sins in any other way than for Jesus to accept sin's punishment upon himself. And if it was not possible for Jesus to save us in any other way than by dying in our place, do you suppose it is possible for you and me to be saved in any other way than by trusting in him?

PRAYER: Father, teach me to pray, "Not my will, but yours be done."

Series: *Jesus' Last Day on Earth*

READ: John 13:1-17, 34

Foot Washing

Then he poured water into a basin and began
to wash the disciples' feet. (John 13:5)

Maundy Thursday, the day before Good Friday, gets its name from the
Latin word *mandatum*, "command," because of the "new commandment"
Jesus gave his disciples in the Upper Room: "that you love one another:
just as I have loved you" (v. 34). Then he offered an illustration of what
he meant.

Apparently there was no servant that evening to wash everyone's
feet—a common act of hospitality offered to guests before a meal. Perhaps
the disciples wondered whether one of them ought to volunteer to do it.
But no one offered—foot washing was a slave's job, too demeaning for the
inner circle of disciples to even consider. How then must they have felt
when they saw Jesus get up and take the towel and wash basin himself?
He, the Master, would serve them and do the slave's work. Philippians
2:8 sums up Jesus' entire life with one phrase: "he humbled himself."

Do we really need it spelled out to us? If our Lord would do this,
then no act of service to others is "beneath" us. Did you notice that a
commissioning statement is included here? In the Great Commission
in Matthew 28, Jesus commands us to make disciples, baptizing them in
God's name and teaching them all that Jesus commanded his disciples.
In the Humble Commission in John 13, Jesus commands us to follow his
example and "do just as I have done to you" (v. 15).

PRAYER: Now that I know these things, Lord Jesus,
thank you that I am blessed if I do them!

Series: *Jesus' Last Day on Earth*

READ: Luke 22:7-23

The Upper Room

*He took bread, and when he had given thanks,
he broke it and gave it to them. (Luke 22:19)*

The single most momentous and dramatic act of Christian worship was instituted on a Thursday evening, in an upper room in a house in Jerusalem, where Jesus celebrated the Passover with his disciples.

While they were still reclining at the table after the meal, Jesus created a new meal to symbolize the new covenant of grace he would make with his disciples. What Jesus did was deliberate and deeply symbolic. He took bread, gave thanks for it, broke it, and gave it to his disciples, saying, "This is my body, which is given for you" (v. 19). When he broke the bread Jesus wasn't just making sure everyone got a piece. He was showing that his body had to be broken and his blood shed on the cross, so that he could offer forgiveness and life to all who receive him.

The best place to do that—to receive Christ—is at the Lord's Table. There we have communion with him. "The bread that we break," Paul wrote, "is it not a participation in the body of Christ?" (1 Cor. 10:16). In the supper we physically experience what occurs spiritually when we trust in Christ: we receive him; he becomes part of us, and we of him. This doesn't happen just by going through the motions. It happens by faith through the operation of the Spirit, who unites us with the risen Christ. "Faith," wrote John Calvin, "is the mouth and stomach of the soul." "Believe," said Augustine, "and you have eaten."

PRAYER: Thank you, Lord Jesus, that you are to our hungry and thirsty souls the true meat and drink of eternal life.

Series: *Jesus' Last Day on Earth*

READ: 1 Peter 2:20-23

Last Words: An Example

*Christ also suffered for you, leaving you an example,
so that you might follow in his steps. (1 Peter 2:21)*

Luke records that as he was being crucified Jesus prayed, "Father, forgive them, for they know not what they do." (Luke 23:34).

To pray for forgiveness is not unusual in the circumstances. If I were facing death, I know I would pray for forgiveness too—for myself. But Jesus, being sinless, had no need of that. The forgiveness he prayed for is for his killers, "for they know not what they do." But is ignorance really an excuse?

Jesus had lots more to forgive than just the torture. He was betrayed by a close comrade, deserted by his best friends, caught up in the machinations of a jealous hierarchy who hated him for his sheer goodness, mocked and spat upon by the crowds he had taught and fed and healed, tortured by the agents of law and justice, and finally condemned by a crooked judge who admitted he was innocent even as he passed sentence upon him. Jesus prayed that they all might be forgiven.

In many of these devotionals we consider the deep theological meaning of the cross. But it's also important to remember the practical lesson the apostle Peter draws from it. Jesus offers us an example of how we are to behave when we suffer unfair treatment. So ask yourself this: Is there anything anyone has done to me that matches what Jesus endured? And if Jesus forgives his tormentors, what should I do about mine?

PRAYER: Lord Jesus, thank you that the "them"
for whom you prayed includes me.

READ: John 19:25-27

Last Words: The Family of God

Woman, behold, your son! . . . Behold, your mother! (John 19:26-27)

John names a little handful of loyal friends who watched and waited at the cross. There were four women and a man—"the disciple whom [Jesus] loved"—John's indirect way of referring to himself (v. 26). And the first named among the women at the cross was Jesus' own mother, Mary. What must have been going through her mind and heart as she watched her son die!

Jesus took pains, even as he hung from the cross, to see that Mary was provided for. I could easily imagine him saying something like, "I'm sorry, but I can't deal with this. I've got a lot on my plate right now." He could have been excused for focusing on more significant matters. But he thought of Mary and her needs and entrusted her to the care of the beloved disciple. There's more to this, though, than just taking care of family matters. Mary and John and the others represent the new community Jesus is bringing into existence through his death.

Have you ever secretly wished you could belong to another family? Kids sometimes do when they find out that in their friend's family, they don't have to eat vegetables or they receive higher allowances or go on better vacations. Have you ever seen a family that was so warm, so appealing, that you wanted to be part of it? But the family of Jesus is exactly that, and it's open to everyone. "Whoever does the will of God, he is my brother and sister and mother" (Mark 3:35).

Jesus created a new family for humankind at the foot of his cross. It's called the church.

PRAYER: Dear God, I give thanks for my fathers and mothers and sisters and brothers in Christ.

READ: Luke 23:39-43

Last Words: The Dying Thief

Today you will be with me in paradise. (Luke 23:43)

That is the most amazing promise in the whole Bible. It was spoken to one of the criminals who died next to Jesus when he turned and humbly asked, "Jesus, remember me . . ." This man could not have known what was happening before his own eyes for the salvation of the world. But he pleads to be remembered when Jesus comes into his kingdom (v. 42). "This is the King of the Jews" read the sign above Jesus' head (v. 38), but he certainly didn't seem like much of a king hanging there on a Roman gibbet. What prompted the thief to reach out in faith to a king on a cross? We can only wonder at the mystery of God's grace.

To this great plea Jesus makes an even greater promise: salvation, immediate and unconditional. What Jesus said to the thief was not a prediction or a hope, it was a guarantee that coming from anyone else would be preposterously arrogant. But from Jesus' lips it rings true. Remember, he has the authority to make such promises: "I have the keys of Death and Hades" (Rev. 1:18). And he has the integrity to keep them: "Jesus Christ is the same yesterday and today and forever" (Heb. 13:8).

"Today you will be with me in paradise." That's not just a promise, it's a definition. The simplest and best definition of heaven is just those two words: "with me." It was the apostle's desire (Phil. 1:23). It is our ultimate hope, the fulfillment of every wish or dream.

PRAYER: "The dying thief rejoiced to see that fountain in his day; and there may I, though vile as he, wash all my sins away."
(*There Is a Fountain Filled With Blood*)

READ: Mark 15:33-39

Last Words: The God-Forsaken God

My God, my God, why have you forsaken me? (Mark 15:34)

This word from the cross made such a powerful impression that it was recorded in Aramaic, the language Jesus spoke. Matthew and Mark both report only this dreadful, difficult word. It was three in the afternoon. Since noon the horrors of Golgotha had been shrouded in an unearthly darkness, as though creation itself did not want to see what was happening. When Christ was born, the night sky blazed with light; when he died, the noonday sun was darkened. Then out of gloom, an anguished cry was heard: "Eloi, Eloi, lema sabachthani?" (v. 34).

What does this mean? The cry of dereliction can't mean what it seems to, it is often argued. God abandon Jesus? The Father forsake the Son? How could that even happen? But though we can't fully understand them, we must take Jesus' words at face value, as expressing reality. He said what he did because God had really abandoned him.

No one can ever truly understand the cross without coming to grips with the meaning of these words: "My God, my God, why have you forsaken me?" (v. 34). Before he died physically, Christ died spiritually, for us. He suffered ultimate death—the utter desolation of being excluded from the presence of the God of life. The Heidelberg Catechism says that this is what is meant when we confess in the creed that "He descended to hell." There was hell for Jesus so that there would be none for those who believe in him. The liturgy that I have used as a pastor for the Lord's Supper reminds us that he was forsaken "so that we might be accepted of God and never be forsaken of him."

PRAYER: Lord, this is such a deep mystery
to me, but thank you forever.

READ: Psalm 42

Last Words: Thirst for God

I thirst. (John 19:28)

Toward the end of his ordeal, Jesus asked for something to drink. Just a couple of syllables gasped out of a dry throat—"I'm thirsty." Why is this one little detail recorded in Scripture for all eternity? It's easy to see why most of the seven last words from the cross were preserved. They raise big issues or express important ideas. But why was Jesus' thirst noted and remembered? For one thing, it reminds us of all he went through for us. And whenever we suffer from thirst, we can identify with him and offer our pain to him as one who understands.

But there is another kind of thirst: spiritual desire. Jesus thirsts for us, and we thirst for him: "Father, I desire that they also, whom you have given me, may be with me where I am" (John 17:24). "As a deer pants for flowing streams, so pants my soul for you, O God. My soul thirsts for God, for the living God" (Ps. 42:1-2).

Have you ever felt that kind of thirst? Maybe you have, but you didn't know what it was. You thought it was dissatisfaction with your job or relationship problems or money trouble or a midlife crisis. You didn't realize that what you were experiencing was really a hunger for God and a thirst for his life. But that's what it was. And there's only one way to satisfy that thirst. On the chapel walls of each convent of Mother Teresa's Missionaries of Charity, two simple sentences are inscribed. Both are spoken by the Lord Jesus. The first is *I thirst*. And the second: *I quench*.

PRAYER: Lord Jesus, you are all I truly want or need.

READ: John 19:28-30

Last Words: All Done

It is finished. (John 19:30)

"It is finished," Jesus cried. *What* is finished? Jesus wasn't just talking about the ordeal of his suffering. If someone has struggled terribly at the end of life, when death comes at last, we often say with relief, "It's over." When Jesus cried out, "It is finished," he did not mean, "It's over." Jesus isn't talking about his life here. He's talking about his *work*, the task that he came into the world to do. This isn't a cry of relief, it's a cry of accomplishment.

He finished his work by his dying. It was midafternoon at Golgotha when the end came. Jesus spoke his last three words from the cross in rapid succession. He said, "I thirst" (v. 28). And someone gave him a drink of wine. He raised his head and shouted, "It is finished" (v. 30). And then he bowed his head and breathed out his life with a quiet prayer: "Father, into your hands I commit my spirit" (Luke 23:46).

So it was with his death that Jesus actually did what he had come to do, which was to save us. Hebrews explains it like this: "When Christ came . . . he entered once for all into the Holy Place, not with the blood of goats and calves, but with his own blood, thus obtaining eternal redemption . . . He has appeared once for all at the end of the age to remove sin by the sacrifice of himself" (Heb. 9:11-12, 26 NRSV).

I don't fully understand how and why Christ's death atoned for sin. I just know that it has. The sacrifice has been offered—fully, finally, completely, once for all. Atonement—"at-one-ment" between a holy God and sinful people—has been made. It's all done. There's nothing left for us to do, except accept it.

PRAYER: "Jesus paid it all, all to him I owe." (*Jesus Paid It All*)

READ: Luke 23:44-49

Last Words: The Final Word

Father, into your hands I commit my spirit! (Luke 23:46)

The moment Jesus died was an awe-inspiring sight; no one who witnessed it ever forgot it. There were signs and portents all around: an eerie darkness at midday, an earthquake, rocks splitting and dead bodies rising and walking about the city (Matt. 27:51-54). The Gospels describe how the temple curtain that divided the Holy Place from the Holy of Holies was ripped in two "from top to bottom," according to Matthew (v. 51)—an obvious symbol of how the way is now open for everyone to access God directly through Jesus. Even the centurion who commanded the crucifixion squad on Golgotha was impressed, though his exact words are reported somewhat differently by the gospel writers.

But for Jesus the end came quietly, even gently. He breathed out his life in a prayer, with his Father's name on his lips. This final word from the cross is another quotation from the Psalms (31:5), but it makes me think of the prayer I learned as a child:

Now I lay me down to sleep.
I pray the Lord my soul to keep.
If I should die before I wake,
I pray the Lord my soul to take.

Jesus died with the confidence of a little child in his Father, whom he had more than once commended to his disciples as an example of faith. The early Christians spoke of death as "falling asleep" in the Lord (1 Thess. 4:13-14). On top of everything else, Jesus, at the end, shows us how to die.

PRAYER: Father, into your hands I commit my spirit—this day and every day.

READ: Matthew 21:1-11

The Crowd That Acclaimed Him

Blessed is he who comes in the name of the Lord! (Matthew 21:9)

Holy Week begins with Palm Sunday and Jesus' triumphal entry into Jerusalem. Notice three things about this familiar story. First, it was a *deliberate* act. As you read the gospel accounts, you can't help but notice a sense of careful planning. Secondly, it was a *symbolic* act. This was a royal entrance, and all the details would have sent that message to the crowd, especially Zechariah's prophecy (Matt. 21:5; see Zech. 9:9). Thirdly, it was a *public* act. It set the crowd off like a slam dunk. Throughout his ministry, Jesus was always trying to keep the crowds quiet, almost trying to hide his messianic identity. But now that the time has come for his death, it's as though Jesus wants everybody to pay attention.

Now think about the reaction of the crowd. They certainly responded positively and favorably. They acclaimed Jesus, welcoming and cheering him as their king. But I can't help hearing an echo of the cries of the crowd just a few days later. They went from hosannas and blessings on Palm Sunday to "Crucify him, crucify him!" on Good Friday (John 19:6). How could that have happened in less than a week? Well, you know how it is with crowds. People get caught up in the excitement and don't really know what the shouting is about. Makes you want to be careful about running with the crowd, doesn't it?

Of course, many in the crowd *did* know what they were shouting for. They were cheering for the Messiah, the King. But they had the wrong idea. They expected a Pizza Parlor Messiah—you know, "He delivers." When we confess Christ we must accept him on his terms, not ours.

PRAYER: Lord, may I greet you with joy
on your coming triumphal entry.

READ: Matthew 26:20-25

The Man Who Betrayed Him

Is it I, Lord? (Matthew 26:22)

Johann Sebastian Bach's *St Matthew Passion* sets Matthew's text of the passion story to dramatic music. When the soloist singing Jesus' words announces to the disciples that one of them will betray him, an agitated chorus immediately breaks in with the disciples' question, "Lord, is it I?" The choir sings that phrase exactly eleven times, because there was one disciple who didn't have to ask Jesus who the traitor was.

What can Judas teach us? For one thing, he shows us the danger of what John Bunyan described in the character he called Formalist. Formalist is outwardly religious but inwardly unconverted. Formalism is having the appearance of faith without the reality; it's talking the talk without walking the walk.

It is sobering to remember that Judas was one of the Twelve, a member in good standing of Jesus' inner circle. He had all the advantages of his position: he had heard Jesus' teaching, seen his miracles, even served in his mission. Judas was present in the Upper Room, had his feet washed, even participated in the communion meal. To all appearances he was another faithful disciple. When Jesus announced there was a traitor in their midst, no one asked, "Lord, is it Judas?" But all this time Judas's heart was unchanged.

Church attendance, Bible reading, charitable giving, works of service—these are all good things. But if your heart hasn't been changed, none of them matter.

PRAYER: Lord, deliver me from every competing love.
Make me wholehearted in my devotion to you.

Series: *Jesus' Last Day on Earth*

READ: Matthew 26:31-35, 69-75

The Disciple Who Denied Him

And immediately the rooster crowed. (Matthew 26:74)

Many of the people who welcomed Jesus with loud "Hosannas" on Palm Sunday must also have shouted, "Crucify him!" on Good Friday. It's perilously easy to betray or deny Christ; all you have to do is fall in with the crowd.

Having done that in the high priest's courtyard, Peter could have gone on with them in rejecting the Lord, and who knows where that would have ended? But then one small, seemingly random thing happened. He heard a rooster's crow. It wasn't extraordinary, it was utterly ordinary. But this little sound was Peter's wake-up call. His soul was pierced by the memory of Jesus' warning (v. 34), and he went outside and wept bitter tears of repentance.

That rooster's crow was a sound of grace. You know how it goes when we get caught up in sin. We stifle our conscience until it finally falls silent. We become deadened—to guilt, to truth, even to God. But then somewhere, somehow, a rooster crows. Maybe it's in a sermon or through a comment in a friend's conversation or a verse of Scripture or a line from a song or an old memory that suddenly flashes through our mind. Whatever it is, something quickens our conscience again, and we realize what we have done.

If you hear a rooster crow in your life, don't ignore it. Recognize in that moment the Lord's voice, calling you to repent. It could be a very small sound. But through such things souls are saved.

PRAYER: Lord, help me to hear your voice in the small things.

.

Series: *Jesus' Last Day on Earth*

READ: John 18:28-19:16

The Judge Who Condemned Him

So he delivered him over to them to be crucified. (John 19:16)

The Apostles' Creed mentions three names among its 100 or so words. The first, of course, is Jesus; the second is Mary; the third is Pontius Pilate. Pilate would have been totally forgotten, just another minor official from a long-dead empire, except for a trial over which he presided. But that was the trial at which Pilate condemned Jesus to death, and now his name lives in infamy forever. How would you like to be eternally remembered as the man who crucified Christ? It only took one cowardly decision for Pilate.

Pilate didn't want to condemn Jesus. Each of the gospel writers takes pains to record Pilate's verdict: Jesus was not guilty (John 18:38). But like so many successful men, Pilate was in love with the world—with his status, his possessions, and especially his career. Set over against all of that was the fate of this one innocent man, Jesus Christ.

The balance was tipped at the decisive moment when someone in the crowd shouted that if Pilate released Jesus, he would be no friend of Caesar. It just wouldn't do for a bad report from Judea to reach the emperor's ears. So Pilate's choice came down to this: he could either be Jesus' friend or Caesar's. He could have the world or he could have Christ, but not both. Though Pilate would like to have chosen Jesus, he just couldn't bring himself to pay what that would cost him.

What about you? Which will you choose today: the world or Jesus?

PRAYER: You may have all the rest; give me Jesus.

Series: *Jesus' Last Day on Earth*

READ: Luke 23:26-33

The One Who Carried His Cross

They seized one Simon of Cyrene . . .
and laid on him the cross. (Luke 23:26)

There is a street in Jerusalem known as the Via Dolorosa, the "Way of Sorrows." It is the route Christ is believed to have followed when he carried his cross—actually the *patibulum*, or crossbeam—from the judgment hall of Pilate to the place of execution. Weakened by beatings, Jesus wasn't strong enough to make it all the way to Golgotha. So the soldiers grabbed a man to help him—one Simon, from Cyrene in North Africa. The fact that Simon's name is noted in the Gospels, and that Mark even mentions the names of his two sons (Mark 15:21), indicates that he and his family were known in the early church. Simon, who literally took up the cross and followed Jesus, came to know him in a deeper way later on and carried the cross figuratively as well.

We all need to emulate Simon. Jesus said that those who would be his disciples must deny themselves, take up their cross daily, and follow him (Luke 9:23). Carrying your cross does not mean putting up with an unpleasant circumstance or annoying people. In Jesus' day, carrying a cross meant a one-way trip to death. It's his way of calling us to die to self and live for him.

It doesn't cost a lot to become a follower of Jesus; it costs *everything*. But if we are willing to join Jesus on the way of the cross, we discover another gospel paradox. The way of sorrows becomes the way of joy, the road to heaven.

PRAYER: Lord, I say no to self,
take up my cross, and follow you today.

Series: *Jesus' Last Day on Earth*

READ: John 19:17-30

Beneath the Cross of Jesus

*And I, when I am lifted up . . . will draw
all people to myself. (John 12:32)*

"Beneath the cross of Jesus I fain would take my stand" (Elizabeth Cecilia Clephane). The truth is that beneath the cross of Jesus was not a nice place to be. The sights and sounds and smells of that place on that day would have been utterly revolting. None of us would really have wanted to stand beneath it. Most of the people who were there kept their distance.

The earliest visual symbols of the Christian faith were the fish and the Good Shepherd. The cross wasn't used until much later, after the reality of a Roman crucifixion had faded from the public imagination. Eventually the cross became the defining sign of Christianity. In medieval Europe, pilgrims flocked to churches and monasteries that claimed to have a piece of the true cross. And still today crosses are popular as decor and personal jewelry.

For us as Christians, to display or wear a cross is not just a matter of personal taste or aesthetics. It's not about the physical object; it's about its meaning. Paul describes the gospel as "the word of the cross" (1 Cor. 1:18), that is, the message of how Jesus died to save us. Jesus himself said that he would be lifted up as Moses had lifted up the serpent in the wilderness, "that whoever believes in him may have eternal life" (John 3:15). When Jesus was literally lifted up on Good Friday, most of those who saw it made fun of him. But when he is lifted up today—in our preaching, our praises, our prayers—he does draw many to himself, me included.

PRAYER: "Far be it from me to boast except
in the cross of our Lord Jesus Christ." (Galatians 6:14)

READ: John 19:31-42

Dead and Buried

Since the tomb was close at hand, they laid Jesus there. (John 19:42)

On Saturday, Jesus was dead. Christians call this day, the day when life itself stopped and Jesus' body lay in the tomb, Holy Saturday. After Jesus died, he was buried. It's a simple statement that we repeat, perhaps unthinkingly, every time we say the Apostles' Creed. But we should think about it.

Corpses need to be disposed of. What makes death so repulsive is not just the fear or the pain; it's the indignity of the thing. This is why Jesus' burial is so comforting. It means he went all the way through the experience of death for us, to the bitter end. He even became a corpse that had to be prepared and then carried away and buried like every other dead body. His identification with our mortality is complete. "He knows our frame; he remembers that we are dust," affirms the psalmist (Ps. 103:14). And we may be sure of it, because he once was dust himself. If Jesus could do that much for me, I know that he will be with me when I too am one day a corpse.

The prayer of committal in the Reformed Church's funeral liturgy says that "by his rest in the tomb, [Christ] sanctified the graves of the saints." No matter how dark the place, our Lord has been there before us—including the grave. So death is not the end for us. Even burial isn't the end. Because after Saturday comes Sunday.

PRAYER: Thank you, Lord, for all you have done for me.
Be near me now and in the hour of my death.

Easter

Easter

As a friend of mine often says, we live in a world where a resurrection happened. There really was an Easter! The miracle of Christ's resurrection changes everything.

Easter Sunday is a high point of the Christian year, but as Christians our celebrations extend much longer than one day. The season of Easter is an ongoing celebration of Christ's redemptive work in the world. Our focus is on the impact of Christ's death and resurrection—in our own lives, and in the testimony of Jesus's first disciples and the early church. It extends to the cosmic testimony of Revelation.

Easter, or Eastertide, lasts fifty days, including forty days from Easter Sunday to Ascension Day (based on the forty days during which the risen Lord appeared to his disciples, according to Acts 1:3) and ten more days up to Pentecost Sunday.

The devotionals in this season are drawn from five series.

* *Colossians*, published in May 2004, shares one of the last letters from Paul. The letter unveils something of the glory, power and authority of the Lord Jesus.

* *Jesus' Last Day on Earth*, published in April 2009, recounts the events leading up to and culminating in Jesus' death and resurrection.

* *Easter*, published in April 2015, looks at the items associated with Jesus' death.

* *Acts*, published in April 2018, examines the development of the early church and the way it continues to shape the church today.

* *Hearing Jesus*, published in October 2020, explores the first three chapters of the book of Revelation and the vision of Christ in glory and power given to us there.

READ: Matthew 28:1-10

On the Third Day

He is not here, for he has risen, as he said. (Matthew 28:6)

I'm guessing you know the story. Several of the women who were closest to Jesus head out to the garden tomb early Sunday morning to finish the job they had not had time to complete on Friday afternoon. As they reach the grave they see to their astonishment that the stone sealing the tomb has been rolled back. The women are even more startled by the angel's incredible news: "Do not be afraid, for I know that you seek Jesus who was crucified. He is not here" (vv. 5-6).

The angel meant that literally. He wasn't speaking the way we sometimes do in funeral homes. ("Grandpa isn't really here. He's in heaven.") The angel's announcement to the women wasn't referring to Jesus' soul; it was referring to his body.

This Easter announcement has never been contradicted. To the angel's "He is not here," no one has ever been able to respond, "Wait! He is over here. There's his body." Jesus' resurrection was a physical event. The New Testament says as clearly as it can that Jesus rose bodily from the tomb. Skeptics who argue that the gospel accounts of the resurrection are really just a symbolic way of saying that Jesus' influence lived on in his disciples' lives simply haven't got the story straight.

As Christians, we base our faith on the fact that Jesus rose. More than that, we are staking our whole future on it. If we're wrong about this, says the apostle, we're wrong about everything (see 1 Cor. 15:14-19). Not to worry; we live in a world where a resurrection has happened. And because it has, something similar will happen to us one day.

PRAYER: Jesus lives, and so shall I.

Series: *Jesus' Last Day on Earth*

READ: John 20:1-10

Who Moved the Stone?

Who will roll away the stone for us? (Mark 16:3)

More than eighty years ago an English skeptic named Frank Morison set out to explain Jesus' resurrection in non-supernatural terms. His study led him to call that project "the book that refused to be written." The book Morison did actually write, which described how he became convinced that Jesus really did rise from the dead, was called Who Moved the Stone?

We know who moved the stone—God did! Perhaps a more interesting question is why God moved the stone. It can't have been to let Jesus out. His resurrection from the dead wasn't a resuscitation. It didn't look like a movie when they shock someone's heart in the ER and the person suddenly starts to breathe again. In the resurrection Jesus did not simply return to this life; his body was mysteriously changed into the life of the world to come. So Jesus didn't come slowly awake on Easter morning, get up, and walk out of the tomb. Rather, he was totally transformed in a moment, "in the twinkling of an eye" (1 Cor. 15:52). The risen, glorified Lord transcended the laws of time and space. Things like locked doors (John 20:19) or sealed tombs presented no obstacle to him.

So why move the stone? Not to let Jesus out, but to let the witnesses in. As John would later write, "That . . . which we have heard, which we have seen with our eyes, which we looked upon and have touched with our hands . . . we proclaim also to you, so that you too may have fellowship with us" (1 John 1:1-3). They were telling what they saw; you can bank on it.

PRAYER: Alleluia! Christ is risen!

Series: *Easter*

READ: Revelation 1:1-3

Blessed Reading, Blessed Hearing

Blessed is the one who reads . . . this prophecy, and blessed are those who hear, and who keep what is written in it. (Revelation 1:3)

Jesus didn't just rise from the dead; he *is* risen. He's alive right now, and he's still speaking to his disciples. The opening chapters of the book of Revelation both describe the risen Lord Jesus and record his continuing message for his church. Jesus sent an angel to pass this message on to John so that all of us, "his servants" (v. 1), can know it too.

Think of John as he appeared now at the end of the New Testament. At this point he was a very old man; all the other apostles were gone—martyrs for the sake of the gospel. Now we must imagine John's body worn out, his eyesight dimmed, his hearing faded. Physically, John has been used up in the cause of the gospel. But spiritually his senses were as keen as ever. John's symbol in the church was the far-sighted eagle. His spiritual sight penetrated to the highest heaven, his vision extended to the end of time. Don't think of him, though, as some sort of seer or prophet. Think of him as a journalist. John called himself a "martyr" in the original sense of that Greek word—a witness. John wasn't making this stuff up. He simply recorded what the angel showed him, in a book that can be read and heard and obeyed.

This raises a question. What do you think of the Bible? Is it just a product of the religious imagination, or is it a revelation from God, given through human witnesses? Blessed are those who read it as the latter, and who hear and keep it accordingly.

PRAYER: Praise God for his Word.

Series: *Hearing Jesus*

READ: Revelation 1:4-6; Revelation 5

To Him Be Glory Forever

. . . to him be glory and dominion forever and ever. (Revelation 1:6)

In Greek doxology means a "word of glory." Doxologies are brief ascriptions of praise that Christians have used in worship since the very beginning. The salutation of Revelation 1:4-5 is Trinitarian: John offers his readers grace and peace from God the Father, from the sevenfold Holy Spirit, and from Jesus. But the doxology in verses 5 and 6 is directed to Jesus, the one who freed and transformed us. The point is simple: we worship God, and we also worship Jesus.

Here's why, according to John. We worship Jesus because he loves us. John said he *loves* us. Not, "I remember how he used to love us way back when." Jesus may no longer be physically present, but he is still very much alive, and his love for his own continues. We also worship Jesus because he's freed us from our sins by his blood. Jesus' death for us on the cross is the ultimate proof of his love. It's the "sacrifice of atonement" (Rom. 3:25 NIV) that puts us right with God by paying sin's penalty. Though we have not yet been freed from sin's presence in our lives, we have been set free from the guilt of sin.

And we worship Jesus because he's given us a new identity and purpose. Peter put it like this: "you are a chosen people, a royal priesthood, a holy nation, God's special possession, that you may declare the praises of him who called you out of darkness into his wonderful light" (1 Peter 2:9 NIV). In a world where lots of people claim to be spiritual, it's pretty easy to spot the Christians. We're the ones praising Jesus!

PRAYER: Glory to the risen Lord!

Series: *Hearing Jesus*

READ: 1 Corinthians 15:22-28

The Alpha and the Omega

"I am the Alpha and the Omega," says the Lord God. (Revelation 1:8)

Alpha and omega are the first and last letters of the Greek alphabet. I'm it, says God. Everything from A to Z comes from me and belongs to me. I'm the beginning and the end—and everything in between.

Nothing exists apart from God or outside of God. Yet things have gone terribly wrong in God's original creation. Some of God's highest and most glorious creatures have turned against him. Angels have become demons, and seek to destroy everything that's good. Human beings, made in the very image of God, rejected God and brought death into the world. In a passage that could serve as the outline of the book of Revelation, the apostle Paul explained how God would set things right again. "For as in Adam all die, so also in Christ shall all be made alive. But each in his own order: Christ the firstfruits, then at his coming those who belong to Christ. Then comes the end, when he delivers the kingdom to God the Father after destroying every rule and every authority and power . . . The last enemy to be destroyed is death . . . When all things are subjected to him, then the Son himself will also be subjected to him who put all things in subjection under him, that God may be all in all" (1 Cor. 15:22-24, 26, 28).

In the beginning, there was only God. In the end, there will only be God. Plus "those who belong to Christ." The creation will be restored, and God will be all in all.

PRAYER: Alpha and Omega, I look forward
to the time you will be "all in all."

Series: *Hearing Jesus*

READ: Revelation 1:4-9; John 16:25-33

Partners in Tribulation

I, John, your brother and partner in the tribulation and the kingdom
and the patient endurance that are in Jesus . . . (Revelation 1:9)

A key word in the book of Revelation is *thlipsis*, meaning distress,
suffering, tribulation. John knew all about *thlipsis*, and so did the
churches he was writing to; they were partners in it. He was on Patmos,
a small rocky island off the coast of Turkey. He had been exiled there
during the reign of the emperor Domitian (in the AD 90s) because of
his faithful ministry of God's Word and his witness to Jesus. The last of
the twelve apostles, John alone would die of natural causes, but he would
likely die in prison.

There is no false advertising in the New Testament. The gospel
promises are clear and repeated. Faith in Christ leads to long-term
glory, but to short-term trouble. As someone once observed, those
who kneel beneath the cross shouldn't be surprised if they get some
blood on them.

Don't believe the gospel because you think it will make your life
easy and happy. Believe it because it's true. Believe that Jesus really did
come from God to give us eternal life. Believe he really did overcome
the world, even as that world crucified him. Believe that when you suffer
hardship or loss you really will have peace in him. "I have said these
things to you, that in me you may have peace. In the world you will have
tribulation. But take heart; I have overcome the world" (John 16:33). If
we are partners in tribulation, let's also be partners in endurance.

PRAYER: Lord, thank you for your great and precious promises.
Help me to treasure them.

Series: *Hearing Jesus*

READ: Daniel 7:9-10, 13-14; Revelation 1:12-17

What Jesus Looks Like Now

When I saw him, I fell at his feet as though dead. (Revelation 1:17)

What's your mental picture of Jesus? Some might think of a painting that once hung in many a church lounge, a portrait of an olive-skinned Jesus with brown hair and beard and a rather dreamy expression on his face. Or there's another picture I once saw—the laughing Jesus, head thrown back and white teeth flashing from a black beard. Then there are the ethnic portrayals: African Jesus, Asian Jesus, Indian Jesus.

These imaginative efforts are legitimate because Jesus was a real human being who looked like us. In the Orthodox tradition of iconography, it is forbidden to attempt a picture of God the Father. The Father has no body. But to refuse to attempt a picture of Jesus is also forbidden, because it is a denial of the reality of the incarnation.

John's portrait of Jesus, though, is completely different. He was not trying to show what Jesus looked like back then, during his life on earth. He was showing us what Jesus looks like *now*. No painter could ever do this figure justice. No video clip, with images flashing fire and a roaring soundtrack of Niagara Falls, could ever convey the awesome glory of the risen Lord. John's reaction says it best: "When I saw him, I fell at his feet as though dead." Later, John responded in a similar way to an angel, but he was told to get up; even an angel is just a creature (Rev. 22:8-9). Here, however, his prostrate worship of the glorified Jesus is entirely appropriate.

PRAYER: Jesus, I give you the glory that is your due.

Series: *Hearing Jesus*

READ: Revelation 2:1; Matthew 18:18-20

Among the Lampstands

*For where two or three are gathered in my name,
there am I among them.* (Matthew 18:20)

The Lord Jesus dictated seven letters to John for distribution among the churches of Asia Minor. Each letter is addressed to the "angel" of the church. Since *angellos* in Greek means "messenger," it could be that the addressee is the pastor of the church rather than a literal angel. Regardless, the Lord's words are intended for the whole congregation. All seven letters follow the same outline: first, an opening statement where the recipients and the sender are identified. In each letter, the glorified Jesus has a message for the church—exhortation plus praise and/or criticism. And finally, the letter concludes with a warning ("Listen to what the Spirit is saying!") and a promise to those who "conquer" by standing firm in faith.

Jesus is standing among seven golden lampstands, and gripping the seven stars in his right hand. The symbolism of Revelation often is difficult to decipher, but not here. Jesus himself explains the meaning: "the seven stars are the angels of the seven churches, and the seven lampstands are the seven churches" (Rev. 1:20). Jesus is present in each of his churches and with each of his ministers. Of all places, this is where he chooses to be! In the sanctuary during worship, in the fellowship hall over coffee, in the Sunday school class, in the nursery with the little ones, in the pastor's study—the Lord is there, unseen but alive; hearing, seeing, caring, holding.

PRAYER: Lord, I remember my church and pastor
before you. Bless them, I pray.

Series: *Hearing Jesus*

READ: Revelation 2:2-6; Luke 7:36-50

Ephesus: Lost Love

*But I have this against you, that you have abandoned
the love you had at first. (Revelation 2:4)*

In the musical *Fiddler on the Roof*, the main character, beset by the uncertainties swirling around his life and family, asks his wife, "Do you love me?" She replies, "Do I *what*? Look what I've been doing for you the past 25 years!" Love is best measured not by words but by actions. The measure of God's love for us is his gift of Jesus (John 3:16), and Jesus' death for us is its ultimate demonstration (Rom. 5:8).

By these measures God's love for us is infinite. But why is our love for Jesus so important? Luke 7 shows the reason. Because Jesus had forgiven her many sins, the woman who washed Jesus' feet with her tears and dried them with her hair felt such overwhelming love for him that she had to demonstrate it somehow, even if that meant embarrassing herself in public. The Ephesians were more like Simon the Pharisee—respectable, doctrinally correct, but cold. Love for Jesus is the measure of our gratitude.

Jesus was a realist. He knew that as time goes on, "the love of many will grow cold" (Matt. 24:12). Often that's because the Christian life is hard, and people drift away. But sometimes love grows cold because Christians get too caught up in church business. The Ephesian church was orthodox, it rejected heresies, it abhorred sinful behavior (Rev. 2:6). But it had forgotten what grace feels like. It had slipped away from where it all begins—Jesus' merciful love for us, and our grateful love for him.

PRAYER: Lord, whether warm or cool,
I ask that my love for you be rekindled.

Series: *Hearing Jesus*

READ: Revelation 2:7; Revelation 22:1-5

The Tree of Life

To the one who conquers I will grant to eat of the tree of life, which is in the paradise of God. (Revelation 2:7)

The original Tree of Life was in the Garden of Eden, along with the Tree of the Knowledge of Good and Evil. After Adam and Eve ate the forbidden fruit, their innocence was lost; their relationship with God and his world was ruptured. Sin not only affected them; it affected the whole creation. Yet God was merciful; he clothed Adam and Eve, and gave them a promise that one day evil would be destroyed by a Son of Eve. Then God drove them out of paradise, and placed an angelic guard at the gate to bar their reentry.

That doesn't sound like mercy. But it was. God himself explained why: "'Now, lest he reach out his hand and take also of the tree of life and eat, and live forever—' therefore the Lord God . . . placed the cherubim and a flaming sword that turned every way to guard the way to the tree of life" (Gen. 3:22-24). Imagine if Adam and Eve had been able to go back and eat of that other tree. Think about it: eternal life in a fallen world, everlasting struggle with our own sins, with dysfunctional relationships, with the frustrating contrariness of nature; above all, everlasting life apart from God. That's not paradise. That's—quite literally—hell.

So there is no way back to Eden. We can only go forward. But for all the faithful, the tree of life awaits in the garden city, the new Jerusalem.

PRAYER: Thank you, Father, for keeping
your promise to send the Savior.

Series: *Hearing Jesus*

READ: Revelation 2:8; Mark 16:1-8

The Living One

The words of the first and the last, who died and came to life.
(Revelation 2:8)

We have already heard God call himself the Alpha and Omega, the first and last (Rev. 1:8). Now Jesus does the same. His second letter, addressed to the church of Smyrna, is introduced as, "The words of the first and the last, who died and came to life." The book of Revelation just can't make this point often enough. All that God is, Jesus is.

It hinges on the truth that Jesus died and came back to life. That's a historical fact. It happened. Jesus really died; now he's really alive. Jesus didn't just rise; he is *risen*. That's the good news the angel proclaimed on Easter morning: "He is not here: for he is risen." Jesus is the Living One. "Fear not, I am the first and the last, and the living one. I died, and behold I am alive forevermore" (Rev. 1:17-18).

Did you catch the "Fear not" there? John had just been blown away by the glory of the risen Lord. He was lying at Jesus' feet like a dead man. And the first thing Jesus said to him was, "Don't be afraid." Someone has noted that this is the most often-repeated command in the Bible. Not "Don't sin." Not "Believe in me." Not "Love one another." Those are all great biblical imperatives. But what Jesus told us more than anything is, "Don't be afraid. I'm alive. Forever." Jesus has passed through death into life. Death has lost its grip; it no longer can hold him. Nor can it hold us.

PRAYER: Give thanks to the Living One.

Series: *Hearing Jesus*

READ: Revelation 2:9-10

Smyrna: Facing Suffering

You will have tribulation. (Revelation 2:10)

"I didn't go to religion to make me happy. I always knew a bottle of Port would do that," quipped C. S. Lewis. "If you want a religion to make you feel really comfortable, I certainly don't recommend Christianity" (*God in the Dock*).

Jesus never said that following him would lead to a trouble-free life. In fact, he said just the opposite. Smyrna was a church under persecution, as are many today. The suffering that Jesus warns the church about is specifically Christian suffering. It is suffering "dishonor for the name" (Acts 5:41), the persecution that comes from identifying with Jesus. This persecution takes a number of forms. It is economic ("I know . . . your poverty"); being members of a despised minority, Christians can be squeezed out of the best jobs or schools or careers. It is verbal ("I know . . . the slander"); believers in John's day were accused of all sorts of antisocial attitudes and behavior, and it's the same for faithful Christians today. And persecution may be physical ("Do not fear what you are about to suffer"). Following Jesus in some places means prison, beatings, even death.

Here's the thing about Christian suffering: it's all voluntary. It's like the grueling qualifying course for the U.S. Navy SEALS. A trainee can drop out anytime just by ringing a bell and "tapping out." In the same way, we can escape the trials of faith at any time. All we have to do is tap out, stop identifying as a Christian, stop holding to God's Word.

PRAYER: Lord, keep me always faithful to you.

Series: *Hearing Jesus*

READ: Revelation 2:11; Revelation 20:11-15

The Second Death

*The one who conquers will not be hurt
by the second death.* (Revelation 2:11)

"Be faithful unto death, and I will give you the crown of life," Jesus told the church of Smyrna (Rev. 2:10). Here the death is physical and the life is eternal. Jesus knew how these Christians would have their faith tested by the suffering they would have to endure for his sake. He knew it wouldn't last forever. So he told them to hang in there. What's a few days of suffering compared to an eternity of joy?

But there is another kind of death, the second death, which happens after physical death—eternal death. This is not something anyone likes to think or talk about, believe me. The images the New Testament uses to describe it—lake of fire, outer darkness, undying worm—are horrifying. Yet they scarcely begin to convey the terrible reality. John Donne aptly described it this way: "when all is done, the hell of hells, the torment of torments is the everlasting absence of God, and the everlasting impossibility of returning to his presence . . . to fall out of the hands of the living God, is a horror beyond our expression, beyond our imagination."

Would God really do that to people? How could anyone who believes in a loving God believe that? We tremble in the face of mysteries we don't fully understand, and trust in the ultimate goodness of God. Meanwhile, be sure of this: faith in Christ delivers from the second death. "Whoever hears my word and believes him who sent me has eternal life. He does not come into judgment, but has passed from death to life" (John 5:24).

PRAYER: Thank God that you have passed from death to life.

Series: *Hearing Jesus*

READ: Revelation 2:12; Hebrews 4:11-13; Revelation 19:11-16

The Sharp Two-Edged Sword

The words of him who has the sharp two-edged sword. (Revelation 2:12)

In Revelation, as throughout the Bible, the two-edged sword is the Word of God. The key is that it issues from the mouth of the Lord Jesus. God does what he does by speaking. It's how he made the creation: "By the word of the LORD the heavens were made" (Ps. 33:6). It's how King Jesus will win the final victory: "From his mouth comes a sharp sword with which to strike down the nations" (Rev. 19:15). The battle of Armageddon won't be fought with planes and tanks; the Lord will simply speak, and every evil power will be overthrown.

Hebrews also compares God's Word to a sharp sword, or perhaps we should say a scalpel, because it cuts open and lays bare the secrets of the heart. The Bible is an instrument of discernment. It can separate truth from falsehood, wheat from chaff, real from phony. If we approach Scripture humbly and openly, it will show us ourselves, what we truly are in God's sight. Sinners, yes; but loved and redeemed sinners, accepted in the beloved Son, and precious to God.

God's Word doesn't just cut, whether to destroy or diagnose. It also heals. I love the story of the Roman officer in the Gospels who came to ask Jesus to heal his servant. Jesus offered to go with him, but the man said no. "Lord, I am not worthy to have you come under my roof, but only say the word, and my servant will be healed" (Matt. 8:8). So he did, and he was.

PRAYER: Lord, speak your healing word into my life today.

Series: *Hearing Jesus*

READ: Revelation 2:13-16

Pergamum: Where Satan Has His Throne

I know where you dwell. (Revelation 2:13)

On the acropolis of ancient Pergamum stood the magnificent Temple of Zeus. Alongside it was another temple dedicated to the worship of the Roman emperor. That hill and its temples dominated the skyline of Pergamum; you couldn't escape the sight of it. Wherever you went, a sort of visual propaganda proclaimed: "Rome rules! Caesar is Lord!" It was as if Satan had settled in Pergamum and made it his capital.

Tough place to be the church, for sure. But the Christians of Pergamum had been doing pretty well. The Lord commended them for holding fast to the faith, even though one of their members had already been martyred, Antipas the "faithful witness." "Witness" in Greek is *martys*; it is because the early church had so many witnesses who were "faithful unto death" (Rev. 2:10) that martyr came to mean a person who dies for the faith.

But not everyone is an Antipas. There were some in Pergamum who were waffling on their spiritual and moral integrity—and inviting others to do the same. We're not sure who the Nicolaitans (v. 15) were, except that they suggested a more lax approach to the two ongoing temptations for the early church—idolatrous feasts and sexual immorality. That's also what Balaam tempted the children of Israel to do (see Num. 25:1-3; 31:16). The Lord hasn't changed. If the church doesn't repent, he'll use his two-edged sword in judgment on it.

PRAYER: Jesus, today I ask for strength to hold fast to you.

Series: *Hearing Jesus*

READ: Revelation 2:17; Isaiah 43:1-7

A New Name

I will give him a white stone, with a new name written on the stone that no one knows except the one who receives it. (Revelation 2:17)

My older sister told me that my parents thought about naming me James. It's weird to think that I might have gone through life as Jimmy rather than Dave. Dave is my name, it's who I am. This version of me is flawed—don't I know it! But the Bible says that one day I will be like Jesus himself. Of all God's promises about the future, this is the hardest for me to imagine. I can sort of picture the new creation: new heavens, new earth, eternal life. I can't even begin to picture the new me.

The Lord promises us a new name that will fit our new nature, written on a white stone. It sounds like a fairy tale.

"Here and there and not just in books," writes Frederick Buechner, "we catch glimpses of a world of once upon a time and they lived happily ever after, of a world where there is a wizard to give courage and a heart, an angel with a white stone that has written on it our true and secret name, and it is so easy to dismiss it all . . . But if . . . our glimpses of it . . . are only a dream, they are one of the most haunting and powerful dreams that the world has ever dreamed" (*Telling the Truth: The Gospel as Tragedy, Comedy, and Fairy Tale*).

The gospel is a kind of fairy tale; just one that happens to be true.

PRAYER: Thank you for my new name.

Series: *Hearing Jesus*

READ: Revelation 2:18; Matthew 17:1-8

Eyes like Flame

. . . the Son of God, who has eyes like a flame of fire. (Revelation 2:18)

When I was a pastor, my church had to fill out an annual report to our classis. In Reformed churches, the classis is the local assembly to which each congregation is accountable. So the classis needed to know what was going on with our church: how we were doing, whether we needed help—or perhaps correction. Jesus didn't need any annual reports from his churches. The first words he spoke to each of the seven churches was, "I know." Whatever is happening, whatever the church is doing or not doing, the Lord knows all about it, the good and the bad. He sees it all.

Why did Jesus' eyes flash with fire? So that "all the churches will know that I am he who searches mind and heart, and I will give to each of you according to your works" (Rev. 2:23). Jesus is not a passive observer. His searching gaze leads to judgment for everyone.

This is the only place in Revelation where the title "Son of God" is given to Jesus. But John had heard it before, long before, during the preview of Jesus' glory he saw on the Mount of Transfiguration. "And a voice from the cloud said, 'This is my beloved Son, with whom I am well pleased; listen to him'" (Matt. 17:5).

So when Jesus looks at us, and maybe through us, and calls us to repent or commands us to hold on, *listen* to him.

PRAYER: Speak, Lord, your servant is listening.

Series: *Hearing Jesus*

READ: Revelation 2:18-25

Thyatira: Hold Fast

Hold fast what you have until I come. (Revelation 2:25)

Thyatira didn't have great cultural importance, like Ephesus; it wasn't a significant religious center, like Pergamum; it didn't occupy a strategic site, like Laodicea. All Thyatira had was trade. But that presented a problem for the church there. Working in business meant belonging to the trade guilds, quasi-religious organizations that controlled all employment. Their gatherings involved sacrifices to the gods, with eating and drinking the sacrificial offerings, and sexual shenanigans following. Could Christians participate in such things?

"Jezebel" (a code name for an influential teacher in the congregation) said yes; Jesus said no; and the church mostly said nothing, hoping the issue would just fade away. Jesus had a lot of good to say about this church, but he criticized them for one thing: their tolerance! We hear a lot these days about tolerance, but tolerance can be a bit tricky. For the church to tolerate people who are different is good. To tolerate false teaching and immoral behavior is not.

During the Civil War a colonel in a beleaguered Union outpost wired for orders. "Hold the fort," the commanding general replied; "I am coming." P. P. Bliss later wrote a gospel hymn based on the incident.

Christ's word to us is, "Hold fast . . . until I come." It's a command that implies a promise. He will come. We can be sure.

PRAYER: Lord, give me wisdom to know
when to tolerate and when to hold fast.

Series: *Hearing Jesus*

READ: Revelation 2:26-29; Psalm 2

The Morning Star

And I will give him the morning star. (Revelation 2:28)

Before we leave Thyatira, give a last thought to Jezebel, because what's said about her is remarkably relevant to our church situation today. Jezebel called herself a prophetess, meaning she claimed the inspiration and authority of the Spirit for her teaching. That teaching urged the Christians of Thyatira to join in what their society approved. It probably went something like this: "You don't have to separate yourselves from the world. Embrace the culture, especially if it's good for business. Go ahead, go to the temples, attend the feasts. Your traditional morality with its fear of 'worldliness' is old-fashioned and naive. Those of us with the Spirit know better." The claim that you can ignore the letter of God's word and be guided by the "spirit" of love is a very old lie.

In Psalm 2, the Lord promised his Son that he would rule over the nations with authority and power, with an iron rod to dash in pieces those opposed to his righteous reign. In Revelation 2, Jesus the Son promised the same thing to those who remain true to him. To the Romans, the morning star was Venus, a symbol of Roman power and sovereignty. (Julius Caesar claimed to be descended from the goddess Venus.) To John's faithful readers, the morning star was Jesus himself—"I am the root and the descendant of David, the bright morning star" (Rev. 22:16). If we hold fast and keep his works, we will share in both Jesus' life and his kingly rule.

PRAYER: Jesus, I am awed by your promise that those who resist the world will rule with you.

Series: *Hearing Jesus*

READ: Revelation 3:1; Revelation 4:1-11

The Seven Spirits

The words of him who has the seven spirits of God. (Revelation 3:1)

In the book of Revelation, *seven* is the number of fullness or completeness. When Revelation speaks of the seven spirits of God here (or in 4:5 or 1:4), it doesn't mean that God has seven different spirits or that the Holy Spirit has somehow multiplied. It's simply a reference to the Holy Spirit in all his fullness.

Throughout his earthly life, Jesus was continually identified with the Holy Spirit. He was conceived by the Spirit in his mother's womb. He was anointed with the Spirit at his baptism. Full of the Spirit, Jesus was led by the Spirit into the wilderness where he was tempted by the devil (Luke 4:1). He undertook his ministry in the power of the Spirit (Luke 4:14). He cast out demons by the Spirit (Matt. 12:28). And at the end of his life on earth, in the upper room, Jesus promised the Spirit to his disciples. He called the Spirit "another Helper" like himself, who would be his very presence with them and would remind them of all his teaching (John 14:16-18, 26).

In John's vision, the same Jesus who had the Spirit also held the stars. We've already been told that the stars represent the seven messengers of the churches (Rev. 1:20). Happy the church whose pastor is filled with the Spirit, who follows Jesus' teaching and faithfully preaches the Word of God. The ministry of the Word in the power of the Spirit can wake a sleeping church up, and make a dead church come alive.

PRAYER: Lord, raise up faithful pastors for your church
and fill them with your Spirit.

Series: *Hearing Jesus*

READ: Revelation 3:1-4; Luke 13:1-5

Sardis: Wake Up!

. . . but unless you repent, you will all likewise perish. (Luke 13:5)

I was driving along and noticed a billboard that had been put up by a local atheists' group. "Millions of Americans are living happily without religion," the sign said. Of course they are, I thought. When you have plenty of money, and good health, and can travel all over, it's hard not to be happy. But what happens when those things are taken away—by a pandemic, for example?

What we call pandemics the ancients called plagues, and Revelation is full of them. Seals are broken, trumpets blow, bowls of wrath are poured out; war, famine, and pestilence are unleashed; a quarter of the world dies, then a third. And the plagues keep coming. What's the point? The point is to get everyone's attention. "God whispers to us in our pleasures, speaks in our conscience, but shouts in our pains: it is his megaphone to rouse a deaf world" (C. S. Lewis, *The Problem of Pain*, p. 81). We might think of plagues as "teachable moments." It's God shouting to the world, "Wake up, people! Repent!"

Millions of people living happily without religion are millions of people living happily without God. But that kind of happiness cannot and will not go on. Unless they wake up to the truth, they're in for a truly rude awakening, and an unexpected and uncomfortable divine visitation. As Christians, we are not immune from slumbering under the illusion of security. Might Jesus be wanting to shake us up, as he did the church in Sardis?

PRAYER: Lord, are you speaking to me? What are you saying?

Series: *Hearing Jesus*

READ: Revelation 3:5-7; Revelation 7:9-17

Dressed in White

*The one who conquers will be clothed
thus in white garments. (Revelation 3:5)*

Revelation 7 describes the church in two different but equally dramatic ways. First, the church is a carefully numbered community of 144,000, drawn equally from the twelve tribes of Israel. This does not mean that only those descended from the original children of Israel are saved, or that the population of heaven is capped at the size of a small city. Revelation's numbers are symbolic. The church consists of 12 x 12 x 1,000, meaning the full total—whatever that may be—of God's redeemed, sealed by him as his own and protected.

Next, John saw this same church as a great, uncountable multitude. It is multicultural, multiracial, multinational, and multilingual, drawn from every place and people. They hold palm branches in their hands as a sign of victory; songs of worship are on their lips; promises of everlasting joy are theirs. The church is one huge, beautiful mosaic. But with all its diversity, there is one way everyone is the same: they are all dressed exactly alike. "They have washed their robes and made them white in the blood of the Lamb" (Rev. 7:14).

Heaven has a dress code: the white robe of Christ's righteousness, purchased by his sacrificial blood, received by faith.

PRAYER: "When he shall come with trumpet sound, O may I then in him be found; dressed in his righteousness alone, faultless to stand before the throne." (*My Hope is Built on Nothing Less*)

Series: *Hearing Jesus*

33

READ: Revelation 3:7-11

Philadelphia: Church of the Open Door

Behold, I have set before you an open door. (Revelation 3:8)

Of all the churches, this one seems to have been the Lord's favorite. It's the only church of which he has no words of either criticism or warning. The same formula ("I know your works") that introduces Christ's judgment on churches like Ephesus or Sardis is used in Philadelphia as a prelude to comfort.

In human terms the Philadelphian church was small and weak. But it was faithful. It held fast to Christ's word and kept proclaiming his name in the face of opposition. It was displaying that very important fruit of the Spirit: patient endurance. So Jesus blessed his church in Philadelphia.

He reminded them of the open door he had set before them. No one could shut out those whom Jesus had invited into the kingdom of God, because he held the only key. In fact, Jesus himself was the open door—the door of the sheep (John 10:7), the narrow gate that led to life (Matt. 7:14). By trusting in him, the Christians of Philadelphia had entered the kingdom, and the Lord promised that their faith would be vindicated. One day their enemies would be made to bow down before them, "and they will learn that I have loved you" (Rev. 3:9). When I read these words, I think of all those who have been persecuted because they decided to follow Jesus. I think of all those living in a secular, post-Christian society who have been ridiculed for their faith. Eventually everyone—especially the persecutors and mockers—will know the Jesus followers were right.

PRAYER: Give thanks for Jesus, the open door.

Series: *Hearing Jesus*

READ: Revelation 3:12-13

Pillars of the Church

I will make him a pillar in the temple of my God. (Revelation 3:12)

The phrase "pillars of the church" calls up faces and voices out of my past—from the church I grew up in, from the churches I have served. It's how we describe those members on whom every church depends—faithful Sunday school teachers, youth leaders, elders and deacons, servants of every kind; the people who are always there, first to volunteer, supportive of leaders, constant in prayer, generous givers. Wonderful folks, those pillars—ask any pastor. But that's not what Jesus means here.

His promises here are for everyone in the church; everybody gets to be a pillar, not just the busy few. This is about privilege, not responsibility. Jesus is offering a reward, not another job to do. The promises relate to the time when there will no longer be a need for workers in the church because the church's work will be finished and its joys just beginning. We usually think of pillars as support structures, but the pillars of the temple were decorative; they were an adornment, made for glory. They even had names: Jachin and Boaz (1 Kings 7:21).

Jesus promises to write a name on us too, his own name, and his Father's name, and the name of the city of God, the heavenly Jerusalem. That is where we will all belong, where we will each have a place prepared for us, forever. "Who is there that would not yearn for that City, out of which no friend departs, and into which no enemy enters?" (St. Augustine).

PRAYER: Lord, may your whole church soon be gathered from the ends of the earth into your kingdom.

Series: *Hearing Jesus*

READ: Revelation 3:14-20

Laodicea: Knocking at the Door

Behold, I stand at the door and knock. (Revelation 3:20)

If you remember any of the seven churches, you probably remember the one Jesus threatened to spit out of his mouth. "Laodicean" became a synonym for half-hearted Christians. The lukewarm temperature of the church probably referred as much to its spiritual usefulness as its spiritual ardor. You can use both kinds of water—cold for drinking and hot for washing. But lukewarm water is like salt that's lost its savor; not much good.

Whatever the spiritual problem, a deeper intimacy with Jesus is the solution. He is always ready, standing at the door. My boyhood church had a stained glass window depicting Christ knocking at the heart's door. The door is overgrown, vines cling to its edges. It looks like it hasn't been opened in a long time. Significantly, there's no handle on it; the door can only be opened from the inside.

It's worth remembering that Jesus doesn't really need a handle to come in; he's already got a key. He's the one "who opens and no one will shut, who shuts and no one opens" (Rev. 3:7). But still he says to each of us, "If anyone opens I will come in." Jesus wants us to want him in our lives. He politely waits for us to invite him in. If we do that, he won't just eat and run; he'll come to stay. "If anyone loves me ... my Father will love him, and we will come to him and make our home with him" (John 14:23).

PRAYER: Lord, please come in and make my heart your home.

Series: *Hearing Jesus*

READ: Revelation 3:21-22; Revelation 12:10-17a

Faith is the Victory

*The one who conquers, I will grant him to sit with me
on my throne, as I also conquered and sat down
with my Father on his throne.* (Revelation 3:21)

Seven times over in his letters to the churches the Lord makes promises
to "the one who conquers." These concluding promises are variations on
a single theme: eternal life. But the promise of life is only made to those
who stay the course. "The one who endures to the end will be saved"
(Matt. 10:22). Not the one who drops out somewhere along the way.
Heaven is for winners; only conquerors need apply.

I trust you want to be among the conquerors. I know I sure do.
The question is, conquer what? Sin in our lives? No one does that
completely, not even in the Holy Spirit's strength. Conquer death, and
the power of evil? Christ has already done that for us. I think the battle
the Lord calls us to win is the battle against opposition and worldliness
and doubt and suffering and all the other discouraging things that can
tempt us to quit.

Here's a second question: conquer how? John tells us. "The accuser
. . . has been thrown down . . . And they have conquered him by the
blood of the Lamb and by the word of their testimony, for they loved
not their lives even unto death" (Rev. 12:10-11). We win the same way
Jesus did, not by human willpower or worldly weapons, but by patiently
enduring suffering with faith. We win by "looking to Jesus . . . who . . .
endured the cross, despising the shame" (Heb. 12:2).

Faith is the victory that overcomes the world.

PRAYER: God, give me the faith that endures.

Series: *Hearing Jesus*

READ: Matthew 13:1-9

Ears to Hear

He who has ears, let him hear. (Matthew 13:9)

Every letter in Revelation 2-3 concludes with this sentence: "He who has an ear, let him hear what the Spirit says to the churches." Jesus added something similar to his parable of the sower. It's not enough simply to hear the Word of God; the Word must take root in our lives and produce lasting fruit.

But doesn't everyone with ears hear? I've noticed something as I have aged and my hearing has degraded. When you don't quite catch a comment, you get tired of saying, "Huh? What did you say?" or, "Could you repeat that?" So you just ignore what was said and hope it wasn't too important.

Jesus is not warning people who are hard of hearing; he's warning people who are good at ignoring. Don't do that with God's Word. Don't let it go in one ear and out the other. Rather, respond to it: do what it's asking you to do. Believe what the Word promises and do what it commands. If we do that, we will live.

The book of Revelation opened with John's beatitude: "Blessed are those who hear, and who keep what is written" (Rev. 1:3). Miles Smith, author of the preface to the King James Bible, offers Bible readers an expanded version of this beatitude: "A blessed thing it is, and will bring us to everlasting blessedness in the end, when God speaks to us, to listen; when he sets his Word before us, to read it; when he stretches out his hand and calls, to answer, 'Here am I; here we are to do your will, O God.'"

PRAYER: Here I am to do your will, O God.

Series: *Hearing Jesus*

READ: Acts 2:42; Acts 4:32-36

The Marks of the Church

They devoted themselves to the apostles' teaching and the fellowship, to the breaking of bread and the prayers. (Acts 2:42)

If our churches were more like they ought to be and could be, we wouldn't know what to do with all the people. They would be breaking down the doors to get in. Why? Because people today are hungry for community. They want to belong somewhere, to experience acceptance that is genuine, nonexploitive, inviting.

People are also searching for something to believe in. Ours is a very "spiritual" age. The problem, though, is that much of the spirituality doesn't distinguish between reality and fantasy. People today believe all right, but in what? In witchcraft and astrology, in crystals and reincarnation, in extraterrestrials and conspiracies. As the popular saying has it, when people stop believing in God, they don't believe in nothing; they believe in anything.

Luke's description of the early church shows how God intends for our desires to be fulfilled in the life of the church. The Jerusalem church was both a welcoming and a worshiping community. It was doctrinally sound, warmly supportive, socially engaged, sacramentally fed, and focused outward in prayer for the world. When the church is living out the life of the Spirit as a new community in Christ, it meets our most basic human needs. Our most basic human needs? Beyond mere physical survival, they are the needs that make us human—the need to be authentically related to God and to each other.

PRAYER: Help my church to be the answer
to someone's deepest need.

Series: *Acts*

READ: Acts 3:1-10

What I Have I Give You

In the name of Jesus Christ . . . rise up and walk! (Acts 3:6)

Good things can happen when you attend the evening service! As Peter and John were heading to worship one afternoon, they passed a beggar who had staked out a good spot by one of the temple gates. His tactics were simple: "Ask them for help while they're feeling religious." When the beggar held out his hand to Peter and John, he must not have been expecting much from those poor-looking fishermen. But Peter got his attention: "Look at us." We don't have any money, Peter told him, but we do have something else we can offer you: "In the name of Jesus Christ of Nazareth, rise up and walk!"

Spiritual power tends to be in inverse proportion to financial wealth. Rich Christians (or rich churches) often depend upon money and technology to solve their problems. But when we no longer have to rely on God alone, we seldom experience God working in powerful and wonderful ways. The story is told of a visit to the Vatican during the Middle Ages by the great theologian Thomas Aquinas. He called on the pope, who was counting out a large sum of money. The pope remarked with considerable satisfaction, "The church can no longer say, 'Silver and gold have I none.'" "True," agreed Thomas. "Neither can she now say, 'In the name of Jesus Christ rise and walk'" (quoted in F. F. Bruce, *The Book of Acts*).

You can trust in money or you can trust in Christ, but it's very hard to trust in both.

PRAYER: Lord, give me the treasure that lasts.

Series: *Acts*

READ: Acts 7:54-8:3

Saul of Tarsus

Saul was ravaging the church. (Acts 8:3)

The man we will come to know as the apostle Paul first appears in Acts as one of those responsible for Stephen's martyrdom. As a junior member of the mob that stoned Stephen to death, Saul was given the job of "holding the coats" of the actual executioners.

According to early Christian tradition, Paul wasn't much to look at—a bald-headed, bandy-legged, little guy. By his own admission, Paul came across as not especially powerful or impressive (1 Cor. 2:3-4). But his passion, intellect, energy, and courage made him stand out. Shortly after Stephen's death we find that Saul has become a leader of the effort to stamp out the Jesus movement. Paul himself summed up his early life this way: "Formerly I was a blasphemer, persecutor, and insolent opponent. But I received mercy because I had acted ignorantly in unbelief . . . Christ Jesus came into the world to save sinners, of whom I am the foremost" (1 Tim. 1:13-15).

Despite all that he would become, Paul never forgot what he once was. To himself he would always be "the chief of sinners." Paul never lost his sense of wonder that the Lord who knew all that he was and everything he had done, still loved him and revealed himself to him. The lesson Paul drew from that was that if God could save him, he could save anybody. "But I received mercy for this reason, that in me, as the foremost, Jesus Christ might display his perfect patience as an example to those who were to believe in him for eternal life" (1 Tim. 1:16).

PRAYER: Fill me with wonder at your amazing grace.

Series: *Acts*

READ: Acts 9:1-9

The Damascus Road

Who are you, Lord? (Acts 9:5)

The zealous young man, born to Jewish parents in the Roman colony of Tarsus in Asia Minor, educated in Jerusalem under Israel's greatest rabbis, was on the fast track to success. He was a rigid defender of Jewish tradition, morally blameless, as he would later describe himself. He zealously hunted down Christians in Jerusalem and dragged them before the authorities, convinced that in so doing he was serving God by punishing heretics. He even got permission to carry on his inquisition elsewhere. So one day he set out for Damascus.

He never made it there. At least, Saul of Tarsus never did. What happened on that journey changed him forever, and altered the course of world history. Think of it. In one dramatic moment Paul's eyes were opened, not only to the truth about Jesus but to the truth about the church. He would not only become a Christian himself, he would be called as a missionary to bring the gospel to the gentile world (Acts 26:16-18).

Years later Paul would say that what he experienced was not a vision or imaginary encounter. It didn't happen inside his head, it happened outside on the road. What Paul witnessed was an actual appearance of the risen Lord, the last such appearance to his apostles (1 Cor. 15:8). Paul's conversion was in one sense unique. But in another sense what happened to Paul is the same thing that happens to every Christian. By God's grace we meet the living Christ, acknowledge him as Lord, and are commissioned in his service.

PRAYER: Jesus, I confess you as Lord and savior of the world, and my Lord and savior too.

Series: *Acts*

READ: Acts 16:25-34

Question and Answer 1

What must I do . . . ? (Acts 16:30)

I once had a friend whose personalized license plate read *QANDA1*. If you are familiar with the Reformed faith you probably caught the reference to the Heidelberg Catechism's much-loved first question and answer: "What is your only comfort in life and in death? That I am not my own, but belong . . . to my faithful Savior, Jesus Christ." That's a beautiful truth. But there's an even more basic question and answer that ought to be considered first by everyone. It's the Philippian jailer's question and the apostle Paul's answer.

"What must I do to be saved?" Our salvation is God's grace from beginning to end; we do nothing to earn it, we take no credit for receiving it. But that does not mean we are passive, that we don't have to respond to the gospel. It's no good sitting around expecting someone else to respond for me. On the contrary, *I must do something* to be saved. Do what?

The jailer's question cried out for an answer, and it got one. "Believe in the Lord Jesus, and you will be saved" (v. 31). Sometimes people say that it is enough just to ask the big questions about life, that it doesn't matter if you find answers to them. The journey is what's important, not the arrival. That's like saying to someone who is having a heart attack, "It's enough that you are looking for the hospital; it doesn't matter whether you actually get there." Asking the question shows a recognition of our need. Acting on the answer means life or death.

PRAYER: Lord Jesus, I believe.

Series: *Acts*

READ: Acts 17:16-34

Mars Hill

What . . . you worship as unknown, this I proclaim to you. (Acts 17:23)

Are you ever bothered by the idolatry of our culture—the consumerism, the obsession with technology, the celebrity worship, the addiction to entertainment and pleasure? When Paul was walking around Athens, "his spirit was provoked" by all the idols. Paul did not look at the city as a tourist, admiring the Parthenon and the other temples, nor did he visit it as an art critic, deriving pleasure from the sculptures and paintings. He viewed it as a Christian, appalled at the ignorance that "exchanged the truth about God for a lie and worshiped and served the creature rather than the Creator" (Rom. 1:25).

But although Paul was very upset by the idolatry, he was very gentle in his approach to the idolaters. He begins by probing the Athenians' vulnerable spot, namely the fear, evident in the altar to the Unknown God, that despite all their religion and philosophy these people still are ignorant of the truth. They worship countless gods, but they are afraid they might have missed one. Sensing their spiritual insecurity, the apostle speaks to that and establishes a point of contact between his beliefs and theirs, even quoting from their own writers to affirm their sense of the divine.

This is all good, but Paul is an evangelist, so he takes it further by preaching the gospel, which in shorthand form is the message about "Jesus and the resurrection" (Acts 17:18, 30-31). At this point there is a division. Some misunderstand, some mock, some want to hear more, and some believe (vv. 32-34). That's how it is with the gospel.

PRAYER: Lord, help me build my life on Jesus and the resurrection.

Series: *Acts*

READ: Acts 18:1-11

God's People

I have many in this city who are my people. (Acts 18:10)

When the apostle Paul moved from Athens to Corinth, it was like going from the frying pan into the fire. Athens, with its sophisticated philosophers and debaters, was tough ground for a missionary. But Corinth was worse. Corinth had grown big, busy, and wealthy. And like many such cities, it was also immoral. In fact, the city's reputation was such that its name was used as a verb in the ancient world: to "corinthianize" was a synonym for sexual promiscuity.

You might think this was a very unpromising place to plant a church, and you'd be right. But the Lord had prepared the way. One night God spoke to Paul, telling him not to be afraid, to go on preaching, and promising to be with him. That must have been wonderfully encouraging for Paul to hear. But what came next was even better—"for I have many in this city who are my people."

Notice the tense of the verb. It's present, not future. God says, "I *have* many people here." Not, "I *will have* many—once your evangelism program starts to bear fruit, Paul." Not, "I *could have* many—if they believe in me." It's simply, "I have many." The Lord knows his own. They are already his, and have been since before the foundation of the world (Eph. 1:4). If you are a Christian, you don't belong to God because you believe in Christ; you believe in Christ because you belong to God. "My sheep hear my voice, and I know them, and they follow me" (John 10:27).

PRAYER: I praise you, Lord, for the wonder of your love.

Series: *Acts*

READ: Acts 22:22-29; Acts 23:12-24

God Moves in Mysterious Ways

Paul resolved . . . [to] go to Jerusalem, saying,
"After I have been there, I must also see Rome." (Acts 19:21)

The last ten chapters of Acts tell the story of Paul's journey to Rome. It takes a long time, and a lot happens along the way. Paul announces his intention to travel to Rome in chapter 19, and immediately all hell breaks loose (literally). There's a big riot in Ephesus, and Paul has to leave town. There's another one in Jerusalem, and Paul's life is only saved at the last minute when Roman troops place him in protective custody. It almost looks like there's an organized campaign to keep Paul from reaching Rome. Who could be behind that, I wonder?

One big thing Paul had going for him through all the turmoil of these years was his Roman citizenship. When the Roman officer who arrested Paul found out he was a Roman citizen by birth, he took extra care to protect him.

Paul's life is saved through Roman intervention, and his innocence—and by implication the legitimacy of the faith he proclaimed—will eventually be declared in a Roman court (Acts 26:30-32). After languishing in prison in Caesarea for more than two years, Paul exercises his right as a Roman citizen and appeals his case to the emperor (25:10-11). So even his transportation to the capital will be in a Roman ship, at Roman expense! God does move in mysterious ways, as William Cowper's hymn says—ways that aren't always comfortable for us. But he accomplishes his purposes without fail, every time.

PRAYER: Lord, use my life too, in whatever way you choose, for your kingdom purposes.

Series: *Acts*

READ: Acts 24:10-27

Felix: The Procrastinator

When I get an opportunity I will summon you. (Acts 24:25)

When Paul arrived in Caesarea, the Roman capital of Palestine, Felix was the governor. His name means "happy" or "lucky," but Felix probably didn't feel like he had drawn the long straw. Judea was especially difficult to govern. The big problem there was the Jews, an independent-minded people who quarreled a lot over religion.

Felix got to see this first-hand when he held a hearing on Paul's case. The high priest accused Paul of causing riots and being "a ringleader of the sect of the Nazarenes" (v. 5). The second charge was true; the first was false. The upheavals that followed Paul throughout his missionary journeys were caused by his enemies' hatred of the gospel. To say that Paul was responsible for them was to blame the victim, not the instigators. Paul was able to refute all the criminal charges against him with a clear and straightforward defense.

Felix didn't condemn Paul, but he didn't release him either. He held Paul in custody, while continuing to speak with him. Felix had "a rather accurate knowledge of the Way" (v. 22); in other words, he didn't need more information about Christianity. What he needed was to make a decision about it. When the apostle talked about urgent things like sin and judgment, Felix dismissed him: "When I get an opportunity I will summon you." Felix is a spiritual procrastinator. He thinks that maybe later on would be the time to respond to the gospel.

But somehow "later on" never comes.

PRAYER: "Today, if you hear his voice,
do not harden your hearts." (Psalm 95:7-8)

Series: *Acts*

READ: Acts 25:1-22

Festus: The Scoffer

Paul, you are out of your mind. (Acts 26:24)

After Felix moved on, a new governor arrived in Caesarea. Now Paul became Festus' problem. For some reason that Festus couldn't quite figure out, the Jews in Jerusalem were still wanting to kill Paul. "They had certain points of dispute . . . about their own religion," explains Festus to King Agrippa, a local prince making a courtesy call on the new governor. The controversy centered on "a certain Jesus, who was dead, but whom Paul asserted to be alive" (25:19). Unlike Felix, Festus didn't know much about Christianity, but he sure got this right. That is indeed what it's all about—it's about a dead man who is alive!

When Paul was invited to explain his views, he took the opportunity once more to gain a hearing for the gospel. Instead of focusing on his personal innocence (while nevertheless proclaiming that), Paul shared his testimony. Not only did he see the risen Lord, he was commissioned by Jesus to take the good news of redemption and forgiveness to the whole world.

As Paul fearlessly preaches the gospel, Festus interrupts with an outburst, "Paul, you've gone mad! Your study has driven you insane!" To this pragmatic Roman politician, taking God seriously enough to believe that he would come in the flesh, die for humanity, and then rise again from the dead was evidence of an unbalanced mind. But Paul was neither crazy nor a wild fanatic: "I am speaking true and rational words" (26:25). If Jesus is God, it's not crazy to believe he rose from the dead. If he rose from the dead, it's not crazy to believe in God.

PRAYER: Jesus, I worship you today, my risen and reigning Lord!

Series: *Acts*

READ: Acts 26:1-29

Agrippa: The Almost-Believer

In a short time would you persuade me to be a Christian? (Acts 26:28)

Paul's speech before Festus and Agrippa is his fifth public defense since his arrest in Jerusalem. As usual, the apostle turns his testimony into a gospel sermon. At the climax, he turns to the king: "King Agrippa, do you believe the prophets?" (v. 27). Paul was asking if he would accept the testimony of God's Word by putting his faith in Christ. Agrippa was not used to being addressed like that. In his *An Open Letter to the Christian Nobility*, Luther insisted that the pope should not sit and receive Communion but like any other "stinking sinner" rise and show respect to his God. The great ones of the world are generally held in such awe that no one tells them they're just another sinner in need of a Savior like the rest of us.

That moment, by God's grace and Paul's holy boldness, was King Agrippa's opportunity to acknowledge himself a sinner in need of Christ. He put it off with a cryptic reply: "In a short time would you persuade me to be a Christian?" (v. 28). Was Agrippa offended by the question? (As in, "How dare you address me personally?") Was he making a joke out of it, trying to laugh it off? Was he honestly asking for more time to think? Whatever it was, Agrippa parried Paul's gospel appeal, and the moment passed. As the King James Version of the Bible puts it, "Almost thou persuadest me . . ."

Never mind Agrippa; he has long since had to appear before the Judge. What I should ask myself is whether *I* believe the Scriptures. Have I responded in faith to the Christ who died and rose for me?

PRAYER: Lord, I do believe.

Series: *Acts*

READ: Acts 28:17-31

Without Hindrance

[Paul] lived there . . . proclaiming the kingdom of God
and teaching about the Lord Jesus Christ with all boldness
and without hindrance. (Acts 28:30-31)

Wait a minute, that's it? This is how Acts ends? Luke says that the apostle spent two years under a loose sort of house arrest, preaching and teaching the gospel boldly and without hindrance. In fact the phrase "without hindrance" is a single word in Greek, and it's literally the last word in the book of Acts.

But how could Luke leave us hanging like that? What happened to Paul? Was he acquitted as he expected (see Phil. 1:25)? Did he reach Spain with the gospel, as he hoped and had mentioned to the church in Rome (Rom. 15:28)? Tradition says yes, that Paul was released by Caesar. Tradition also says that he traveled for two more years before he returned to Rome, was rearrested, and executed during the violent persecution of the church by Nero in AD 64.

But that's tradition talking. Luke doesn't tell us. He simply ends with Paul still in custody, preaching the gospel day in and day out. Perhaps he did that because Acts really isn't *Paul's* story, it's the *gospel's*. And the story of the gospel is open-ended. Gospel ministers come and go, even the greatest ones. But the gospel goes on and on, without hindrance. There is a church-planting network in the United States today called Acts 29. That's a good reminder. Now it's our turn to carry on the story of the gospel, with all boldness and without hindrance.

PRAYER: I praise you, Lord, that nothing stops your Word.
Use me as part of Acts chapter 29.

Series: *Acts*

READ: Acts 1:9-12

He Ascended into Heaven

We have this as a . . . steadfast anchor of the soul, a hope that enters . . . where Jesus has gone as a forerunner. (Hebrews 6:19-20)

"He ascended into heaven." We say that every time we recite the Apostles' Creed. But can we actually believe this? Maybe in Bible times people could believe that heaven was a place up in the sky, and that Jesus flew up there after his resurrection, but modern people can't.

Yes we can. The point of the ascension is not that heaven is "up there." The point is that Jesus Christ in his resurrection body has left the physical universe and entered the presence of God. In his ascension, Jesus signals that he no longer will be physically present here in the world, but that his body will now be in the realm where God reigns—the place we call heaven.

Nor does it mean that Jesus floated up like a balloon or took off like a rocket. As Martin Luther supposedly said, "It didn't happen the way you climb up a ladder in your house. It means he is *above* all creation and *in* all creation and *outside* of all creation."

Jesus' glorified body is in heaven, at the right hand of the Father. He has gone there as our forerunner. He is our anchor of hope. We're tied to him by faith, like a ship chained to its anchor. So we can be sure that where he is now we one day will be. Hallelujah!

PRAYER: Lord, confirm us in the hope
that we will one day be with you.

Series: *Acts*

READ: Colossians 3:1-4

Living on a Higher Plane

Set your minds on things that are above. (Colossians 3:2)

Have you ever thought about where Jesus is right now? If we are believers he is both with us and within us. "I am with you always," he promised (Matt. 28:20). Wherever two or three gather in his name, he is there (Matt. 18:20). Jesus and the Father come and make their home with those who love him and keep his word (John 14:23). That's a lot of places to be, all at once. Christ keeps all these wonderful promises through his Spirit—that is, in the person of the Holy Spirit. Jesus himself in his physical, resurrected body is, as we confess in the Apostles' Creed, "seated at the right hand of God the Father almighty," sharing God's glory and rule. So we are right in thinking of Christ as being everywhere present. But strictly speaking, he isn't here on earth. He is in heaven. That's "where Christ is, seated at the right hand of God," (Col. 3:1).

Does this distinction really matter? Certainly! And here's why. As Christians our lives have been incorporated into Christ's (vv. 3-4). So we need to start living on a higher plane. We must "set [our] minds on the things that are above." Up to this point in Colossians Paul has been talking mostly about what Christians should believe about Jesus. Now the apostle is going to turn from Christian belief to Christian behavior. And the first step in *living* Christianly is *thinking* Christianly. If we're going to live the new life of Christ we're going to need a new mindset, a new focal point for our thoughts, because what our bodies do is mostly determined by where our minds are set—either on earthly things, or the things that are above.

PRAYER: Lord, help me remember that my true life is with you.

Series: *Colossians*

READ: Colossians 3:5-12

Playing Dress-up

Therefore, as God's chosen people, holy and dearly loved, clothe yourselves with compassion, kindness, humility, gentleness and patience. (Colossians 3:12 NIV)

When I was a student and we were living in California, my wife worked in an office where one individual was especially disliked. "I'm not going to be nice to her," another co-worker announced. "If I did that I would be a hypocrite." But there is a kind of hypocrisy that we *ought* to practice; it's called "good manners." We should treat people better than we feel about them. In fact, we should always act better than we are, because that's how we actually *become* better than we were.

Watch children sometime when they play at being grown-ups. They dress up in adult clothes that are far too big for them, they try to talk like adults, they pretend to do that kinds of things adults do. But just this sort of pretending is what eventually helps them turn into adults. They act their way into reality. If we are immature Christians, we have to act our way into holiness. What we must do is pretend that we're more spiritually grown-up than we really are. Dress up in Jesus' clothes. Walk and talk like him. Put on a mask with Jesus' features and wear it in front of everyone you meet. If you do that long enough, one day you'll discover that you actually do look just like him! How cool would that be!

If you *act* holy, you will *be* holy.

PRAYER: Jesus, I want to think, speak, and act just like you. Please help me.

Series: *Colossians*

READ: Colossians 3:12-17

What the Well-Dressed Christian is Wearing

Above all, clothe yourselves with love. (Colossians 3:14 NRSV)

In Colossians 3 Paul uses the metaphor of changing clothes to describe the new way of living to which Christ calls his followers. When people joined the early church, the beginning of their new life was marked by the ceremony of baptism, in which they would strip off their old clothes before going down into the water and then put on white robes afterwards. The change of clothing symbolized the new life they were entering and the new behavior they would be exhibiting from then onwards.

"Over all these virtues put on love, which binds them all together in perfect unity" (v. 14 NIV). Paul is thinking of love as rather like an overcoat or a cloak. It goes on over everything else and makes our wardrobe complete.

There is a law of physics which says that in a closed system all physical bodies move toward a state of increasing entropy. That's just a fancy way of saying that, left to themselves, things tend to run down and fly apart. But love is a greater power than any force of physics, and it's just the opposite. Love builds up and binds. Love pulls everything and everyone back together.

Love is the uniform that identifies members of the body of Christ, the new community of God's redeemed people.

PRAYER: Lord, more than anything help me
to put on love—today and every day.

Series: *Colossians*

READ: Colossians 4:2-17

Relationships

Give my greetings to the brothers
and sisters. . . (Colossians 4:15 NIV)

The first impression I get when reading the chatty paragraph that closes
Paul's letter to the Colossians is one of cheerfulness. That's surprising
when you realize Paul was just then in prison awaiting trial for his life.
You might think he would be preoccupied with his personal future. But
that seems to be far from his mind. Instead, it's all news about others
and instructions for various workers. Even when he requests prayer for
himself, Paul asks his friends to pray not for his release, but for God to
use him in prison to spread the gospel (vv. 3-4). When someone asked
E. Stanley Jones, the great missionary to India, why he still worked so
hard in his old age, he replied, "Because with my last breath I wish to
commend the Lord Jesus." Paul would have agreed.

What else comes through here is how much Christians care about
each other. Some who don't know Paul very well think of him only as
a gigantic intellect: all brain and no heart. Paul actually had a huge
capacity for friendship. He was greatly loved—notice all the people
who voluntarily shared captivity with him—because he loved greatly!
Relationships within the church are more important than the work of
the church. Actually, the relationships *are* the work, because institutions
and organizations come and go, but people are forever.

PRAYER: Lord, thank you that you place me in a community—family,
friends, church—through whom your love can touch and support me.
Help me be that support to others.

Series: *Colossians*

READ: Colossians 4:2-4, 18

Famous Last Words

Remember my chains. (Colossians 4:18)

We tend to pay special attention to someone's last words. Sometimes they are inspiring. When the English reformer Hugh Latimer was burned at the stake, his last words were addressed to his fellow martyr Nicholas Ridley: "Be of good cheer, Master Ridley, and play the man. By God's grace, we shall this day light such a candle as shall never be put out." Sometimes they are deeply moving, like Paul's last words to the Colossians: "I, Paul, write this greeting with my own hand. *Remember my chains.*"

The apostle dictated this letter to a helper while he was imprisoned in Rome. But he took up the pen himself to add this postscript, as he often did (Gal. 6:11, 1 Cor. 16:21, 2 Thess. 3:17). The chains to which he refers here were real ones, binding him to a Roman guard.

Paul is not asking for pity when he urges the Colossians to remember his chains. As he said earlier, "I am now rejoicing in my sufferings for your sake" (Col. 1:24 NRSV). So what does he want? Paul is asking or two things. First, this is an appeal to *listen to him.* Paul's chains bear witness to the authenticity of his ministry. They underscore his authority. He is "an ambassador in chains" (Eph. 6:20) for the sake of his Lord. They are a reminder that he has paid the price for his service and has earned the right to be heard. Second, Paul is asking for *prayer.* "Remember my chains" means: "Remember where I am. Remember my situation, and pray for me."

PRAYER: Lord, I remember all those suffering for your sake today.

Series: *Colossians*

READ: Acts 1:1-8

Witnesses

You will be my witnesses . . . (Acts 1:8)

The great biblical scholar N. T. Wright has remarked that the answer to the question, "Lord, will you at this time restore the kingdom to Israel?" was, as usual with the disciples, "Yes. But not the way you think." Jesus' kingdom was spiritual in nature, not political. Even after the resurrection, the disciples found it hard to give up the idea that Jesus would set up an earthly kingdom centered on Jerusalem, with himself on the throne and they as his senior staff. Furthermore, the "Israel" whom Jesus would rule wasn't just the Jewish people. It would include all who would come to acknowledge Jesus as Lord. We too are part of that Israel.

And we too are commissioned to be witnesses. Acts 1:8 is a foundational verse. It functions as an outline of the book; think of it as Luke's "Table of Contents." As we follow the action in Luke's story, we will see the gospel going first to Jerusalem (chapters 1-7), then to Judea and Samaria and other nearby regions (chapters 8-12), and finally, with the conversion of Saul of Tarsus in chapter 9, to the ends of the earth (chapters 13-28).

But we could also read Acts 1:8 as a blueprint for every church that seeks to be faithful to Jesus' final instructions. The Lord's command to all his disciples is the same: "Wait for power, then go out and witness to me, both locally and globally." Is your church doing that?

PRAYER: Lord, I want to be part of what you are doing
in the world. Please give me power.

Series: *Acts*

READ: Acts 4:1-22

No Other Name

There is no other name . . . by which we must be saved. (Acts 4:12)

In C. S. Lewis' novel *That Hideous Strength*, a character makes a commonplace observation: "I suppose there are two views about everything." "Eh? Two views? There are a dozen views about everything," comes the rejoinder—"until you know the answer. Then there's never more than one."

The commonplace view today is that, if we actually do need saving, there are a dozen ways that can happen. The apostolic rejoinder is that there's only one. This claim is offensive to many. People don't like to hear that they have to be saved, that they're lost and alienated from the life of God apart from Jesus Christ. People also don't like to think that Jesus is the only name that saves, that no other religion under heaven, no moral system, no good intentions, no human efforts, can atone for sin and bring forgiveness.

"To preach Christ as the world's only Savior" was Words of Hope's original mission statement, chosen in 1945 when the ministry was started. It is still what the organization is doing today. That may seem intolerant. But it's the truth. The bad news is that we all need saving. The good news is that there's a name that saves. "Everyone who calls on the name of the Lord will be saved" (Rom. 10:13). And the name of the Lord is Jesus. As far as salvation goes, it's Christ or nothing. Not a dozen ways, just one.

PRAYER: Come, Lord Jesus, and save your people.
My faith and hope are in you alone.

Series: *Acts*

READS: Acts 13:44-52

A Light to the Nations

I have made you a light for the Gentiles. (Acts 13:47)

Have you ever reflected on the fact that, while nothing is too big for God to do, some things are too small? Speaking of his Servant, the Messiah, God declared it was "too small a thing" for him to save only the lost house of Israel. He must also be "a light for the Gentiles," to all nations and peoples, "that my salvation may reach to the ends of the earth" (Isa. 49:6 NIV). It's not enough for God to be merely an ethnic deity for one particular group. His light is for all the nations; his salvation must reach to the ends of the earth.

As was his normal practice, when Paul came to preach the gospel in the city of Antioch of Pisidia he began in the synagogue. When he announced that he would continue his message the following sabbath, Luke says the whole city showed up to listen. It was a dicey moment. The synagogue was filled with gentiles eager to hear the gospel, and the Jewish congregation was upset. They turned against Paul, who then shifted his focus to the outsiders, justifying his decision with Isaiah's prophecy.

Paul's quotation of Isaiah 49:6 comes with one significant change. In Isaiah the words were addressed to the Messiah. But when Paul quotes the verse he introduces it by saying, "For so the Lord has commanded *us.*" "I have made you a light for the Gentiles" means Paul himself and all Christians. It's what Jesus told his disciples: "You are the light of the world" (Matt. 5:14). Christ's light must shine through us to the whole world. Anything less would be too small a thing for God.

PRAYER: Lord, make us a light.

Series: *Acts*

READ: Acts 28:11-16

A Tale of Two Cities

And so we came to Rome. (Acts 28:14)

Luke devotes a huge chunk of Acts to the story of Paul's journey to Rome, so there must be something significant in getting him there. When the apostle finally reached Rome, Nero was emperor—a chilling thought, considering that he was the Caesar to whom Paul had appealed his case. But Paul's arrival looks something like a triumphal entry, which is no less encouraging to the apostle.

Rome is so much more than just another stop on Paul's missionary itinerary. It marks the climax of Paul's career, as he finally is able to realize his long-time ambition of preaching the gospel in the capital of the empire. But Paul's arrival in Rome is also the fulfillment of Luke's plan for the book of Acts.

We could read Acts as "A Tale of Two Cities." The book begins in Jerusalem and ends in Rome. Luke's agenda for Acts is spelled out in Jesus' final instructions to his disciples, recorded in Acts 1:8: "You will be my witnesses in Jerusalem and in all Judea and Samaria, and to the end of the earth." So why does Rome serve as the climax? There was a well-known saying that is still familiar to us: "All roads lead to Rome." That was literally true. A golden post set in the middle of the Roman Forum was "Mile Marker 0" for every road throughout the Empire. But if all roads led *to* Rome, then roads *from* Rome led everywhere! Paul's arrival in the capital represented the goal of taking the gospel to the ends of the earth. It should still be our goal today.

PRAYER: Lord, may the good news of Jesus continue to go
to the ends of the earth, until your triumphant return.

Series: *Acts*

READ: Acts 2:1-12

The Mighty Works of God

We hear them telling in our own tongues
the mighty works of God. (Acts 2:11)

In serving as Words of Hope's president for nearly 23 years, I often had the joy of traveling to other countries to preach. But I always felt like a dumb American. Our international ministry leaders could speak two or three or six different languages; I could only speak one. Sometimes I would joke that I wanted to become a Pentecostal—if that meant being instantly fluent in another language without having to learn it!

Rushing out into the streets of Jerusalem on Pentecost, Jesus' followers began to proclaim in the Spirit's power all the mighty things God had done for salvation—especially Jesus' death on the cross and his resurrection from the dead. The international crowd gathered in the city was filled with astonishment, amazed as much by the medium as by the message. The tongues truly were amazing, but it was the message of the saving power of God through Jesus Christ that mattered most.

On Pentecost, the Holy Spirit enabled the disciples to preach the gospel in other languages as a miraculous sign of what was to come. For us, the task is longer and more laborious. We use translators, interpreters, and teachers. Missionaries spend years learning another language and culture. But the purpose and result is the same as on Pentecost: people hearing the good news in their own native tongues.

PRAYER: Lord, may your whole church be "pentecostal" in proclaiming the gospel in the languages of the world's peoples.

Series: *Acts*

Ordinary
Time

Ordinary Time

The longest season in the church's liturgical calendar is called Ordinary Time. The name comes from the word "ordinal," which refers to the church practice of numbering Sundays through the year.

However, it's fitting that we call this season ordinary, since most of life is ordinary most of the time. Holidays are great, special seasons of anticipation and preparation are very useful, but what really matters is following Christ through all the ups and downs of our ordinary, day-to-day lives. In the words of Eugene Peterson, the Christian life is a life of discipleship, "a long obedience in the same direction."

Ordinary Time is sometimes divided in two parts, the first between Epiphany and Lent (if you follow the shorter Epiphany season), and the second from Pentecost to Advent. Some traditions emphasize that while the other seasons tell the story of Jesus, Ordinary Time tells the story of the people of God. Our focus in this season is living the life of faith, sharing in the mission of God, following Jesus' example through suffering, and accepting his gift of salvation.

The devotionals in this season are drawn from eleven series published from 1984-2022, and also includes several new devotionals.

* *Walking with Christian: Pilgrim's Progress*, published in November 1984, studies the Biblical roots of the great Christian allegory *The Pilgrim's Progress* by John Bunyan, and its lessons

of faith, courage, and sacrifice.

* *Faith's Hall of Fame*, published in May 1990, looks at the heroes of faith listed in Hebrews 11.

* *What to Believe*, published in December 1999, defines the robust theological words that capture the vital basic meanings of Christian faith.

* *Habakkuk*, published in February 2004, studies the message of the ancient prophet and his enduring questions.

* *Trustworthy Sayings*, published in January 2008, shares "trustworthy sayings" from Paul, things that we can be especially sure of as we face an unknown future.

* *Galatians*, published in January 2011, studies Paul's letter to the Galatians and its message of the centrality of Christ.

* *Jonah and the Heart of God*, published in January 2012, studies the challenge God gives us in the book of Jonah.

* *The Mission of God*, published in November 2016, shares the great mission God is embarked on to save his people and restore the world he loves.

* *Acts*, published in April 2018, examines the development of the early church and the way it continues to shape the church today.

* *Psalms of Ascent*, published in March 2019, takes us on the road to Jerusalem with the songs travelers sang as they made their annual pilgrimage to the temple.

* *Walking in the Way of Wisdom*, published in July 2022, studies Proverbs and the practical teaching it provides in helping us live day-to-day as God intended.

READ: 1 Timothy 6:11-21

The Good Fight

Fight the good fight of the faith. (1 Timothy 6:12)

When I was a boy, Veterans Day was known as "Armistice Day." It was a commemoration of the moment World War I ended, at the eleventh hour of the eleventh day of the eleventh month of 1918. Each year our classroom would fall silent and we listened to the sound of "taps" echoing down the empty corridors. As a sixth-grader with two years of cornet lessons behind me, I got to go out and play the song for the whole school (a nerve-wracking experience). Though we may not have realized all that it meant, the solemn ceremony was a reminder that in this world nothing good can be won without a fight.

That is important to remember. "Fight the good fight of faith!" Paul urged Timothy. Why? Because we're in a spiritual war, and we have a fearsome enemy. Peter describes him this way: "Your enemy the devil prowls around like a roaring lion, seeking someone to devour. Resist him, firm in your faith" (1 Peter 5:8-9). Even when not stirring up literal persecution, the devil attacks believers with fear, doubt, and temptation. His goal is to make us give ground morally and spiritually, to fall away from faith. But thankfully, the Lord gives us weapons with which to fight back (see Eph. 6:10-18). And don't forget the weapon Jesus used against the enemy in the wilderness—the sharp sword of the Word of God.

Do you recognize doubt, discouragement, and fear as the devil's flaming darts being fired at your faith? Fight back with the promises of God's Word!

PRAYER: Lord, thank you for giving us what we need to overcome fear and resist temptation.

Series: *Walking with Christian: Pilgrim's Progress*

READ: 2 Timothy 4

A Strong Finish

*I have fought the good fight, I have finished the race,
I have kept the faith. (2 Timothy 4:7)*

There's something quite moving about people's last words, especially if they testify to faith. When John Wesley was near death he asked for help to sit up. He wanted to sing a hymn—Isaac Watts' paraphrase of Psalm 146. "I'll praise my Maker while I've breath, and when my eyes shall close in death, praise shall employ my nobler powers." The next day he was too weak to sing, but those who were with him heard him repeat "I'll praise, I'll praise," until he breathed his last.

2 Timothy 4 contains the apostle Paul's last words. The time of his departure is at hand, he says, like a ship that is about to set sail from the harbor (v. 6). Unlike John Wesley, Paul wouldn't die in bed. He would be executed; according to tradition, through beheading. His life's blood would be his final sacrifice for his Lord, poured out like an Old Testament drink offering. Then come the three simple statements of verse 7 which make up his testimony. He's fought the good fight, he's finished the race (see Heb. 12:1-2). And he has kept the faith.

The apostle's testimony is not just that he's been faithful, that he's kept faith with the Lord—though that's true. But Paul says he has kept *the* faith. There is a difference between faith and "the faith." Faith is trust or belief. *The* faith is the truth of the Christian gospel, more broadly, the truth of the whole of the Word of God. In a time when so many in the church are abandoning basic Christian teaching, keeping the faith is more important than ever.

PRAYER: Lord, help me to keep the faith.

READ: Psalm 23

The Shadow of Death

*Even though I walk through the valley of the shadow
of death, I will fear no evil. (Psalm 23:4)*

I was eating lunch with a group of friends in a Chinese restaurant, and we had just come to the most fun part—the fortune cookies. We were all cracking our cookies open and looking at the messages inside them, when suddenly one of us said, "Listen to this!" He held up his tiny slip of paper and read: "Courage is fear that has said its prayers." What an extraordinary sentence! Who would ever expect to hear something like that in a fortune cookie?

"Courage is fear that has said its prayers"—that really is a word from God. When God calls us to walk through hard times, when our way lies through the valley, when death casts its terrible shadow over us, then we remember and pray the words of this best-known and best-loved Psalm. The Lord is with us, no matter what. When it's so dark we cannot sense his presence, he is there. He is there to guide us with his staff and protect us with his rod, even when the rod falls on us. "I feel the hand of a father upon me when you stroke me, and when you strike me I feel the hand of a father too" (St. Augustine, *Confessions*).

The greatest Christian heroes aren't necessarily those who are famous or perform great deeds. They are those who, when called to pass through the Valley of the Shadow of Death, refuse to turn back.

PRAYER: "Yea, though I walk through death's dark vale, yet I will fear no ill; for Thou art with me, and Thy rod and staff me comfort still."
(*Scottish Psalter*)

Series: *Walking with Christian: Pilgrim's Progress*

READ: Luke 11:1-4, 9-13

God the Father

When you pray, say: 'Father . . .' (Luke 11:2)

How is this for an assignment: describe God, in 300 words or less. That's like trying to summarize the works of Shakespeare on a postage stamp.

So how might we talk about God? We could speak of God like the philosophers do, as "the Ground of Being" or "the Unmoved Mover." Better are the majestic words of a great poet:

> *Thee, Father, first they sung, Omnipotent,*
> *Immutable, Immortal, Infinite*
> *Eternal King; thee, Author of all being,*
> *Fountain of light, thyself invisible*
> (John Milton, *Paradise Lost*)

Best of all is the way Jesus taught us to think of God. He didn't need 300 words to do it; he needed only one. Jesus told us to call God "Father." Infinitely better than the best of earthly fathers, God is great and good, caring and compassionate, wise and powerful—all that and much more. But most important of all, he loves us. He wants us to come to him, talk to him, entrust ourselves to him, not as an abstract idea or a set of attributes, but the way a little child leaps into her father's outstretched arms. Do you know God that way?

PRAYER: Dear God, thank you for being my Father for Jesus' sake. Amen.

Series: *What to Believe*

READ: Hebrews 1:1-4

God the Son

In these last days he has spoken to us by his Son. (Hebrews 1:2)

One of the most basic biblical ideas is the idea of revelation. God must reveal himself to us if we are to have any real knowledge or understanding of him. We can't get there on our own. We can't find God through reason or science or exploration. When the Soviet cosmonaut Yuri Gagarin returned to earth after becoming the first man to orbit the planet, he toed the atheist line by reporting, "I looked and looked but I didn't see God." Of course he didn't! Where would we be if all it took to find God was a spaceship? If we are to know God at all, he must make himself known to us. And he has. He has caused the truth about himself to be written in a book, the Bible.

The Bible leads us to a person. When the magi showed up in Jerusalem looking for the newborn king of the Jews, the scriptures directed them to a baby in Bethlehem. When Jesus' critics wanted proof of his authority, he pointed them to Moses, "for he wrote of me" (John 5:46). When the writer to the Hebrews wanted to stress the supremacy of Jesus, he referred to God's revelation in the Old Testament, but described the Son as God's ultimate revelation. The English reformer William Tyndale put it this way: "The scripture is that wherewith God draweth us unto him. The scriptures sprang out of God, and flow unto Christ, and were given to lead us to Christ. Thou must therefore go along by the scripture as by a line, until thou comest at Christ, which is the way's end and resting place."

PRAYER: Thank you God, for sending your Son.

READ: John 14:1-18, 25-27

The Holy Spirit

. . . you have received the spirit of sonship. (Romans 8:15 RSV)

Jesus' disciples were understandably troubled. He had just told them in the Upper Room that he was leaving them (John 13:33). For three years he had been their teacher, helper, friend. But don't worry, Jesus told them. I'll come back for you. What's more, I'll come back *to* you, and I will do that by sending you another Friend, Helper, and Teacher—the Holy Spirit (14:16-18).

Both the Hebrew (*ruach*) and Greek (*pneuma*) words for Spirit also mean "breath" or "wind." As the wind fills our bodies when we breathe, so the Holy Spirit, the third person of the Trinity, is the invisible, life-giving, life-sustaining presence of God within us.

The Holy Spirit is the Spirit both of Christ and of God (Rom. 8:9). He is the one through whom Christ lives within us (Rom. 8:10-11). On the night before Jesus' death on the cross, he gave his disciples some of his richest and deepest teaching ever, much of it focused on the person and work of the Spirit. The primary purpose of the Holy Spirit is to convince us of the truth about Jesus and enable us to put our trust in him, to convict people of sin, to inspire faith and obedience, and to be the presence of Jesus in us.

The Holy Spirit is the power source for Christian life and ministry. He gives gifts (1 Cor. 12) and cultivates fruit (Gal. 5:22-26) for individuals and churches so that the lives of both may be holy and productive of good.

PRAYER: "Come, Holy Spirit, heavenly Dove,
with all Thy quickening powers." (*Come, Holy Spirit, Heavenly Dove*)

Series: *What to Believe*

READ: John 10:22-33

The Holy Trinity

. . . in the name of the Father and of the Son and of the Holy Spirit. (Matthew 28:19)

God is one. There is only One who is supreme, the Lord God of Israel. Yet God is also three. As the ancient Creed of St. Athanasius declares: "The Father is God, the Son is God, and the Holy Spirit is God. Yet they are not three Gods, but one God, not three Lords, but one Lord."

This is all the more astonishing when you remember that the apostles, who first taught this idea, were all devout Jews. They recited from infancy the *Shema*, Israel's bedrock confession of faith: "Hear, O Israel: The LORD our God, the LORD is one" (Deut. 6:4). But in the New Testament we see these Jewish followers of Jesus responding to further revelations of the nature and being of the one true God. So Thomas, falling in worship before the risen Jesus, cries out, "My Lord and my God!" (John 20:28). Paul states that the Spirit is both the Spirit of God and of Christ" (Rom. 8:9-11). Jesus himself says: "I and the Father are one" (John 10:30).

The Sunday after Pentecost is celebrated as Trinity Sunday in many churches. Though the word *Trinity* may not appear in the New Testament, the fact of it shines out of every page. The triune nature of God is not a theory devised by Christian theologians. It is an understanding of God's essential nature which the events of Easter, Pentecost and subsequent Christian experience demanded.

PRAYER: "Holy, holy, holy . . . God in three Persons, blessed Trinity." (*Holy, Holy, Holy!*)

Series: *What to Believe*

READ: Hebrews 11

Faith's Hall of Fame

These all died in faith. (Hebrews 11:13)

In 1936 somebody came up with the idea to build a museum that would honor the game of baseball and its greatest players, managers, and others. The location chosen for the museum was Cooperstown, New York. The name they gave it was the Baseball Hall of Fame. Since then, hundreds more "Halls of Fame" have been built to commemorate all sorts of people and activities, some of which are pretty weird!

But did you know there is also a Hall of Fame in the Bible? It's not literally called that of course, but it is there, in Hebrews 11. In this chapter many great men and women of the Old Testament are singled out for honor not because of their athletic achievements or scientific discoveries or worldly importance, but because of their faith.

What a list it is! The famous and prominent are there (Abraham, Moses, David), together with some who are not so well known (Barak, Jephthah). Some are questionable moral exemplars (Samson? Jephthah?), and many others are not even named specifically. Some did things which were clearly heroic, suffering torture and even martyrdom for their faith. Others qualified for mention by living quiet lives of everyday obedience. What is most striking to me about this list is that anyone is eligible for inclusion. While you may not have the natural ability to enter any other Hall of Fame, you *can* trust God and live for His glory, and that makes you a potential candidate for Faith's Hall of Fame.

PRAYER: Lord, help me strive for the honors you bestow, rather than merely human recognition.

Series: *Faith's Hall of Fame*

READ: Hebrews 11:1-16

Are You a Traveler?

These all died in faith . . . having acknowledged that they were strangers and exiles on the earth. (Hebrews 11:13)

John Bunyan's classic allegory of the Christian life, *The Pilgrim's Progress*, begins with a poem which is called, "The Author's Apology for His Book." That does not mean Bunyan was ashamed of his book and wanted to apologize to everybody for writing it. The word *apology* originally meant a defense or explanation, literally a "word on behalf of." In this poem Bunyan is telling everyone why he wrote this kind of book. Some people in his time didn't like *The Pilgrim's Progress*; they thought it was not serious enough, they didn't like telling Bible truth in the form of a story. But Bunyan, like every good teacher, knew that describing the Christian faith in this fresh new way would not only help people understand it better, it would also help them remember it.

The most important thing in this Apology is its explanation of the purpose of *The Pilgrim's Progress*: "This book will make a traveler of thee, If by its counsel thou wilt ruled be." Bunyan wrote not just to teach us about pilgrims but to turn us into pilgrims ourselves. In this way, his book is like the Bible—especially Hebrews chapter 11—which also does that. While we're not to abandon this world, we are meant to live for the world to come. I once heard someone ask a great preacher where his home was. He smiled, and instantly replied, "Heaven." Is that true for you?

PRAYER: Almighty God, you called Abraham, Sarah, Isaac and Jacob to be pilgrims and exiles on the earth, and to desire a better country. Help us seek the same, and to find it.

Series: *Walking with Christian: Pilgrim's Progress*

READ: Hebrews 11:1-3

What Is Faith?

By faith we understand . . . (Hebrews 11:3)

Hebrews 11 begins with a classic definition, one of the clearest answers the Bible gives to the question: "What is faith?" "Faith is the assurance of things hoped for, the conviction of things not seen" (v. 3). Faith is an attitude of trust concerning those things you cannot personally verify. How do you know something is true? For some things you can use your senses: Is it raining? Go outside and check. For others you use reason: Does 2 and 2 make 4? Add it up! But there are many things lying beyond the realm of our senses and our mental faculties that require a different way of knowing. You can't confirm such things by seeing for yourself or through logical deduction.

The Bible calls these "the things not seen." Several kinds of things fall into this category. Some things are not seen because they are invisible, like God or love. Some things are not seen because they happened in the past, when there was no one around to look, like the creation of the world. Some things can't be seen because they are future—the "things hoped for"—like heaven and Jesus' return. The point is that you can only be sure of such things by faith. It's not that particularly gullible people have to operate by faith, while the more intelligent among us can use another means of knowing. No, when it comes to the things not seen, everyone—scientist, skeptic, or saint—can only know by faith. The question is, faith in what—or whom?

PRAYER: Lord Jesus, help me to live by faith in you, especially in those areas where I cannot see or prove things.

Series: *Faith's Hall of Fame*

READ: Genesis 1; Hebrews 11:3

By Faith We Understand

By faith we understand that the universe
was created by the word of God. (Hebrews 11:3)

During the Middle Ages a theologian called Anselm of Canterbury coined the phrase: "I believe in order to understand." He meant that you cannot wait until all your questions are answered before you put your faith in God, because all your questions will never be answered. Rather, you must first be willing to believe in him, and then your questions will begin to be answered.

That's how faith operates, according to Hebrews. Our key verse today uses the creation of the world as an example. Scientists develop theories about the development of things, but they cannot answer the ultimate questions, especially: Why is there something rather than nothing? Science can explore *how*, but it has nothing to say about *who* or *why*. That's where faith comes in.

"By faith we understand that the universe was created by the word of God," writes our author, referring to Genesis 1. Faith, according to the Bible, isn't just belief or trust. It's belief in *God* and trust in his *Word*. Think about this: faith in itself has little value; it all depends on the trustworthiness of its object. You can have great faith, but if it's faith in a lie or illusion, you will be cruelly disappointed. The reason Hebrews 11 commends all these people is because their faith was in the God of the Bible. They believed what he said and acted accordingly. We can do the same.

PRAYER: God, help me to accept your Word
as true, and live accordingly.

Series: *Faith's Hall of Fame*

READ: Genesis 4:1-10; Hebrews 11:4

Abel

And through his faith, though he died, he still speaks. (Hebrews 11:4)

Have you ever turned off the news in disgust, wondering why they never seem to report anything but tragedies? Well, the Bible isn't much different. One of the first stories it tells is of a murder within the first family.

Abel and Cain were brothers, one a herdsman, the other a farmer. Both gave sacrifices to God from what they raised, but God accepted one offering and not the other. Why? Some have suggested the reason was the nature of the different offerings. Cain brought produce, while Abel offered an animal; that is, he made a blood sacrifice. But grain offerings were perfectly acceptable according to the Law (see Leviticus 2).

The true explanation is found in Hebrews 11:4: "*By faith* Abel offered to God a more acceptable sacrifice." The basis of Abel's acceptance with God was his faith, his trust in God's grace. Faith was the key; "through this he received approval as righteous" (v. 4, NRSV). His sacrifice to God was an expression of his gratitude, not an attempt to buy God's favor. God didn't accept Abel because of his sacrifice; he accepted the sacrifice because it was Abel's, as a sign of his gracious acceptance of Abel himself. That same acceptance could have been Cain's, even after his offering was rejected, if only he had shared his brother's spirit and motivation in worship (Gen. 4:7). But instead, Cain killed him.

There is a world of difference between worshiping God in order to make him accept you and worshiping God because he has accepted you.

PRAYER: "Nothing in my hands I bring,
Simply to thy cross I cling. . . Rock of Ages, cleft for me,
Let me hide myself in Thee." (*Rock of Ages*)

Series: *Faith's Hall of Fame*

READ: Hebrews 11:5-6

Walking With God

Enoch walked with God, and he was not,
for God took him. (Genesis 5:24)

The difference between biography and obituary is that the former tries to explain the meaning of a life while the latter just gives the bare facts. Enoch was a man whose scriptural biography is as brief as an obituary, but it speaks volumes about what it means to be a person of faith.

"Enoch walked with God." This means first of all that he enjoyed intimacy with God. The early chapters of Genesis tell the story of humanity moving further and further from God, both literally and spiritually. Enoch, by contrast, drew ever closer to him. Enoch's greatest delight was to walk in fellowship with God, to live each day with a sense of the presence of God.

To say that Enoch walked with God also means a life of ever greater obedience to God. In Scripture, "walk" is a natural metaphor for the way we live our lives (see Psalm 1, Eph. 4:1). The picture of our lifestyle as a "walk" suggests the two ideas of exertion and progress; we are both working at obedience and advancing in it. "Enoch walked with God, and he was not, for God took him." He drew closer and closer to God, and grew more and more like God, until one day God simply by-passed death and took him home to be with himself. To be at home with God is the reward of all who walk with God by faith.

PRAYER: "In your presence there is fullness of joy, at your right hand are pleasures for evermore" (Psalm 16:11).

Series: *Faith's Hall of Fame*

READ: John 8:12-30; Hebrews 11:6

How to Please God

And without faith it is impossible to please him. (Hebrews 11:6)

Think of all the people you try to please. Employees try to please the boss; their careers depend upon it. People in sales want to please their customers because their income is tied to it. Boys want to please girls and vice versa. Some people choose to please themselves. But for a Christian, there is only one who really matters. Jesus said of the Father, "I always do the things that are pleasing to him" (John 8:29). Every believer longs to be able to say the same.

How do you please God? Though you might think that would be hard, it actually isn't. Pleasing God starts with faith. Faith makes us acceptable to God (Heb. 11:2) because it trusts in what he has done in Christ, not in our efforts to earn his favor. Faith also pleases God because it trusts his promises. Faith pays God the compliment of saying, "Your word is good with me."

Faith also motivates us to do the things that are pleasing God, however imperfect our performance. And "he rewards those who seek him" (v. 6). When our children were little, they would often bring home pictures they had drawn school. We proudly displayed this work on the refrigerator. Those pictures were very pleasing to me, not because of artistic merit but because the artist was my child. That's how it is with the good works we do to please God. They're never what they ought to be. Yet God is pleased by them; he even rewards them. If God were a critic, he would reject our works. But he isn't a critic; he's a Father.

PRAYER: Thank you, Father, that you reward those who seek you.

Series: *Faith's Hall of Fame*

READ: Genesis 6:5-22

A Man and an Ark

*By faith Noah . . . in reverent fear constructed an ark
for the saving of his household. (Hebrews 11:7)*

In thinking about the story of Noah, it's important not to get hung up on details of naval architecture, animal husbandry, or flood geology. The Old and New Testaments present Noah and his story as history, and other ancient Mesopotamian cultures have similar tales of a cataclysmic flood. But many of the hows, whens, and wheres of Noah's fantastic voyage are left unanswered.

The important lesson of Noah and his ark is the one Hebrews 11:7 emphasizes. It's the lesson that faith means obeying the word of God. God spoke to Noah about judgment and salvation. He announced the coming destruction of the world and he explained how Noah and his family could escape. "By faith Noah . . . took heed" (RSV), that is, he listened to what God said and acted accordingly. He couldn't see the rain clouds when he started to build, but he was convinced of what was coming because he believed the word of the Lord, and so did as he was told.

God still speaks about judgment and salvation. Jesus (Matt. 24:37-39) and Peter (2 Peter 3:3-7) refer to Noah and the flood as a preview of the end. This world will be brought to a halt and all its inhabitants will be judged. Only those in Christ, who by faith in him have "entered the ark" of his church, will be saved from destruction. Many see no signs of the approaching end and scoff at the idea, as Peter says. But that doesn't matter; God said it will be so. Those who take him seriously will make sure of their salvation today.

PRAYER: Maranatha! Lord Jesus, come quickly.

Series: *Faith's Hall of Fame*

READ: Genesis 12:1-9; Hebrews 11:8-10

The Father of the Faithful

By faith Abraham obeyed when he was called. (Hebrews 11:8)

The 20th century British biblical theologian James Denney once commented that whenever a New Testament writer wished to make a point about religion, he said, "Look at Abraham." Abraham is the great example for believers, the prototype of the life of faith—at least until the coming of One greater than he.

Abraham shows us that faith is responsive. When God called him to leave his home, Abraham went. Faith is courageous. "He went out, not knowing where he was to go." Faith is persistent. Abraham never settled down, not even in the promised land; he remained a tent dweller all his life. Faith is expectant. Abraham spent his life looking forward, because by faith he understood that God's ultimate provision for him would be better than an earthly country.

When the Lord first appeared to Abraham, telling him to pull up stakes and move out to an unknown place, he gave him two specific promises: a land to live in and descendants to fill it. But both those promises were subordinate to a more basic one: "I will bless you . . . and all . . . will be blessed through you" (Gen. 12:2-3 NIV). The literal fulfillment of God's promises in the land and people of Israel was for the sake of their spiritual fulfillment in the Christian church and our inheritance in glory. Abraham's true descendants are those who have a faith like his (see Rom. 4:16). If you are a believer, he's your father too.

PRAYER: Lord, help me to walk by faith, not sight.

Series: *Faith's Hall of Fame*

READ: Genesis 18:1-14; Hebrews 11:11-12

The Last Laugh

So Sarah laughed to herself. (Genesis 18:12)

Hebrews 11:11 reminds us that there are great women of faith, such as Sarah, as well as great men. The prominence the New Testament gives to women of faith is remarkable. It was women who stood with Jesus under the cross, women who discovered the empty tomb, and women who first saw the risen Lord. Praise God for faithful women!

The Old Testament incident which lies behind this reference in Hebrews was the promise of a son to Abraham and Sarah. That promise had been made repeatedly by God, but each succeeding year brought no fulfillment. Then one day three strangers visited Abraham's camp. In what evidently was a pre-incarnation appearance of Jesus, one of the three "men"—identified as "the Lord"—made the promise specific. Within a year the son would be born. Sarah, eavesdropping on the men's conversation from inside the tent, burst out laughing at the thought. For all those years she had longed for a baby and had nothing but bitter disappointment. Now she was nearly 90 (Abraham was almost 100); the idea of her bearing a child was ludicrous!

It was a physical impossibility to be sure, but the same God who created the universe out of nothing had determined to make a baby where none could be expected. "Is anything too hard for the Lord?" was the question that brought Abraham and Sarah up short. By faith, they answered "No," and so were blessed with a son who was first in the line which produced the Messiah.

PRAYER: Lord, help me always to remember that, whatever I may be facing, nothing is too hard for you. You will see me through.

Series: *Faith's Hall of Fame*

READ: Revelation 21:1-7; Hebrews 11:13-16

Strangers and Exiles

These all died in faith . . . having acknowledged that they were strangers and exiles on the earth. (Hebrews 11:13)

Say the word "pilgrim" and most Americans think of a man in a tall black hat with a buckle on it, carrying a blunderbuss and hunting for turkeys. But it's actually a great Bible word, and an even greater thing to be. Pilgrims are travelers, people passing through on their way to somewhere else, "strangers and exiles on the earth." I've already referred to John Bunyan's title for his great description of the Christian life: *The Pilgrim's Progress.*

Let's think a bit more about what it means to live as a pilgrim. Pilgrims maintain an attitude of detachment. Without opting out of involvement in the world and its problems, they realize that they don't really belong here. They do not define their meaning by the world's wisdom; they do not measure achievement with the world's yardsticks; they do not set their hearts on the world's values; they do not seek their destiny in the world's goals. They never settle down here to permanent residence.

The 2nd century Christian writer of the Epistle to Diognetus described his fellow believers this way: "They dwell in their own countries but simply as sojourners. As citizens, they share in all things with others, and yet endure all things as if foreigners. Every foreign land is to them a homeland, and yet every homeland is a foreign country."

PRAYER: Lord Jesus, give me a pilgrim's heart and a pilgrim's mind. Help me to be in the world, but not of it.

Series: *Faith's Hall of Fame*

READ: Revelation 22:1-5; Hebrews 11:13-16

God Is Not Ashamed

God is not ashamed to be called their God. (Hebrews 11:16)

It's one of a parent's most stinging rebukes. A child who has done some mischief and who should have known better, is met with these hard words: "I'm ashamed of you."

How often we do things of which God must be ashamed! Like a child who embarrasses his or her parents, our behavior can bring dishonor upon the family name. This is actually the point of the commandment not to "take" the Lord's name in vain. As people who bear the Lord's name—"Christians"—when we go wrong in some public way we can damage Jesus' reputation. "Let not those who hope in you be put to shame through me, O LORD GOD of hosts" (Ps. 69:6).

But there is a flip side to all that. There are those of whom this wonderful statement is made: "God is not ashamed to be called their God." What sort of people qualify for that accolade? People who die in faith, who "were still living by faith when they died" (Heb. 11:13 NIV). They didn't receive all the things God promised them. It looked like time ran out on them before they enjoyed his best blessings. But that didn't cause them to waver or turn back. They were still moving forward when they died.

Some say that faith means getting all you ask for from God. That's not true. Faith means trusting God even when you don't get what he has promised. God is proud to be the God of people with that kind of faith, and he has prepared a city for them where they will finally receive all they could ever wish for, and more.

PRAYER: Father, answer my prayer in the way
that you know is best. For Jesus' sake. Amen.

Series: *Faith's Hall of Fame*

READ: Genesis 22:1-14; Hebrews 11:17-19

The Mountain of the Lord

By faith Abraham, when he was tested,
offered up Isaac. (Hebrews 11:17)

How could he and why would he? That's what we want to know when we read that God ordered Abraham to offer Isaac as a sacrifice. We know very well that such a thing is abhorrent to God. The Old Testament from beginning to end rejects the pagan practice of human sacrifice. Then why did the Lord give this command to Abraham?

Hebrews 11 offers two clues. First, Abraham's faith was being tested, specifically his trust in God's promise that his line would continue through Isaac. There never seems to have been any doubt that Abraham would obey God, the story has no hint of struggle within him. The issue for Abraham was reconciling God's *demand* for Isaac with his *promise* about Isaac. This he did by concluding God would raise Isaac from the dead after he was sacrificed. Faith is tested when God's hard demands upon us seem to conflict with his good promises to us. We must submit to the first without giving up the second.

The other thing Hebrews tells us is that this story was a parable (that's the literal meaning of the phrase "figuratively speaking" in verse 19). We cannot read of Abraham and Isaac on the mountain without thinking of another father "who did not spare his own son, but gave him up for us all" (Rom. 8:32), and another day when that son carried the wood of the sacrifice up a hill and laid down his life as the perfect atonement for sin.

PRAYER: Thank you, Father, that when the time
came you gave up your son for our salvation.

Series: *Faith's Hall of Fame*

READ: Genesis 27:1-29; Hebrews 11:20

Father and Sons

By faith Isaac invoked future blessings
on Jacob and Esau. (Hebrews 11:20)

What a sorry story Genesis 27 tells. It reads like a soap opera. Here's Isaac, old and blind, drooling in anticipation of another feast, doting on the son who supplies him his fresh meat. Over there is Rebekah, his once loving wife, whose life is now devoted to deceitful schemes for the advancement of her own favorite child. Don't forget Jacob, putting on Esau's clothes, sticking hair on his arms, and doing a poor imitation of his brother's voice. Or Esau, crying like a baby and screaming for revenge. This scene has everything Hollywood could ask for: ambition, conflict, sensuality, treachery, and the threat of violence running just below the surface like a rip current.

So of course, the writer of Hebrews selects this scene as an outstanding example of faith! "By faith Isaac blessed Jacob and Esau" (NIV). That statement omits a considerable amount of detail, to say the least. But it says something important. You can be deeply flawed, and at the same time a person of faith. Isaac had made a mess of his life. He had lost his wife's affection, failed as a father, given in to self-indulgence. But he still believed in God's future; he still looked forward with sightless eyes to the things that cannot be seen. So he blessed his sons to bring them into line with the promises of God, and when even that didn't turn out as he intended, he recognized the overruling hand of God and let the blessing stand.

PRAYER: Thank you, Lord, that I don't have to be perfect to have faith. Help me trust in you more.

Series: *Faith's Hall of Fame*

READ: Genesis 48:1-21; Hebrews 11:21

Cross Purposes

By faith Jacob, when dying, blessed each
of the sons of Joseph. (Hebrews 11:21)

Joseph had brought his sons to visit his dying father. Jacob, lost in memories of the past, looked up as they entered the room. "Who's that?" asked old Jacob. "These are my boys," Joseph answered. And Jacob took them up, and stretching his arms out over them, he blessed them.

But there was something odd about the blessing. Normally the eldest son received the chief blessing as an indication that the family line would continue through him. When Joseph brought his sons forward he made sure that Manasseh, the first-born, was in position for Jacob to lay his right hand—the symbol of the primary blessing—upon him. But Jacob crossed his arms and reversed the natural birth order. Joseph thought his father had made a mistake and tried to correct him, but the old man's action had been deliberate. By faith, looking ahead to the future God promised, Jacob knew Ephraim was destined to play the larger role. That is exactly how it turned out. As he did with Jacob and Joseph, as he did with Moses and David, the Lord upset the natural order by choosing the younger brother.

God is not bound by our human conventions in the way he accomplishes his purposes. What matters most is not birth or natural ability, but faith.

PRAYER: Thank you, Lord, that you can use me to do
your work. Help me accomplish something for you.

Series: *Faith's Hall of Fame*

READ: Genesis 50:22-26; Hebrews 11:22

Homeward Bound

By faith Joseph . . . gave directions
concerning his bones. (Hebrews 11:22)

Of all the events in Joseph's life, what a thing to single out as a sign of faith. Not his boyhood dreams, not his integrity in Potiphar's house, not his faithfulness in prison, not his magnanimous forgiveness of his brothers, but the final instructions he gave concerning his bones!

But what eloquent instructions they were! How we die can say as much about us as how we live. In Joseph's case, his insistence that the descendants of Israel take his body back to Canaan spoke volumes. It told who he really was. Joseph looked like an Egyptian and talked like an Egyptian; after all, he had lived there for 93 of his 110 years, most of them as Pharaoh's right-hand man. But in his heart he was still an Israelite. He was part of the people of God, and he wanted to identify with them even in death. Joseph's act of faith also said something about where he really belonged. Egypt had been good to him, showering him with honors. But it wasn't home. Home for Joseph was in the promised land. Finally, this shows what Joseph really hoped for. He looked for the great day when God would finally deliver his people. And through the centuries, as Joseph's instructions were passed from generation to generation, that hope was kept alive.

As Christians we too testify to the same things Joseph did. We claim our citizenship, not in this or that country, but in heaven (Phil. 3:20). Our bodies are buried the way seeds are planted (1 Cor. 15:37), in hopes of a future glorious harvest of life.

PRAYER: Lord, help me to live by faith in your promises.

Series: *Faith's Hall of Fame*

READ: Exodus 2:1-10; Hebrews 11:23

Faith Dares

They were not afraid of the king's edict. (Hebrews 11:23)

The world was shocked in 1989 when tanks rolled into Beijing's Tiananmen Square to crush the lives and hopes of unarmed students demonstrating for democracy and freedom. In the 21st century we've seen thousands of young Iranians protesting the brutality of their theocratic regime—and paying a fearful price. In Russia critics opposing an unjust war risk prison or worse. It's thrilling to see individuals daring to defy a powerful state on behalf of justice. I wonder if I would have that kind of courage.

Hebrews says that it's produced by faith. When a Pharaoh arose who did not know of Joseph and who looked upon the growing Hebrew population in Egypt as a security risk, he took decisive action against them. It was the first time, though far from the last, that genocide would be practiced against the Jews. But two brave people defied his edict and protected their son. They acted in part out of natural affection—"because they saw that the child was beautiful" (v. 23)—but also because of faith. Faith is convinced that God is sovereign, and that even the mightiest humans are under his control. It is not afraid of their attacks. "You would have no authority over me at all unless it had been given you from above," Jesus calmly replied to Pilate's threats (John 19:11).

For many believers in the world today, the issue of defying evil edicts of the state is very real. What if my commitment to Christ cost me my job, my child's education, my freedom, my life? Would I have the courage to stand with him? By faith, the answer can be "yes."

PRAYER: Pray for Christians living under oppression.

Series: *Faith's Hall of Fame*

READ: Exodus 2:11-15; Hebrews 11:24-27

Faith Chooses

. . . choosing rather to be mistreated with the people of God than to enjoy the fleeting pleasures of sin. (Hebrews 11:25)

He was the adopted son of an Egyptian princess, destined to be a prince himself. He was raised in all the luxury of Pharaoh's house, enjoying every advantage of position and education. But he gave it all up for the life of a wilderness wanderer. His name was Moses.

He was born in Victorian England to a wealthy family. Educated at Eton College and Cambridge University, he achieved distinction as the greatest cricket player in Britain. He was destined for a life of ease at the top of aristocratic society, but he left it all to answer a call to missionary service, in China, India, and Africa. His name was C. T. Studd.

Why do people walk away from a life that seems to have everything for one of apparent hardship and deprivation? The answer is—faith. Moses chose against worldly status, comfort and wealth. He gave up the place of a prince for that of a slave. He traded the pleasures of sin for ill treatment with the people of God. He exchanged the treasures of Egypt for abuse suffered for God. But he didn't consider it a sacrifice, "for he was looking to the reward" (v. 26). Faith gave him the ability to "see" what was invisible—salvation, heaven, even God himself (v. 27). That kind of vision puts the values of the world in perspective. In the memorable words of missionary and martyr Jim Elliot, "It is no sacrifice to give up what you cannot keep in order to gain what you cannot lose."

PRAYER: God, grant us the faith and courage to choose Christ over the world.

Series: *Faith's Hall of Fame*

READ: Exodus 12:1-13, 21-28; Hebrews 11:27-28

The Lord's Passover

By faith he kept the Passover and sprinkled
the blood. (Hebrews 11:28)

The symbolism of Passover must have seemed odd to the first Israelites. Some of the careful directions that God gave Moses would have made sense. The people were to eat their meal of unleavened bread and roasted lamb quickly, with their bags packed and coats on. These details call to mind the haste of Israel's departure from Egypt, when they were pushed out of the land so fast they didn't have time to add yeast to their bread dough (Exod. 12:34). Then there were the bitter herbs which accompanied the meal, a symbol of the cruel bondage the people had known in Egypt.

But what about the unblemished lamb, and the blood that had to be sprinkled on the doors? Surely God knew where his people lived; his angel didn't need their houses identified to avoid a mistake! According to the New Testament, these details pointed to things the Israelites could not yet see. They were object lessons whose meaning became clear with the coming of the Lamb of God. "Christ, our Passover lamb, has been sacrificed," wrote Paul (1 Cor. 5:7). "Whoever feeds on my flesh . . . has eternal life," said Jesus (John 6:54). Faith is the hyssop brush by which we apply the blood of Jesus to our sins. "If the blood of a lamb then preserved the Jews unhurt in the midst of so great a destruction, much more will the blood of Christ save us, for whom it has been sprinkled not on our doorposts but in our souls" (John Chrysostom).

PRAYER: Thank you, Lord, for the precious blood
of the Lamb that covers all my sin.

Series: *Faith's Hall of Fame*

READ: Exodus 14:10-31; Hebrews 11:29

A Way Out of No Way

*By faith the people crossed the Red Sea
as on dry land.* (Hebrews 11:29)

They were, as the saying goes, between a rock and a hard place. Shortly after dismissing Moses and the people Pharaoh had a change of heart, and set out in hot pursuit with his army. He caught up to Israel on the shore of the Red Sea, and it seemed as though revenge was within his grasp.

The Exodus looked like it was going to be one of the shortest flights on record. Ahead of the people was an impassable sea, behind them an implacable foe. How did they ever get into such a predicament? Had they made a wrong turn somewhere? It's not surprising if we find ourselves in trouble when we fail to walk in God's way. But this wasn't a case of disobedience—God himself had led Israel there, guiding them with a pillar of cloud and fire.

The truth is, there's no guarantee that our walk of faith will not pass through dangerous places or reach apparent dead ends. The Lord has delivered us from bondage to sin, redeeming us by his blood and blessing us with his leading and presence. It doesn't necessarily follow, though, that we won't meet serious difficulties in life. But when we do, he will get us through. There's a saying in the African American church: God can make a way out of no way. There's also a promise in the Bible: "Fear not . . . when you pass through the waters, I will be with you; and through the rivers, they shall not overwhelm you" (Isa. 43:1-2).

PRAYER: Thank God for his power and promises.

Series: *Faith's Hall of Fame*

READ: Joshua 6:1-5,12-21; Hebrews 11:30

The Walls Come Tumbling Down

By faith the walls of Jericho fell down. (Hebrews 11:30)

It was an odd order for a commander to issue to his troops. They were all supposed to march quietly around the city, day after day; then on the seventh day they would march around seven times, blow on a bunch of horns, and have everybody yell a lot. Those tactics would not be found in the training manual of any army, then or now. Not that military expertise would have helped them much. The people of Israel were facing an impossible assignment: possessing no trained army, with no heavy equipment or siege weapons, they were to destroy a large, strongly defended walled city. God's instructions may have sounded crazy, but the people didn't have many alternatives other than to trust and obey. God said march and blow and shout, and the walls would fall down. So they did. And they did!

The early church fathers saw in the story of Jericho an illustration of the power of preaching. The walls of sin may appear to be impregnable, but when the Word of God is sounded, they fall in ruins. It seems like such an odd thing: just get up and talk about the Bible. Tell the story of Jesus. Yet when we do, unbelief can totter and faith spring up.

Modern readers tend to get caught up in questions about the walls of Jericho. Did it actually happen? Would God really order the extermination of an entire population? But Hebrews reads it as a story of faith. If God's people will believe his Word and do as he says, then nothing can stand against them.

PRAYER: Praise God that by faith the walls
you face can come tumbling down.

Series: *Faith's Hall of Fame*

READ: Joshua 2:1-15; Joshua 6:22-25; Hebrews 11:31

Rahab

By faith Rahab the prostitute did not perish
with those who were disobedient. (Hebrews 11:31)

Now here's an unlikely candidate for inclusion in Faith's Hall of Fame. It would seem like Rahab had three strikes against her. First, she was a woman. With the exception of a passing reference to Sarah, Rahab is the only woman named in Hebrews 11. Second, she was a Canaanite, a member of the nation which Israel was commanded to eliminate from the land of promise. "God," ran an ancient rabbinic prayer, "I thank Thee that I am neither a woman nor a gentile." Well, Rahab was both! That's not all. She was also a prostitute. Some people are embarrassed by the Bible's forthrightness. For example, the ancient Jewish historian Josephus explained that Rahab was actually a female innkeeper. But Hebrews doesn't mince words. It describes Rahab with the Greek word *porne*, and if you think you know what that means, you're right. It's the sick who need a doctor, said Jesus. "I did not come to call the righteous, but sinners, to repentance" (Mark 2:17 NKJV).

Whatever she was and had been, when the decisive moment came, Rahab chose faith. As the spies appealed to her for help, she cast her lot with Israel. By faith she chose to identify with the people of God, and that decision was her salvation. If you tend to think of salvation as a reward for being good, the example of Rahab is a powerful reminder that God's grace will save anyone who trusts him.

PRAYER: We praise you, Father, that people of any nation, race, or sex, and sinners of every description, can come to you and by faith receive salvation.

Series: *Faith's Hall of Fame*

READ: Hebrews 11:32-38

Time's Running Out

Time would fail me to tell of Gideon, Barak,
Samson, Jephthah . . . (Hebrews 11:32)

Our guide through Faith's Hall of Fame just checked his watch and
realized he still has dozens of exhibits to show us and only a few minutes
until the museum closes. "What more shall I say? I don't have time to tell
about . . ." He's used up 31 of his 40 verses and only has progressed as far
in Old Testament history as the book of Joshua!

So our writer quickly introduces the judges, rattling off four
representatives: Gideon, Barak, Samson, and Jephthah. The judges were
heroic leaders who were raised up by God at a time of crisis to deliver
the tribes of Israel from foreign oppression. But as heroes they left a lot
to be desired. Gideon was so unsure of himself that he insisted on special
proof from God before he would do what he was told; when God passed
his test, he demanded a repeat performance (Judg. 6:36-40)! Barak
was Israel's army commander, but he wouldn't go into battle unless the
prophetess Deborah—who was twice the man Barak was—went along
(Judg. 4:4-10). Everyone knows about Samson's problems with women
(Judg. 14-16), and Jephthah was a rash and violent man whose unholy
vow cost him his daughter (Judges 11). More evidence that people of
faith can have feet of clay.

Faith is not an award God bestows on special people. It's the way
sinners can live before him and be used by him. If the Lord could
only employ perfect people to accomplish his work, where would that
leave him?

PRAYER: Thank you, Lord, that faith is the pathway to true greatness.

Series: *Faith's Hall of Fame*

READ: Psalm 27; Hebrews 11:32-34

A Man After God's Own Heart

Time would fail me to tell of . . . David. (Hebrews 11:32)

Having mentioned the judges, our writer now passes on to the period of the kings. The kings were those "who through faith conquered kingdoms, enforced justice . . . became mighty in war, put foreign armies to flight" (vv. 33-34).

While there were many kings, with widely different levels of piety and performance, there was just one who set the standard. David was *the* king of Israel. He was the great conqueror of kingdoms, and it was to him that God gave the greatest promise: that out of his house would come a ruler who would sit on his throne forever. Each subsequent monarch in Jerusalem was judged according to this criterion: whether or not he "walked in the ways of his father David."

The Bible doesn't gloss over David's moral failures. Although a great man of faith, David was guilty of great sins as well. Desire for a woman led David astray. But that wasn't the desire that defined him. What defined David was that he desired God more than anything. Despite his lapses, the supreme thing in David's life was always his relationship with God. His heart's desire was for God, to know him, to be with him, to delight in him. "To behold the beauty of the Lord" was the one thing he sought after.

A lot of things can measure our faith—the gifts that we give, the words we speak, certainly our actions and activities. But the main indicator, the one that God especially pays attention to, is the desire of our heart.

PRAYER: One thing I desire, Lord: that I may
dwell with you forever. (see Psalm 27:4)

Series: *Faith's Hall of Fame*

READ: Daniel 6:1-23; Hebrews 11:33

Faith in the Lions' Den

Who through faith . . . stopped the mouths of lions. (Hebrews 11:33)

Here's a familiar Bible story. Daniel had been taken to Babylon as a youth and had risen to a high position there. Now the Medes and Persians had taken over the city, and there was a new emperor. But Daniel kept his place. In addition to his obvious talent, what distinguished Daniel was his devotion to the Lord. When jealous enemies sought to destroy him, they chose Daniel's piety as their weapon. When King Darius issued an edict banning any worship other than worship of himself, they only had to watch and wait.

There are different kinds of courage. Physical courage can be stimulated by an instinctive reaction or a rush of adrenalin. Someone may simply react without thinking, and end up doing something heroic. But Daniel's courage was of a more difficult type. It was moral courage. Knowing what he ought to do, and knowing ahead of time what it would cost him, he calmly proceeded to do it.

Daniel's courage came from his belief that God was in control. He was confident that if he honored God, God would honor him. Daniel knew that the God who had created lions would either deliver him *from* them or else *through* them from death into life. The other key to Daniel's courage was that from his youth he had made it a principle to obey God in all things (see Dan. 1:8). Daniel knew by experience that the secret of faithfulness in great tests is a lifetime of faithfulness in little ones.

PRAYER: Lord, help me to be faithful to you in the small things so that, if I face a big thing, I will be true.

Series: *Faith's Hall of Fame*

READ: Daniel 3:13-30; Hebrews 11:34

But If Not . . .

Our God whom we serve is able to deliver us . . .
But if not . . . we will not serve your gods. (Daniel 3:17-18)

The heroic faith of Shadrach, Meshach, and Abednego "quenched the power of fire" as Hebrews puts it (11:34). That faith is embodied in their refusal to worship King Nebuchadnezzar's golden statue, even though such defiance was certain to cost their lives.

When the band blared, all in the crowd fell on their faces—except for the three Hebrew friends. The king decided to offer them another chance, but the three Hebrew youths didn't waver. They didn't argue with themselves that they could bow outwardly while withholding inward consent, or that they owed it to their people to do what was necessary to maintain their positions of influence. They simply remembered God's command: "You shall not bow down to them or serve them" (Exod. 20:5). And they obeyed.

Their response to Nebuchadnezzar reveals the elements of biblical faith. Faith is confidence in God's power ("Our God . . . is able to deliver us"), plus trust in God's wisdom to determine whatever happens ("But if not . . ."), plus resolute obedience ("we will not serve your gods"). I especially love those three words, "But if not." They are the essence of faith. God is able to heal me, *but if not*, I will still trust him. God can fix my problem . . . rescue me from my predicament . . . heal me . . . *but if not*, I will praise him anyway.

PRAYER: Loving Father, help us to praise you
by thankfulness when you deliver us from trouble,
and by patient endurance when you do not.

Series: *Faith's Hall of Fame*

READ: 2 Kings 4:8-37; Hebrews 11:35

From Death to Life

*Women received back their dead,
raised to life again. (Hebrews 11:35 NIV)*

The writer of Hebrews may have been thinking of this story from 2 Kings 4 but hadn't been able to conceive. Then, when she had given up hope and resigned herself to barrenness, God's prophet promised her a son. In due time the child was born and he became the light of his mother's life. And then one day he suddenly died. "Did I ask for this?" the heartbroken mother cried out to Elisha. Sometimes it seems as though God teases us by giving us a temporary happiness which only makes our subsequent loss the more unbearable by contrast.

Faith has the power to see through the tears and beyond the hurt. "By faith . . . women received back their dead, raised to life again." That is literally what happened with the Shunammite woman and her son. But it will happen with all God's children someday. In our fallen world, all happiness is transitory. Life here is a process of ever-increasing loss: we lose our innocence, our youth, our strength, our beauty, our loved ones, eventually our health, our senses, our memory, our lives. But in God's mercy these losses are only temporary. We will receive it all back again, and then some, when his kingdom comes. "What's lost is nothing to what's found, and all the death that ever was, set next to life, would scarcely fill a cup" (Frederick Buechner, *Godric*).

PRAYER: Lord, help me to view all things in the light of eternity, and to bear both gains and losses, with the strength of faith.

Series: *Faith's Hall of Fame*

READ: Hebrews 11:35-38

Heroes of Faith

. . . of whom the world was not worthy. (Hebrews 11:38)

Reading these verses near the end of Hebrews 11 reminds me of a remark made by Theresa of Avila with reference to her own personal suffering: "Lord, if this is how you treat your friends, I do not wonder that you have so few of them!"

In this section our writer makes no mention of specific individuals. He is probably thinking not only of Old Testament saints but countless men and women who suffered and died for their faith in the centuries between Old Testament and New Testament times, particularly during the Maccabean period. Most of us know little or nothing about that ancient history, just as few details of the widespread persecution of Christians today make the newspaper. The heroes of faith are mostly anonymous. But we may be certain their names are known to God, and that every one of them will be remembered by him.

Looking back . . . remembering . . . honoring . . . is what our writer invites us to do throughout Hebrews 11. We should bear in mind those who gave their lives for values that can't be seen, who looked ahead to things hoped for, who refused to relinquish their faith in God no matter what it cost. We should also recognize that it's not just Christians who suffer for conscience' sake. Today there are many thousands of courageous men and women who are experiencing painful consequences for opposing evil regimes. These too are people "of whom the world was not worthy."

PRAYER: Lord, few of us face persecution. But whatever may come, help us to endure hardship as good soldiers of Jesus Christ.

Series: *Faith's Hall of Fame*

READ: 2 Peter 3:1-9; Hebrews 11:39-40

Something Better for Us

And all these, though commended through their faith,
did not receive what was promised. (Hebrews 11:39)

What a disappointment it must be to wait your whole life for your heart's desire and die without receiving it. That seemed to be the fate of faith's heroes. They were living for the promises, convinced about what they were hoping for. For them, the promises were mostly about physical Israel—the land and its fruits, the Messiah who would conquer and rule it. For God, the promises were ultimately about spiritual blessings: forgiveness, salvation, the joy of fellowship with him, deliverance from death, eternal life. And they were all summed up in a person, Jesus Christ (see 2 Cor. 1:20). Though they didn't realize it, he was what all these heroes of faith were looking for. And every one of them died without seeing him.

Hebrews 11 gives a remarkable explanation for that. It wasn't because they were somehow found to be unworthy of God's blessings that they were denied seeing their fulfilment; on the contrary, they were "commended" because of their faith. But God withheld the fulfillment so that he could include in the covenant promises those who came later; namely, us. And Peter says the reason God continues to delay the Lord's return, when every promise will be fulfilled, is to allow time for still others to repent so they can share in the blessing as well. Even God's seeming slowness is really grace in disguise.

Remember, the Lord may delay in keeping his promises, but he will never fail to keep them. And we have to believe that God's time is best.

PRAYER: Help us to use our time to bring
ourselves and others to repentance.

Series: *Faith's Hall of Fame*

READ: Hebrews 12:1-3

On Track

. . . looking to Jesus, the founder and
perfecter of our faith. (Hebrews 12:2)

Imagine what the crowd in an Olympic stadium must look like to a
runner who is standing at the starting line of a gold-medal race. That's
the image our writer conjures up here in Hebrews 12. We are athletes
down on the track, surrounded by a great cloud of witnesses, a crowd
so vast the individual faces blur and we cannot pick them out. The
people in the crowd are not mere spectators, though. They're all former
athletes themselves, veterans of the race we are running. They are the
saints of Hebrews 11—plus 2000 years' worth more since then—and
their appearance in our mind's eye is an incentive to stay on the course
as they did.

We started these meditations by talking about Faith's Hall of Fame. It's
appropriate that we should end them in Hebrews 12, because none of us is
ready yet for Hebrews 11. To be eligible for the Hall of Fame, you must be
retired. But we're still on the track, running the race. The "race that is set
before us" (12:1) is a marathon, not a dash, and for it we need endurance,
determination, and perseverance. We can't afford to be weighed down by
entanglements, especially sins. Above all, we must concentrate on Jesus,
who is both the source and model of our faith. He himself has finished the
course in triumph, and by looking to him we will find the power to reach
heaven where he is. Nothing short of that will do.

Just running in the race of faith isn't enough. What matters is
finishing it.

PRAYER: Lord, however long or short my remaining
race may be, help me to finish strong.

Series: *Faith's Hall of Fame*

READ: Galatians 1:1-5

It's All Grace

Grace to you and peace from God our Father
and the Lord Jesus Christ . . . (Galatians 1:3)

We've just spent several weeks looking at how faith worked in the lives of God's saints. But while faith transforms the way we live, we're not saved by what we do. To remind us of that, we turn now to the Bible's great proclamation of salvation by grace, Paul's letter to the Galatians.

When my daughter was studying in France, I would occasionally look at her Facebook page to see what was new with her. One day I noticed that under the heading "Religious views," she had written *Tout est grace*. I don't understand French, but I could figure out this much. What she said was, "It's all grace."

The apostle Paul would agree. It—our salvation, our faith, our "religious views"—is all grace. Paul's opening salutation is front-loaded with this greatest of Christian terms: "Grace to you and peace from God our Father and the Lord Jesus Christ." We often skip past those familiar words, but we shouldn't, because this is actually a stupendous announcement. God the Father and the Lord Jesus Christ are *gracious*. (Notice how Paul names these two together and side by side, calling Jesus Lord and equally the source of grace.) God's first word to us in Christ is not judgment or anger or commandment. It is *grace*.

Grace means that God is on our side. The best four-word summary of the gospel that I know is this phrase from Romans 8:31: "God is *for* us." It's all grace! It's all a gift!

PRAYER: Thank you, Father, that my salvation
is a free gift from you.

Series: *Galatians*

READ: Galatians 1:1-9

No Other Gospel

I am astonished that you are so quickly deserting him who called you in the grace of Christ and are turning to a different gospel. (Galatians 1:6)

You can still hear Paul's agitation clearly, even after two thousand years. How could these new believers in Galatia, people to whom Paul himself had brought the gospel just a short time before, already be turning away from the truth and embracing a different "gospel"? The apostle asserts in no uncertain terms that there is only one genuine gospel, the one he himself had preached to them. If anyone confuses people by teaching another way of salvation besides simple faith in Christ, Paul cries, "Let him be accursed!" (v. 9). Whoever contradicts the gospel of salvation by grace alone through faith alone stands under God's judgment.

Paul's passionate outcry sounds a jarring note in our tolerant day, a day in which the church no longer thunders anathemas against false teaching. Most people today prefer to think that all ideas are equally valid, especially when it comes to religion, just as any belief is acceptable as long as it is sincerely held. Even in the church serious doctrinal or ethical differences are treated as if they were merely personal preferences. Everything is tolerated except intolerance.

But Paul had no tolerance at all for those who perverted the gospel, because he was convinced that beliefs have consequences and that non-Christian or sub-Christian beliefs would have bad consequences—eternally bad consequences. We may not like to think that way, but Paul did. What else could his strong language mean?

PRAYER: Lord, preserve your church in the truth of the gospel.

Series: *Galatians*

READ: Ephesians 2:1-10

By Faith Alone

By grace you have been saved through faith.
And this is not your own doing. (Ephesians 2:8)

"The difference between the right word and the almost right word," remarked Mark Twain, "is the difference between *lightning* and *lightning bug.*" In much the same way, the difference between the authentic New Testament gospel and the almost gospel of human religion is the difference between salvation through Christ alone and salvation through Christ plus something else.

It is not faith in Christ *plus* anything else that saves; not faith plus good works, not faith plus religion, not faith plus rituals and observances. The apostolic gospel is faith in Christ plus *nothing*. We are justified by faith *alone*. Paul's words in his letter to the Galatians, said Martin Luther, "are very thunderclaps from heaven against all kinds of self-righteousness."

The word "gospel" means "good news." The real gospel announces that salvation is by grace alone (pure gift) through faith alone (received simply by trusting). The almost gospel of Paul's opponents wasn't good news at all. The preachers who followed Paul in Galatia had proclaimed to them "a different gospel" (Gal. 1:6). They were teaching that in addition to believing in Christ you had to be circumcised as a Jew in order to be saved (see Acts 15:1). The question between Paul and his opponents was one of grace versus law, and it would determine whether Christianity would be a message with power to save, or just one more religion teaching salvation by rules-keeping.

PRAYER: Thank you, Father, that you have done everything for our salvation, and that all we need do is to receive your grace with trust in Christ.

Series: *Galatians*

READ: Galatians 1:11–2:10

Man's Gospel, or God's?

. . . the gospel that was preached by me is not man's gospel. (Galatians 1:11)

Wouldn't you love to know what Paul was doing all those years between his conversion and the beginning of his missionary journeys? The closest we have to a biography is these few verses in which he offers a sketch of his life over some fifteen years. But his purpose is not autobiography, much as we might wish it had been. Everything Paul says about himself he says to underscore this one basic point: he did not get his gospel message from any human being, not even from the other apostles. He got it straight from the Lord.

It's not hard to guess how Paul's opponents sought to discredit him in the eyes of the Galatians. "Well, you know, he wasn't one of Jesus' disciples. He never even met him. Who knows how he came up with his message?" Paul takes his critics head-on. The gospel he proclaimed was God's message of salvation, not man's, and this is the major difference between Paul and his opponents. Their message came from themselves, from their own minds and ideas; Paul's came "through a revelation of Jesus Christ" (v. 12). Their message was man-centered, focusing on what people had to do in order to be saved; Paul's was Christ-centered, focusing on what he did in order to save us.

What Paul had proclaimed to the Galatians was "the gospel of Christ" (Gal. 1:7). It came from Christ, it consisted of Christ, it led to Christ. This is the gospel that saves.

PRAYER: Thank you, Lord for the good news of salvation in Christ. May I believe it and live it today.

Series: *Galatians*

READ: Galatians 2:11-14

Confrontation

I opposed him to his face . . . when I saw that their conduct was not in step with the truth of the gospel. (Galatians 2:11, 14)

It's hard to stick up for the truth. Correcting someone is very tricky. You can be criticized. You can even damage a friendship. That's why we so often avoid confrontations. I tend to look the other way when I see a Christian brother or sister who is going wrong in faith or life. After all, my interfering with them probably wouldn't do any good, and it would just make them angry with me. So I keep quiet.

I'm glad that Paul didn't keep quiet. Galatians 2 describes a face-to-face showdown he had with Peter in the city of Antioch. Peter's withdrawal from table fellowship with gentile believers under pressure from the Judaizers implied that faith in Christ alone was not enough to gain acceptance into the church (and, by extension, acceptance with God). Paul confronted Peter publicly, saying to him in effect, "You have been saved by grace and set free from the law; why would you impose it upon others?"

Peter knew better, but he was afraid of what others thought and said about him. His problem wasn't doctrinal; Peter knew that faith in Christ made gentiles part of the church. The Lord had taught that lesson to him at the house of Cornelius (see Acts 10). His problem was that fear made him fail to live out the implications of the doctrine he believed.

It takes courage to live consistently with the gospel of grace. Maybe we can help each other do that.

PRAYER: Lord Jesus, show where my life is not in step with the truth of the gospel.

Series: *Galatians*

READ: Galatians 2:15-16

Justification by Faith

A person is not justified by works of the law
but through faith in Jesus Christ. (Galatians 2:16)

When the writer David Thoreau lay on his deathbed, a devout aunt asked him if he had made his peace with God. "I was not aware that we had quarreled," he replied. I wonder if he was quite so flippant when he stood before the Judge in eternity.

Ask people today how they expect to be put right with God, and they'll look at you in amazement. "What makes you think I'm not already?" Or they will mumble about how they try to live a decent life, and surely God accepts all good people, doesn't he? Everyone assumes they're good with God, but the day of judgment will reveal otherwise.

In Galatians 2:16 Paul gives classic expression to what Luther called "the chiefest article of Christianity," the doctrine of justification by faith. We are declared righteous by God—accepted by him now and forever—simply on the basis of our trusting in Christ, and not by virtue of anything we do. And lest we should miss the point Paul repeats this point three times in verse 16. The starting point is this: "knowing that a man is not justified by the works of the law but by faith in Jesus Christ."

That may seem like overkill, but the reason Paul hammers at this point is because the idea of earning salvation through religion (the law) or good works is one of the most deeply ingrained of all human instincts. It's very hard for people to believe that they need Christ in order for God to accept them. But they do. Good works are not enough.

PRAYER: I praise you, Father, for accepting me for Jesus' sake.

Series: *Galatians*

READ: Galatians 2:17-21

New Life

*The life I now live . . . I live by faith in the Son of God
who loved me and gave himself for me. (Galatians 2:20)*

Won't all this talk about justification by faith alone make people careless and indifferent to morality? If bad people are saved just by believing in Christ, then what's the point of being good? There is a hint of this objection in verse 17, where Paul asks whether the teaching on justification makes Christ "a servant of sin."

You can just hear the incredulous questions, can't you? "You mean if I just put my faith in Christ I don't have to do anything else? I don't have to go to church, I don't have to tithe, I don't have to keep the Ten Commandments? Are you kidding, Paul?" You can also hear his gentle reply: "No, you don't *have* to do any of those things. But if you truly know Christ, you *will want to.*" Believing in Christ unites us to him in a whole new way. Our old self dies with him on the cross, and we rise to live by faith in him. What matters now are not rules or rituals, but only "faith working through love" (Gal. 5:6).

Justification by faith in Christ gives us a new life, not a license to sin. Like Paul, I ought never to lose my sense of grateful wonder for the Son of God who loved me, and gave himself for me. That realization makes me want to live for him always. The great apostle understood this truth, and so did the great reformer. "If someone knocked on the door of my heart and asked who lived there, I would not say 'Martin Luther' but 'Jesus Christ.'"

PRAYER: Lord, live in my heart today!

Series: *Galatians*

READ: Galatians 3:1-9

Hearing with Faith

Did you receive the Spirit by works of the law
or by hearing with faith? (Galatians 3:2)

When Abraham Lincoln was nominated for a second presidential term in 1864 despite the fact that the U.S. Civil War was then going badly for the Union, he wryly remarked that it wasn't because people thought him the best man for the job. It was more that, as the saying went, they didn't want to "swap horses in midstream."

That's exactly what the Galatians were now trying to do. When the apostle says that Jesus was publicly portrayed to the Galatians as crucified (v. 1), he is referring to the content of the preaching that had converted them. Paul should know; he had been the preacher! His preaching was so focused on the cross—and so powerful and real—that it was as if Jesus had been crucified right in front of the Galatians' eyes. The Galatians were saved when they heard the story of the cross and its message of Christ's atoning sacrifice and believed in him through the work of the Holy Spirit. But having received the Spirit and all the blessings of salvation by faith, they now were thinking of switching back to "works of the law" (v. 2) as the basis of their relationship with God. Paul thinks that's nuts! "Are you going to continue this craziness? For only crazy people would think they could complete by their own efforts what was begun by God" (v. 3 MSG).

"Hearing with faith"; it's the secret of the Christian life from beginning to end.

PRAYER: Lord, teach me what it means to walk
with you by faith, from beginning to end.

Series: *Galatians*

READ: Galatians 3:10-18

The Curse

*Christ redeemed us from the curse of the law
by becoming a curse for us. (Galatians 3:13)*

You hit your thumb with a hammer, and the air around you turns blue. To us, a curse is just a string of naughty words. People don't even think about what they are saying, let alone intend the literal meaning of the words they spew out.

But God's curse is a very different matter. His curse is actually a pronouncement of his judgment upon all who break his law (v. 10). And this is God's curse, God's judgment upon sin: the price of sinning is death (see Rom. 6:23). As preachers are fond of pointing out, the word *gospel* means "good news." But the gospel does not begin with good news. It begins with the bad news that we are cursed. As lawbreakers we live under the judgment of God.

When Paul proclaimed the message of the cross in the synagogue— the place where he usually started in a new city—many of his Jewish listeners must have concluded that Jesus was cursed by God. This is what the law declared: "Cursed is everyone who is hanged on a tree" (v. 13, quoting Deut. 21:23). That's right, said the apostle, Jesus was cursed— but not the way you think. The good news is that Christ the sinless one has taken our curse upon himself and paid the price of our law-breaking on the cross.

Here's a thought. Do you suppose when God included Deuteronomy 21:23 in his law, he knew how his Son would one day die?

PRAYER: Lord Jesus, show me how
I can say thank you to you today.

Series: *Galatians*

READ: Galatians 3:19-29

All One in Christ

*There is neither Jew nor Greek, there is neither slave
nor free, there is no male and female, for you are all one
in Christ Jesus. (Galatians 3:28)*

More than one hundred years ago, a young Indian lawyer travelled to work in South Africa. There, he experienced both the best and worst Christian examples—working alongside a Christian pastor in a clinic serving very poor people, but also blocked from entering a church because he was Indian and oppressed in every way by a government which claimed Christian faith. Mohandas Gandhi never became a convert, though he remained throughout his influential life an admirer of Jesus.

As Christians we should lament the gap between our profession and our practice and be continually striving to close it. Sins like racism, sexism, nationalism, and tribalism have no place in our societies, let alone in our churches. It ought to trouble us more than it does when we find them there. Most of all it should trouble us that prejudice remains in our own hearts. The apostle says that "now that faith has come" (v. 25) we are all children of God, we have all put on Christ, and we are all one in Christ. His point is not that there are no longer any differences of gender, race, or status at all among Christians; his point is that these differences should no longer matter.

Now that faith has come, we are no longer living B.C. (Before Christ). We're living A.D. (Anno Domini, in the year of our Lord). Shouldn't that fact be more obvious in our churches, in our relationships, in our lives?

PRAYER: Forgive us, Lord, for the way our lives
and communities fail to reflect our new life in Christ.

Series: *Galatians*

READ: Galatians 4:1-7

Children of God

And because you are children, God has sent the Spirit of his Son into our hearts crying, "Abba!" (Galatians 4:6 NRSV)

John Wesley, the founder of Methodism and one of the greatest Christian evangelists, said that in spite of his early religious training, in spite of his good works, in spite of the fact that he was an ordained minister, even a missionary, he only really knew salvation when he "changed the faith of a slave for that of a son."

There is a spirit of slavery that can only view God as a fearsome authority or cosmic Judge. But the Holy Spirit speaks to us on a level deeper than words or arguments, driving home the understanding that in spite of our sinfulness we are loved by God and accepted in Christ, the Beloved. He causes a filial love to flood our hearts in response, so that we cry out to God, "Abba . . . Father . . . Daddy." At that moment we truly know ourselves to be God's very children.

Life magazine once published a photograph of John F. Kennedy in the Oval Office. An aide stands to one side, almost at attention. But underneath the big presidential desk, Kennedy's young son John-John is happily playing. The change that the Holy Spirit works in us when he gives us new birth is like the difference in that picture between the servant and the child. One is on duty, tense. The other is a little boy at home with his daddy.

Is yours the faith of a slave, or of a son?

PRAYER: Abba, Father, I love you!

Series: *Galatians*

READ: Galatians 4:8-20

Labor Pains

My little children, for whom I am again in the anguish of childbirth until Christ is formed in you! (Galatians 4:19)

Sitting with my wife through her labor and the delivery of our first child, I had occasion to reflect on God's wisdom in having women give birth rather than men. They're so much tougher!

Childbirth is hard work, even for those of us who only watched from the sidelines. Paul uses it as a metaphor for the anxiety he feels as he watches the Galatians' spiritual struggles. Once already Paul had "given birth" to them spiritually when he first brought the gospel to them (v. 11). But now they are in danger of slipping back into a sub-Christian mindset. So the apostle has been thrown back into the whole painful experience again. He won't finally be delivered "until Christ is formed in you."

This is Paul's goal because this is the definition of Christian maturity. The Christian life is not a matter of keeping lists of rules or observing special ceremonies, days and seasons (v. 10). Such things may be helpful aids, but we must not become slaves to them. The end of the Christian life is Jesus Christ. Our goal is simply to live—and love—as he did. The purpose of the gospel is not merely to improve us but to transform us.

"Mere improvement is no redemption," wrote C. S. Lewis. "God became man to turn creatures into sons: not simply to produce better men of the old kind but to produce a new kind of man" (*Beyond Personality*).

PRAYER: May the goal of my life be nothing
less than to reproduce the life of Jesus.

Series: *Galatians*

READ: Galatians 5:1-15

Christian Freedom

You were called to freedom . . . only do not use your freedom as an opportunity for the flesh. (Galatians 5:13)

Luther begins his treatise on Christian Liberty with this statement: "A Christian man is a perfectly free lord of all, subject to none. A Christian man is a perfectly dutiful servant of all, subject to everyone."

This is the paradox of the gospel. We are free, truly free. "For freedom Christ has set us free" (v. 1). Jesus said, "You will know the truth and the truth will set you free" (John 8:32). "Where the Spirit of the Lord is, there is freedom," added Paul (2 Cor. 3:17). Christ has set us free from sin's binding power and guilt, from Satan's dominion, from merit-based religion, from rules and rituals and good works as the way to win salvation, from never being quite good enough or being able to do enough to earn God's approval. When we realize that God loves us as we are for Jesus' sake, not because of what we are, we are freed from doubt, shame, obsession, compulsion or whatever else would destroy our peace.

But freedom in Christ is not just freedom *from*, it is also freedom *for*; freedom for doing good and becoming holy. It is freedom to be the people God created us to be, people who look and act just like Jesus. Without having to agonize over whether we've earned enough religious merit, we're free to serve Christ gladly. Freedom in Christ is freedom for obedience, for service; above all, it is freedom to love.

PRAYER: Help me to see my freedom
not just as freedom from, but as freedom for.

Series: *Galatians*

READ: Galatians 5:16-26

Keep in Step with the Spirit

Since we live by the Spirit, let us keep in step with the Spirit. (Galatians 5:25 NIV)

Watching a marching band in a great parade is a wonderful experience, one that I really enjoy. Maybe you do too. One thing you'll notice is that when the band isn't playing, the drums keep on beating so that everyone can stay in step. Because a bunch of people walking around in various directions at their own pace isn't a parade, it's just a crowd milling about. Or perhaps you've seen the half-time show at a major university football game, where the band takes marching to amazing new levels. As someone who is rhythmically challenged, I wonder how they can achieve such precision. The answer? Practice, practice, practice.

The Christian life is all about practicing keeping in step with the Spirit of Christ. The sin in our lives (and in our societies) won't be overcome just by our striving to improve ourselves. Sin will only be defeated as we live by the Spirit and are led by the Spirit, marching in conformity with him each day. The answer to the problem of evil is not to be found in trying to become better people but in becoming new people, people who consistently walk in the presence and by the power of the Spirit of God. The key to doing that is daily faithfulness in study of God's Word and prayer. You might choose to begin by memorizing Galatians 5:22-23.

PRAYER: Holy Spirit, may your fruit ripen in my life this day: love, joy, peace, patience, kindness, goodness, faithfulness, gentleness, self-control.

Series: *Galatians*

READ: Galatians 6

The Marks of Jesus

*From now on let no one cause me trouble, for I bear
on my body the marks of Jesus. (Galatians 6:17)*

The apostle Paul got a lot of grief during the course of his many years of missionary service. Much of it was abuse suffered at the hands of hostile opponents of the gospel. Then there were the injuries and illnesses caused by the rigors of travel in the first century. Paul gives a partial catalogue of his personal sufferings in 2 Corinthians 11—beatings, whippings, stoning, shipwreck, cold, hunger, dangers of every imaginable kind. Think of what his body must have looked like! But much of the grief and hassle Paul suffered was at the hands of members of his own churches. The Corinthian letters especially are filled with objections and criticism leveled at the apostle.

Paul's response to his critics is this moving little statement at the end of Galatians: "From now on let no one trouble me, for I bear on my body the marks of Jesus." Leave me alone, he says. I have been faithful to the Lord, and I have the scars to prove it.

A colleague in the Middle East once sent me a picture of a young Christian who had been arrested and interrogated by the secret police. The picture showed the young man's back, crisscrossed with stripes from the beatings. I realized I was looking at "the marks of Jesus." My friend in the picture later told me it was actually quite easy to be a Christian believer in his country. "All you have to do is keep your mouth shut," he said.

PRAYER: Lord, today I remember before you all those
who are suffering for their testimony to you.

Series: *Galatians*

READ: Jonah 1:1-2

A Call from the Lord

Now the word of the LORD came to Jonah the son
of Amittai, saying, "Arise, go . . . and call out." (Jonah 1:1-2)

We've been hearing from the New Testament's greatest missionary, the apostle Paul. Now we turn to the Old Testament's most infamous missionary, Jonah.

If we were playing a word association game and I said "Jonah," what would you say? Most folks would blurt out, "whale," and they'd be right; we know the story as "Jonah and the Whale." But in a way that's too bad because if we only think of Jonah as an incredible fish story, we could miss the point of this very important book. In a sense, Jonah offers the key to understanding the whole Bible. It shows us God's heart for the world, and it prompts us to feel the same way about the world that God does.

In the Bible, a prophet was not so much someone who foretold the future as someone who "forth-told" the word of God. Prophets were publicly commissioned by God to speak for him. God called different kinds of people to this difficult and sometimes dangerous ministry of proclaiming his word to Israel and the world. Some of their messages were put into writing and included in the Hebrew scriptures, giving us the prophetic books.

The opening words of Jonah are typical of these prophecies. The prophet is identified and his commission is stated: The word of the Lord came to Jonah and said, "Go and preach." It is of the utmost importance for our life and faith that when God speaks through his commissioned representatives, we listen.

PRAYER: Speak, Lord, your servant is listening.

Series: *Jonah and the Heart of God*

READ: Nahum 1:1-8; Nahum 3:1-7

Go to Nineveh

*Arise, go to Nineveh, that great city,
and call out against it. (Jonah 1:2)*

Picture yourself as an ancient Israelite. Someone has come to your village with a new book, *The Story of Jonah*. You and your neighbors gather to hear this fresh word from the Lord. The scroll is opened. Everything is in order. Then comes this outrageous statement, "Go to Nineveh."

Hold on! Just a minute! Nineveh? There were two very large reasons why Jonah's fellow Israelites would have been upset by his commission to go to Nineveh. The first was that Nineveh was foreign. Its inhabitants were gentiles, outsiders, strangers to the covenant promises. They had no right to the word of God: that was for the Lord's people, Israel.

The other reason Jonah's audience would have been bothered was because Nineveh was the enemy. Israel and her neighbors were like a school of little fish being threatened by a large and very hungry shark. The shark was Assyria, and its head was Nineveh. As far as the Israelites were concerned, Nineveh meant disaster. They didn't want God's word to go to Nineveh. They wanted him to send an enemy army to destroy it completely (as would happen eventually in fulfillment of Nahum's later prophecy).

The problem was that Israel had grown self-centered in its relationship with the Lord and didn't really care about a world filled with people who didn't know him. It's an easy thing to do.

PRAYER: Lord, let me never think your love
is only for me and my kind.

Series: *Jonah and the Heart of God*

READ: Jonah 1:3-6

Running from God

*But Jonah rose to flee to Tarshish
from the presence of the LORD. (Jonah 1:3)*

If Jonah's commission to take God's word to Nineveh would have been shocking to his contemporaries in Israel, then what comes next in the story is even more disturbing. Jonah simply disobeys. He doesn't just hesitate or make excuses as other prophets sometimes did. He does what no other prophet in the whole Bible ever did. He runs away.

Jonah went down to Joppa and boarded a ship for Tarshish, an area in southern Spain at the opposite end of his world. Instead of heading toward Nineveh, Jonah traveled as far as he could away from it. It was like a person in America being told to go to Africa and instead flying to Australia.

Why did Jonah try to run away? Did he really think that going to Tarshish would let him escape from the presence of the Lord? (Not if he had ever read the 139th Psalm!) Was Jonah afraid? Did he feel like the mission he had been given was a hopeless one? Was he just lazy? We'll have to wait until near the end of the story to find the real reason, but for now, let's just say that Jonah's problem wasn't in his backbone. It was in his heart. What he lacked wasn't courage, but compassion.

The lesson Jonah had to learn was to get his heart in tune with God's heart and to care as much about lost people as God does. It's a lesson many of us have trouble with.

PRAYER: Lord, tune my heart to yours.

Series: *Jonah and the Heart of God*

READ: Jonah 1:4-10

The Most Reluctant Missionary

I fear the LORD, the God of heaven,
who made the sea and the dry land. (Jonah 1:9)

In his autobiography *Surprised by Joy*, C. S. Lewis says that on the day of his conversion he was the most reluctant believer in all England. I think it's fair to call Jonah the most reluctant missionary in history! He should have known he could never run away from God. But that didn't stop him. The story of his attempted escape is a wonderful illustration not only of the power of God but also of what I can only conclude is God's sense of humor. Notice how everyone and everything in this whole experience serves the ultimate purpose of God. Jonah, the sailors, the storm, the fish—all are agents whom God uses to accomplish his will.

God's will for Jonah is that Jonah must bear witness to him. God called Jonah to preach God's word to the world. Jonah may have been history's most reluctant missionary but preach he would, whether willingly or not. If he refused to preach to the Ninevites, then God arranged for him to preach to the sailors. So Jonah became an involuntary evangelist of the ship's crew. "What have you done?" they asked him; "Who are you?" He told them, and his answer was a witness to them about the real God, the God who made the sea and the land.

God is "no respecter of persons" (Acts 10:34 KJV). God doesn't discriminate. He doesn't prefer one nationality or race to another. God loves all groups and classes of people (even sailors!). His plan is to reach out to all of them with his saving word.

PRAYER: Whether reluctantly or eagerly, Lord,
let me take part in your plan.

Series: *Jonah and the Heart of God*

READ: Jonah 1:11-16

Man Overboard!

So they picked up Jonah and hurled him into the sea. (Jonah 1:15)

When Jonah told the sailors to toss him overboard, it looked like a noble thing to do. But I wonder if this wasn't just one more act of defiance against God. If Jonah can't run away to Tarshish, he'll escape by having himself thrown into the sea. In the few moments he had left, Jonah no doubt consoled himself by reflecting that, while it was not the end he would have chosen, at least it meant he didn't have to go to Nineveh! But he was mistaken. Jonah's life wasn't finished yet because Jonah's God wasn't finished yet—with him.

You may be thinking: This is all very interesting, but what does it have to do with me? Consider this. God doesn't just have a plan for saving the world; he has a plan for your part in saving the world. Of course, he first wants you to respond to his love for you by loving and following him in return. But his plan also includes a specific role for you to play in advancing the gospel. Just as it did to Jonah, the word of the Lord comes to us, telling us to "arise and go." Or if not that exactly, then at least to help send those who have been called to go.

We each must choose whether we will obey God's call or try to evade it, whether we'll go to the world with God's word or run away from it. Many have chosen to go. Will you join them by sharing the word in your community? Will you send and support those who go further away?

PRAYER: God, show me what I can do to help reach the world.

Series: *Jonah and the Heart of God*

READ: Jonah 1:17; Matthew 12:38-42

Jonah and the Whale

And the LORD appointed a great fish
to swallow up Jonah. (Jonah 1:17)

I was once talking about the story of Jonah to a group of children. "When Jonah was told to go to Nineveh, why did he run the other way?" one of them asked. Small children find it hard to believe that someone would dare to disobey God in such a spectacular fashion. "If Jonah was a prophet," another one wanted to know, "why didn't he trust God?" That's a good question. I don't know why I don't always trust God either. But the question on every child's mind was the one about the whale. How in the world could that ever have happened?

Actually, the answer is fairly simple. The Bible says that the Lord provided a great fish (not necessarily a whale) to swallow Jonah. This was obviously not a natural occurrence. It was a miracle from start to finish. Either God created a unique creature to swallow Jonah, or he must have modified an existing one in some fairly significant ways.

Of course, many people read this story today and conclude that it has to be a fairy tale. But Jesus didn't seem to think that. He referred to Jonah's story as something that actually happened; in fact, as a preview of his own burial and resurrection.

A 19th-century Scottish preacher called Patrick Fairbairn said of Jonah's whale, "The devourer is transformed into a house of safety." And ever since Easter the grave—the ultimate devourer—has been transformed into a house of safety for all who are in Christ.

PRAYER: Thank you, Lord, for a greater One than Jonah.

Series: *Jonah and the Heart of God*

READ: Jonah 2:3-6; Psalm 42

Sinking Down

You cast me into the deep. (Jonah 2:3)

The whole story up to this point is really a tale of Jonah's decline. From the very beginning Jonah has been going downhill, both literally and figuratively. He first went "down to Joppa" (1:3), traveling from the hill country of Israel down to the coast. Then he went down into the hold of the ship (1:5). Eventually he went overboard into the sea (1:15) where he sank down, down, to the very roots of the mountains (2:5-6).

Jonah's physical descent mirrors his spiritual decline. Jonah is being degraded. Aside from everything else, his experience is profoundly embarrassing. Imagine a prophet being called to prayer by sailors—a class not generally noted for piety. See Jonah sitting there while they cast lots to determine the guilty party, and he is marked. Watch as they drop him overboard like a sack of garbage. How far we can sink when we turn from God!

You can't ignore reality forever. Sooner or later, reality catches up with you, and God is the Ultimate Reality. Have you ever seen a little child playing the game where they hold their hands up in front of their face and cry, "You can't see me"? That's cute in a toddler, but it's not so cute in an adult. You can't live as if God doesn't see you, as if he has no claim upon you or authority over you. People who try to do that begin to slide into the depths; their lives unravel, and eventually they hit rock bottom.

PRAYER: Lord, let me never fall away from you.

Series: *Jonah and the Heart of God*

READ: Jonah 2:1-2; Psalm 130

Out of the Depths

Out of the depths I cry to you, O LORD! (Psalm 130:1)

"Then Jonah prayed to the LORD his God from the belly of the fish" (Jonah 2:1). It seems like a minor detail but it's not. This is a turning point marking the moment when Jonah stopped running from God and turned back toward him for help.

Jonah's prayer reads very much like one of the psalms. (Someone has counted 16 different allusions to the psalms here.) When Jonah was in trouble, he found comfort and strength from the words of Scripture. He calls to the Lord "out of the belly of Sheol" (Jonah 2:2)—from the realm of death itself.

Have you ever been down so low, in so deep, that you were sure there was no escape? What did you do then? Jonah had only one option left. He called to God for help. But wait a minute! God was the very one Jonah had been disobeying. What right did Jonah have now to suddenly remember the Lord and turn to him for help?

The answer is: he had no right at all, any more than any of us does. But here's an amazing thing: whatever we may have done, however deep the hole into which we've gotten ourselves, however far we've gone from God, if we turn back to him and call on his name really meaning what we say, God will hear and save. You might think God would be offended at being used like that, but he's not. He really is amazingly gracious.

PRAYER: Thank you, Lord, for hearing us when we cry out to you.

Series: *Jonah and the Heart of God*

READ: Jonah 3:1-2; Psalm 87

That Great City

Arise, go to Nineveh, that great city. (Jonah 3:2)

Now the Lord re-commissions Jonah, giving him a second chance to deliver God's message to Nineveh. Ancient writers describe the city of Nineveh in tones of awe, noting its size, the strength of its walls and gates, the splendor of its palaces and temples. The ultimate testimony to Nineveh's significance lies in the fact that three times in the book of Jonah God himself calls Nineveh "that great city." It is one thing for people to be impressed with a place, but when God calls a city great, it must really be something.

God cares about the city. Think about that. He doesn't just speak to the church, to people who are actively paying attention to him. His word is also for the great cities of our world, where human culture—and human wickedness—reaches its pinnacle. God's call to the city should dispel the misconception that he is concerned only about the personal life of individuals, that his only business is saving people one by one to be with him in heaven when they die. That's not all there is to biblical faith or to the agenda of the living God. He is not just a private God. He is the God of the whole earth. He is not interested only in individuals. He also cares about cities, societies, cultures, and nations. The Lord is the God of everything and everyone; his concern is to turn earthly cities into the City of God.

It must be ours too.

PRAYER: I pray for my city, state, and nation, Lord, that they would know and fear you.

Series: *Jonah and the Heart of God*

READ: Jonah 3:3-4; Amos 1

Doom

Yet forty days, and Nineveh shall be overthrown! (Jonah 3:4)

Jonah finally arrives in Nineveh and proclaims God's message of judgment on the city "because its evil has come up before me" (1:2). What sort of evil, we might wonder? We are given a hint later in Jonah 3 in the king of Nineveh's call to his people to repent of their "evil way" and "violence" (v. 8). When God pronounced judgment upon Israel's pagan neighbors, it was not just because of their idolatry but also because of their inhumanity. They were idolatrous societies, to be sure. But they didn't know any better because they didn't have God's Word. What they did have was the universal law written in the human conscience. So they were called to account for their pitiless brutality and violence, things everyone knows to be evil.

A full catalog of Nineveh's sins would sound very modern: war crimes and atrocities, torture, infanticide, ethnic cleansing. Such sins deeply offend God the creator, who is angered when the creatures he made in his image are mistreated.

Some people think that God is mostly interested in religion, that he cares about things like sermons, hymns, and liturgies, but not things like economics or politics, as if God is a pious old gentleman who keeps up with theology but doesn't know anything about hedge funds or genetic research. These are often the same people who think that as long as they offer God the proper pious sacrifices, they are free to ignore him when it comes to business. They couldn't be more wrong.

PRAYER: Bring justice and righteousness to the nations, Lord.

Series: *Jonah and the Heart of God*

READ: Jonah 3:5-10

Repent and Believe

Let everyone turn from his evil way. (Jonah 3:8)

What Jonah preached to the people of Nineveh was bad news, not good news. As far as we know, the message he delivered was the simple announcement of impending doom, unmixed with any hope or offer of escape. "Forty days and you're toast!" Yet there was something else there. After all, why should God have sent him to warn the city at all if there wasn't at least the chance of an alternative to judgment and death?

The people of Nineveh took that chance. They responded in an amazing way: they "believed God" (v. 5) and repented. In this case, all they had to believe was that God would indeed destroy them for their sins, as he had declared through Jonah. But they thought that at least they could repent and see what might happen.

Repentance does not just mean to feel sorry for what you have done or to express remorse. Biblical repentance means to turn and to change. It means to turn your life around, turning away from sin and back toward God. It means to change your mind about God and yourself, and to change direction, to set your back to things like dishonesty, injustice, or cruelty, and to set your face toward God and the good. The people of Nineveh did this without a lot of hope, but they discovered just how merciful God is. Even when he speaks of wrath and coming destruction, what the Lord really wants is to show mercy. His warnings are always conditional. Those who believe him and turn to him will be saved.

PRAYER: I turn to you today, Lord, in repentance and faith.

Series: *Jonah and the Heart of God*

READ: Jonah 4:1-2; Exodus 34:5-6; Psalm 103:6-13

Angry with God

That is why I . . . [fled] to Tarshish; for I knew
that you are . . . gracious. (Jonah 4:2)

Jonah has just proclaimed the word of God to a mighty city and the entire population has repented and turned to the Lord. No other preacher in history ever experienced success as dramatic and complete as this.

So what is Jonah's reaction: Awe at the power of God's word? Gratitude and praise for this demonstration of the Lord's wonderful mercy? Hardly. Jonah is angry with God for sparing the penitent Ninevites. Jonah gives vent to his anger in what is perhaps the most embarrassing prayer in the Bible. In it he rehearses Israel's great confession of faith: the Lord is "gracious . . . and merciful, slow to anger and abounding in steadfast love." A friend who is a biblical scholar calls that statement the "John 3:16" of the Old Testament. But instead of confessing these wonderful truths to God's praise, Jonah recites them as a complaint. Now he reveals his real reason for fleeing to Tarshish. It wasn't because he was afraid of failing in his mission but because he was afraid of succeeding! He rails at God: "It's just as I thought. You are such a pushover, such a knee-jerk forgiver! These evil people show a little bit of sorrow and you let them off. I can't stand it!" Maybe Jonah is mad because now Israel's enemy won't be destroyed. Maybe he's one of those people who doesn't like to share with others the good things he himself has been given.

Or maybe his anger is just ridiculous, and we're meant to see it that way.

PRAYER: God, show me the ways that I reject your mercy
for my enemies, and guide me to repentance.

Series: *Jonah and the Heart of God*

READ: Jonah 4:3-5

Sitting and Sulking

Now, O LORD, please take my life from me. (Jonah 4:3)

Jonah's prayer continues in verse 3, as he asks for death. It's a parody of the famous scene from Elijah's life where, having fled from wicked Queen Jezebel's rage, Elijah prays that God will let him die in the wilderness. But where Elijah was depressed because he believed he had failed in his ministry, Jonah was depressed because he had succeeded. Elijah wanted to die because it seemed to him that God's cause was finished. Jonah wanted to die because God's grace had triumphed.

Bit by bit, we are being given an unmistakable picture of the absurdity of Jonah's behavior. From beginning to end there is no justification for anything Jonah has done. Slowly the natural prejudices of the audience against the pagan Ninevites and in favor of the prophet Jonah are being completely reversed. You find yourself approving of the conduct of the people of Nineveh and of God's treatment of them, and condemning Jonah.

When we look at Jonah, we can only wonder how any "man of God" could be so mean-spirited, narrow-minded, and hardhearted. How is it possible that someone who has received from God an undeserved gift of life should become so upset when others are given the same thing? Could it be that when God looks at me, he does not see me as the basically kind, generous, and noble person I imagine myself to be, but rather that he sees me the way I see Jonah?

PRAYER: Help me to see myself as you see me:
flawed and undeserving, but still loved.

Series: *Jonah and the Heart of God*

READ: Jonah 4:6-11

Wonderful Pity

And should not I pity Nineveh, that great city? (Jonah 4:11)

"Do you do well to be angry?" God asks Jonah (v. 4), inviting him to take a look in the spiritual mirror and check his attitude. But Jonah is in no mood to listen. So he gets a little object lesson. Jonah wants destruction for Nineveh, death dealt out on a vast scale. God decides to give a small taste of it to him to let him see how it feels. A plant springs up but dies in a day. Back comes the Lord with the same question: "Is your anger appropriate, Jonah?" "Yes," says Jonah, "I have a right to my feelings. I cared about the plant and now it is gone."

God shows us his innermost heart in the question he then asks Jonah. "You pitied the plant; shouldn't I pity Nineveh, that great city?"

God's heart of love is moved today for the millions of people in our world who do not know him. He feels compassion for those who live from day to day without a thought about eternity or about God himself, people who don't know their right hand from their left, who do not know Jesus Christ, the only one in whom there is life and hope. God has pity for all such, and he longs that they should turn to him in faith and be saved.

Maybe you have been living in ignorance like one of the Ninevites. Maybe you have been living like one of their animals. Whoever you are, God cares about you. His compassion is for you too.

PRAYER: For your wonderful pity, I thank you, Lord God.

Series: *Jonah and the Heart of God*

READ: Jonah 4:10-11

A Question without an Answer

And should not I pity Nineveh, that great city? (Jonah 4:11)

Let's look again at the striking conclusion of the book of Jonah. Perhaps you have noticed it is a question without an answer. I can't help but wonder about Jonah's response to God's question. Was he embarrassed by the contrast between his heart and God's heart? Did he go on to serve with gladness the gospel of grace?

We don't know. But I think the book's ending is intentionally ambiguous. The reason Jonah does not answer God's question is because we each have to answer it for ourselves. Do I care about the world the way God does? Do I have compassion for the people who do not know him, who have not learned about his love, who have never heard of Jesus? Do I share God's heart? What answer would you give?

Here is a little poem that sums up the message:

> And Jonah stalked
> to his shaded seat,
> and waited for God to come around
> to his way of thinking.
> And God is still waiting
> for a host of Jonahs
> in their comfortable houses
> to come around
> to his way of loving
> (Thomas John Carlisle, "You! Jonah!")

PRAYER: God of all peoples and nations, help me
to come around to your way of loving.

Series: *Jonah and the Heart of God*

READ: Genesis 3:1-19

The Missionary God

And they heard the sound of the LORD God walking
in the garden in the cool of the day. (Genesis 3:8)

Having spent some time with the story of Jonah the reluctant missionary, let's trace the story of God's mission through the rest of the Bible—the mission he invites us to share in, like Jonah. Genesis 1 and 2 show the world as it originally was, perfectly beautiful, harmonious, and good. From chapter 3 verse 7 onwards we are in our world, the world where we are naked and ashamed, where thorns and thistles grow when we sow good seed, where daily life is a sweat-drenched struggle against futility and frustration, the world where even the greatest joys are accompanied by pain, and where every hope-filled birth ends in death. Adam and Eve didn't quite realize all this yet, though they were starting to suspect that what they'd done wasn't such a good idea.

But then God comes into the story. Adam and Eve heard him walking in the garden. What was *that* like, I wonder? However it happened, it meant that God had come personally, looking for his lost children. The Bible is not the story of humanity's search for God; it's the story of God's search for humanity. The God of the Bible is on a mission, and the first missionary he sends into the world is himself. God's mission of salvation began in the garden of Eden, but ultimately it would lead him into another garden—one with an empty tomb. If he weren't this kind of God, the Bible would be a very short book. It would have ended at Genesis 3:7.

Thankfully, it doesn't!

PRAYER: We bless you for being a missionary God.

Series: *The Mission of God*

READ: Genesis 3:8-15

Where Are You?

But the Lord God called to the man . . .
"Where are you?" (Genesis 3:9)

As God came looking for them, Adam and Eve turned and ran the other way! "And the man and his wife hid themselves from the presence of the Lord God among the trees of the garden" (v. 8).

How do you picture this? I think of a toddler holding his hands up in front of his face and saying, "You can't see me!" Did Adam and Eve really think they could hide from God, that trees and shrubs could shield them from the searching gaze of omniscience? Did they really believe they could escape from the presence of the One who is always present everywhere?

The first time God speaks after the fall is to ask a question of his hiding children: "Where are you?" I suggest that this is not a request for information. God is not trying to locate Adam and Eve because somehow he has lost sight of them in the bushes.

God questions Adam and Eve not in order to gain a fix on their location but to offer an invitation. God is opening a conversation with them. In other words, he wants to communicate with them. "Communicate" comes from the same root word as "communion." What God is really saying is, "What have you done? Where have you gone? Tell me. Confess to me. Return to me."

In reaching out to a lost world, God always has the first word.

PRAYER: Here I am, Lord. Speak to me.

Series: *The Mission of God*

READ: John 20:19-23

Another Great Commission

As the Father has sent me, even so I am sending you. (John 20:21)

The word mission comes from the Latin verb *missio*, meaning "send." A missionary is a person who has been sent. By whom? To where? For what? Sent by Christ to the ends of the earth to make followers of all peoples. Only Christ has the right to make such demands. In a famous passage at the end of Matthew's gospel the risen Jesus claims that all authority in heaven and on earth belongs to him. Because Jesus is Lord, "There is not one square inch in all creation of which he cannot rightfully claim, 'This is mine!'" (Abraham Kuyper).

Christ is Lord of the nations and Savior of the world. The Good News must be proclaimed to every person under heaven—and not just with words. In another great post-resurrection commission, Christ sends his followers into the world to continue what the Father sent him to do: to practice deeds of justice and mercy, to convey the love of God in the midst of human misery, to announce the good news of forgiveness. The ultimate goal of Christian mission is not merely to win decisions for Christ but to make disciples of Christ who incarnate his love.

The mission Christ gave us is a staggering one. There is no place we are not sent. There is no person to whom we need not bring the gospel. There is no act of service to which we may not aspire.

PRAYER: Lord, I accept my part in carrying out your mission to the world.

Series: *What to Believe*

READ: Genesis 12:1-3

Blessing the Nations

In you all the families of the earth shall be blessed. (Genesis 12:3)

Why did God choose Abraham? What made him so special? As far as we know, he was just a guy living in Mesopotamia, like any other guy living anywhere else in the world. But then God revealed himself to Abraham and invited him to step out by faith on a journey to an undisclosed location. So why did God choose him?

Perhaps because he had to start somewhere, and Abraham was as good a place as any. God was on a mission to redeem his broken world and reclaim his wandering children. He began with a single family, but from the beginning it wouldn't be about just that family, or even about their physical descendants. Right from the start God had the endgame in view. He will use Abraham and his family to bless all the families of the earth by producing from them a Messiah who will do what is needed to offer salvation to the whole world.

God made two promises to Abraham: numberless offspring (v. 2) and a land to dwell in forever (v. 7). Both were fulfilled literally to some extent. But the ultimate fulfillment of both promises is spiritual. The true Promised Land is heavenly (Heb. 11:13-16). And Abraham's descendants are all who are justified by faith in Christ. As an old saying puts it, God always fulfills his promises, "either in the letter or in the better."

PRAYER: Father, bless me to be a blessing to others.

Series: *The Mission of God*

READ: Isaiah 2:1-5

The Coming Nations

. . . and all the nations shall flow to it. (Isaiah 2:2)

A common assumption is that in the Old Testament God cares about the people of Israel, but in the New Testament he cares about all people. A second-century heretic named Marcion went so far as to suggest they were two different Gods: an angry Jewish one and a loving Christian one.

A closer reading of Scripture explodes this notion once and for all. The God of the Bible is one—holy *and* gracious, concerned for his chosen people *and* for all nations. He is the God of Abraham, Isaac and Jacob—*and* Jesus.

Isaiah foresees the day when Mount Zion will be lifted above the surrounding hills, and the nations of the world stream into Jerusalem to worship the Lord. But the emphasis falls just there—on their *coming*.

Jesus will turn this exactly around. He will send his disciples *from* Jerusalem *out* to the ends of the earth. In Isaiah, Jerusalem is a magnet, attracting all peoples to Israel's God. For Jesus, Jerusalem is a launching pad, rocketing his followers out to reach the nations. We have to take our message to the nations, not wait for the nations to come to us.

That's why Words of Hope takes the gospel to "the hard places." Today millions of people are not Christians for the most basic reason: they've never heard of Jesus Christ. The God of the Bible cares about that. Shouldn't we?

PRAYER: Pray for one of the hard places.

Series: *The Mission of God*

READ: Isaiah 49:1-6

A Light to the Nations

It is too small a thing for you to be my servant to restore the tribes of Jacob. (Isaiah 49:6 NIV)

"Is anything too hard for the LORD?" the angel asked Abraham when Sarah laughed at the idea that she would bear a child in her old age (Gen. 18:12-14). No, nothing is too hard for God. But some things are too small.

It is too small a thing for the servant of the Lord merely to be the Savior of Jacob and Israel. Yahweh is the God of Israel, but he's no mere tribal deity. He is also the God of all the earth. Therefore he says to his servant, "I will make you as a light for the nations, that my salvation may reach to the end of the earth" (Isa. 49:6). Jesus clearly understood this to refer to himself when he declared, "I am the light of the world" (John 8:12).

Paul quoted Isaiah 49:6 in a sermon he preached during his first missionary journey. Speaking in the local synagogue in Antioch of Pisidia, he used this verse to justify his sharing the gospel with gentiles as well as Jews. So he made a small but important change: "We are turning to the Gentiles. For so the Lord has commanded us, saying, 'I have made you a light for the Gentiles'" (Acts 13:46-47).

Did you catch that? Isaiah said the Lord's Servant (i.e. Jesus) was a light for the nations. Paul says the Lord has made *us* a light for the nations. We are *commanded* to proclaim Christ as universal Savior and Lord. Anything less would be too small for him.

PRAYER: Jesus, Light of the world, all glory is due to you!

Series: *The Mission of God*

READ: 1 Corinthians 3:5-9

Synergy

We are God's fellow workers. (1 Corinthians 3:9)

A popular term floating around today is the word *synergy*, which literally means "working together." That's the word Paul uses to describe himself and Apollos—and by extension all Christians. We are God's fellow workers, God's *synergoi*.

Does God require co-workers? I don't think so. After all, he created the entire universe all by himself, without any help from us. But then why does he take us on as his partners in mission? If it is not for his sake, then it must be for ours. Have you ever let your young child or grandchild help you out with a household project? You surely didn't do it for the sake of greater speed or efficiency. You did it because you love the child, because you want him to learn and grow and stretch himself, because you know it will help her to feel important.

No doubt employing us as his partners is a very inefficient way for God to accomplish his work of salvation. After all, God could have used angels to convince everyone of the truth about Jesus. How impressive would angelic preachers be! God could choose some night to rearrange the stars in the heavens so that they spell out "Jesus is Lord!" Then everyone would know the truth. But he chooses instead to use us—our words and actions, our halting, faulty, often awkward witness to Christ—in order to bring life to the world.

In doing that God gives our lives eternal significance.

PRAYER: Lord, help me to work with you today.

Series: *The Mission of God*

READ: 2 Corinthians 5:17-21

Christ's Ambassadors

We are ambassadors for Christ. (2 Corinthians 5:20)

Arriving in India in the middle of the night after a long journey, I shuffled zombie-like through a huge jam of people in front of the Immigration Control desks, looking with envy at the empty line marked "Diplomatic Passports Only." Ambassadors enjoy VIP perks because they really are important people. Their job is to speak authoritatively on behalf of the government they represent. In order to do this, ambassadors must be sure they know what their leaders want them to say.

Who are we as servants of Jesus Christ? Here is another answer given by Paul to the church in Corinth: We are Christ's ambassadors. And we know what our King wants us to say. It's "the message of reconciliation," namely, that "God was reconciling the world to himself in Christ" (v. 19 NIV). Notice that God is the subject here, the one doing the work of reconciling. It's not just that we must be reconciled to God; God also must be reconciled to us. Sin has caused problems on both sides of a broken relationship, and only God can accomplish the great act of reconciliation—Christ's death on the cross—which clears the way to restored fellowship with him.

But there are some things for us to do: we must first believe the gospel ourselves and accept what God has done for us. "We implore you on behalf of Christ, be reconciled to God" (v. 20). And then we must proclaim this message as ambassadors to the whole world.

PRAYER: Thank you, God, for the work and message of reconciliation.

Series: *The Mission of God*

READ: Romans 1:1-15

Eager to Preach

*I am eager to preach the gospel to you
also who are in Rome. (Romans 1:15)*

Paul's excitement for God's mission crackles like lightning across the page, even after more than 19 centuries. It is all the more impressive considering he wrote these words after some 20 years of hard missionary labor. All those miles traveled, the toil, dangers, physical suffering, personal attacks, conflicts, and controversies—could you have blamed Paul if he had said he'd had enough? But no. "I am eager to preach the gospel to you also who are in Rome!"

Paul's eagerness has several sources. His gospel ministry was part of his worship, his spiritual service to God (v. 9). He looked for pleasure and mutual benefit from fellowship with the Christians in Rome (vv. 11-12). His enthusiasm is also explained by his sense of obligation (v. 14). The Lord had transformed his life, turning him from an enemy of the gospel into a lover of Christ and his church. Paul felt a debt of gratitude, and he wanted to "pay it forward" so others could experience the gospel's saving power (vv. 16-17).

But there's one more reason why Paul was eager to preach to the Christians in Rome. He looked for their help to aid him in his ultimate goal of reaching as far as Spain on his missionary journeys (15:23-24). The book of Romans isn't just a theological treatise. It's a missionary support letter, and any church that takes it seriously will commit to supporting modern-day missionaries who share the gospel like Paul did.

PRAYER: Lord, make me eager to share your good news.

Series: *The Mission of God*

READ: Romans 1:16-17

The Gospel the Power of God

I am not ashamed of the gospel. (Romans 1:16)

The gospel of Jesus Christ arouses ridicule, opposition, even hatred. A little religion, especially if it's kept private and quiet, is one thing; it's even quite respectable. Entire university departments are devoted to the study of religion.

But the gospel is another matter. At the center of the gospel, as Romans explains it, is the message of the cross, which proclaims that human sin has cut us off from God, and human religion can't bring us back again. Only the death of God's own Son can make us right with God. That message offends human pride and human wisdom, and it's very tempting to soft-peddle it in order to avoid embarrassment. Oh yes, I know what it's like to be ashamed of the gospel. Don't you?

But Paul was not ashamed because he knew from experience that "it is the power of God for salvation to everyone who believes" (v. 16). The gospel is not *about* the power of God; it *is* the power of God for the specific purpose of saving us from sin, death, judgment, and hell. To experience this power we must receive the gospel with faith. Paul says that the gospel is the power of God for salvation, not to everyone, but "to everyone who believes." If you don't believe it, the gospel is nothing to you. Many today assume that those who don't believe the gospel will nevertheless somehow be saved by it. I don't think the apostle would agree.

PRAYER: Lord, help me to always glory in the gospel.

Series: *The Mission of God*

READ: Acts 7:54-60; Revelation 2:12-13

Faithful Witness

Antipas my faithful witness, who
was killed among you. (Revelation 2:13)

There is often a high cost for being "not ashamed of the gospel." On a visit to a small Bible college in a rural district of India, I heard the story of Navin Doman. The students at the college were from the Kuruk people and Navin was the first Kuruk Christian, converted through the witness of German Lutheran missionaries in the 19th century. When Navin accepted Christ and was baptized in 1850, the tribal elders seized him, bound him, and told him he would be killed on the spot if he did not renounce Christ. Navin replied, "I will not deny my faith. If you kill me, from each drop of my blood a thousand Christians will spring." The Kuruk leaders were so impressed with Navin's courage they allowed him to go free. He became an evangelist, and spent the rest of his life bearing witness to Christ.

The Greek word for "witness" is *martyr*. It is because so many of the early Christian witnesses were faithful to the death—like Stephen at the beginning of the New Testament and Antipas at the end—that *martyr* gained its modern meaning. The African church father Tertullian famously said that the blood of the martyrs was the seed of the church. In God's providence Navin Doman was not called to seal his testimony with his life's blood. But his prophecy has come true in other times and places. From every drop of martyr's blood, a thousand Christians have sprung.

PRAYER: Lord, give me the strength to be a faithful witness.

Series: *The Mission of God*

READ: Revelation 12:7-17

The Blood of the Martyrs

They have conquered him by the blood of the Lamb and by the word of their testimony, for they loved not their lives even unto death. (Revelation 12:11)

At Namugongo, just outside of Kampala, stands a memorial to the Ugandan martyrs. There, on June 3, 1886, the king of Buganda put to death 26 young men who had angered him by their Christian commitment. Some were cut to pieces, others were burned alive; all refused to renounce their faith in Christ.

The church in Uganda at the time was very small. The gospel had come there a decade earlier, when missionaries were sent from England at the invitation of the prior king. But the martyrdoms in Namugongo became a turning point. The example of these martyrs, who walked to their deaths singing hymns and praying for their enemies, so inspired many of the bystanders that they began to seek instruction from the remaining Christians. Within a few years the original handful of converts had multiplied many times and spread far beyond the court.

Today Uganda has a higher percentage of Christians than any other African country. The Anglican Church of Uganda, Words of Hope's partner in radio ministry, alone has more than 10 million members. And every year on June 3 hundreds of thousands of Christians, both Protestant and Catholic, walk to Namugongo from all over East Africa to honor the martyrs whose blood was the seed of the church.

PRAYER: Lord, I praise you for faithful witnesses. Strengthen those who face persecution today.

Series: *The Mission of God*

READ: Luke 6:20-23

Blessed Are the Persecuted

Blessed are you when people hate you . . . and revile you . . . on account of the Son of Man! (Luke 6:22)

"Blessing" and "persecution" don't sound like they belong in the same sentence. But Jesus puts them there. "Blessed are you when others revile you and persecute you and utter all kinds of evil against you falsely on my account" (Matt. 5:11).

Some years ago I met an Iranian man who as a young university student was disturbed by the injustice and inequality of the Shah's regime. He joined the Communist party to work for revolution. He was arrested, imprisoned, and tortured by the Shah's secret police. But when the Islamic revolution came to Iran, it turned out to be very different from the Communists' dream. The new Iran was even more brutal and repressive than it had been under the Shah.

Dejected, despairing of the future, wondering if he even wanted to go on living, my friend was sitting on a park bench one day when he noticed a windblown piece of paper at his feet. Glancing down, he saw that it had English words printed on it. It was a page from a Bible. He picked it up and his eyes fell on these words: "Come to me, all who labor and are heavy laden, and I will give you rest." My friend accepted the invitation then and there, and became a follower of Jesus.

Eventually he would go to prison again, this time for the gospel. He told me he found it more enjoyable to be jailed as a Christian than as a Communist. Actually, I don't think "enjoyable" was the word he used; it was something like "more blessed." We do have Jesus' word on that.

PRAYER: Pray for the church in Iran.

Series: *The Mission of God*

READ: Romans 10:1-18

How the Gospel Works

How are they to believe . . . ? (Romans 10:14)

According to Paul, being saved is easy. All anyone has to do is "[call] on the name of the Lord" (v. 13). But he's not talking about some sort of magic incantation. The call has to come out of faith in Christ and an understanding of his saving work. Furthermore, the call must be accompanied by public confession; it can't just be some kind of private deal we do with Jesus. "If you confess with your mouth that Jesus is Lord and believe in your heart that God raised him from the dead, you will be saved" (v. 9).

Okay, Paul says, now think through this with me. Salvation is simple to receive. You don't have to climb all over heaven and earth to get it. Just call on the name of the Lord. But the name of the Lord is "Jesus." People have to believe in Jesus in order to call upon him. But how can they believe in him if they've never heard of him? And how can they hear unless someone tells them? And how can anyone preach unless they are sent? There it is in a nutshell. That's how the gospel works. It's the rationale for missions. Those who know Jesus as Savior must tell others about him.

If we proclaim the gospel throughout the world and people don't believe, that's on them. But if we don't proclaim it and people don't hear, well, that's on us.

PRAYER: Lord, send your gospel out to the world today.
In fact, use me to send it.

Series: *The Mission of God*

READ: 1 Thessalonians 2:9-13

Faith Comes by Hearing

Faith comes from hearing . . . the word of Christ. (Romans 10:17)

So here is how the gospel works. As missionaries—or for that matter any Christians—share the message of Christ, some people hear it and believe. They receive it not merely as human information but as the very Word of God (1 Thess. 2:13). And this results in changed lives, as hearers of the Word also become doers, and "walk in a manner worthy of God" (v. 12).

Albert Dosti is a pastor in Albania. As a young man serving in the Albanian military, he was assigned the task of monitoring foreign radio broadcasts being transmitted into the country in the Albanian language. One of the programs he monitored, listening to it in case it contained subversive political messages, was called "Words of Hope." No politics there, but a truly subversive message nevertheless! After listening for some time, Albert discovered that a strange and unexpected thing had happened—he had become a believer. Eventually Albert would become the radio pastor for Words of Hope Albania, and would write and record almost 2,000 programs in which he faithfully preached the Word of God.

Jesus once said that the hour is now here when the dead will hear his voice, and those who hear will live (John 5:25). He was speaking of spiritual death and spiritual life. Many listen to the gospel but they don't really *hear* it. To hear it in such a way that new life is born in you is a sort of miracle. Has that happened to you?

PRAYER: Lord, give me the kind of hearing that results in life.

Series: *The Mission of God*

READ: John 10:14-30

Jesus' Other Sheep

My sheep hear my voice . . . and they follow me. (John 10:27)

Who are the "other sheep" to whom Jesus refers (v. 16)? They are all those people, in every time and place, from every tribe and language and race, who belong to him and who will be brought eventually to salvation through him.

Notice the present tense: "I *have* other sheep." Jesus doesn't say, "I will have other sheep someday, once my missionary forces go out and win converts." His sheep already belong to him. He knows who they are, every last one of them. When we proclaim the gospel to the world, it's not in the uncertain hope that someone, somewhere, will believe it. It's in the sure confidence that Jesus' sheep are everywhere, and when they hear his voice they will follow him.

For a number of years Words of Hope partnered in broadcasting the gospel to Southeast Asia in the Hmong language. I was visiting the producer of those programs in his office. "Let me show you something," he said, handing me a stack of pages with hundreds of names written on them. "These came in the mail, with a simple request: 'Pastor, we heard you speaking on the radio about the Lamb's Book of Life, and we would like you please to record our names in it.'" Of course, the pastor assured his listeners that they need not worry. Their faith in Jesus was evidence that their names had already been recorded in the Book long ago, by the Lamb himself.

PRAYER: Thank you for writing my name in the Lamb's Book of Life.

Series: *The Mission of God*

READ: Revelation 6:9-11

How Long?

How long before you will judge and avenge our blood? (Revelation 6:10)

Walking through the old market district of a city in eastern Turkey, my guide mentioned that all the shops and businesses around us had once been owned by Armenians. A century ago the majority of people in that region were Armenian Christians; today almost none are left. My companion lowered his voice and added, "There are deep caverns north of the city where they say the bodies were thrown." In Turkey, it's not safe to talk about such things except in a whisper.

What is the mission of God in a world of such horrors: genocide, persecution, exploitation, sex slavery, poverty, terrorism, and corruption? Jesus said that his mission was to give his life as a ransom for many (Mark 10:45) and to build his church (Matt. 16:18). So we proclaim the gospel to the world and invite people everywhere to become followers of Jesus.

But followers of Jesus must also witness to and work for the coming of God's kingdom, God's reign of justice and peace here on earth. The Hebrew prophets called it shalom—the state of things where all is right, where humans and even nature itself flourish together in joyous harmony.

I was talking with a wise Christian about our struggle to understand all the evils of life. He said, "I don't ask God *why* anymore, I ask him *when*. When are you gonna come and *fix* things?" We may be sure that he will; meanwhile, we join him in working on the fix.

PRAYER: Come, Lord Jesus!

Series: *The Mission of God*

READ: Acts 1:8

Power, and a Plan

You will be my witnesses. (Acts 1:8)

The job the Lord gave his disciples was huge—to reach the whole world with the gospel. But he didn't expect them to do it on their own. Jesus promised a resource more than adequate for the work: the power of the Holy Spirit.

Then he added that they would be his witnesses "in Jerusalem . . . Judea . . . Samaria, and to the ends of the earth" (v. 8 NIV). In one sense, this is a simple historical description of how the gospel spread throughout the world. It is effectively the table of contents of the book of Acts.

But it is also possible to read this as a plan for us to follow. Witness begins with local outreach; proceeds to those nearby, including people from different cultures; and doesn't stop until "the ends of the earth."

Past generations made that last step a priority and were willing to pay the price it took to do it—not just the cost in dollars, but in prayer, hard work, and sacrifice. The ends of the earth are filled with missionary graves. Samuel Zwemer, the great Reformed Church missionary to the Muslim world, took his young family to the Middle East in the 1890s. Within a few years, Zwemer lost two young daughters to illness. What did he think then of his decision to go to that hard place with the gospel? A clue is given in the phrase from Revelation he inscribed on their graves: "Worthy is the Lamb to receive riches."

PRAYER: Pray for a missionary today.

Series: *The Mission of God*

READ: Matthew 28:16-20

Go Make Disciples

Make disciples of all nations. (Matthew 28:19)

I heard about a megachurch in the United States that wanted to obey the Great Commission. In fact, they wanted to fulfill it all by themselves. They read online that there are 195 countries in the world. So they organized teams to go and do a weeklong evangelistic blitz in each of them. Makes me think of the apostle's words concerning his fellow Jews: "they have a zeal for God, but not according to knowledge" (Rom. 10:2).

There are two problems with this approach to the Great Commission. One is that it misunderstands the meaning of "nation." Jesus wasn't talking about countries as we think of them—those different colored shapes on the world map, separated by lines and symbolized by flags. He was talking about *ta ethne*: ethnic groups, tribes, peoples. Uganda, with 30 million people, has 51 different tribal groups, each with its own language or dialect. Indonesia, another Words of Hope ministry field, has more than 700. And still another country where we work, India, has more tribes and languages than those other two countries put together. The Lord intends that every one of those "nations" should be reached with the gospel.

The second mistake is in thinking that our goal is to evangelize the world. But proclaiming the gospel is only the first step. Jesus didn't say, "Win converts who believe in me." He said, "Make disciples who obey me." A Persian Christian leader put it to me bluntly: "Don't evangelize if you won't disciple."

PRAYER: Lord, use me in your mission to the nations.

Series: *The Mission of God*

READ: Romans 16:25-27

A Gospel for the World

. . . to bring about the obedience of faith. (Romans 16:26)

The apostle closes Romans, fittingly, with a doxology—"Now to . . . the only wise God be glory forevermore through Jesus Christ!" (vv. 25-27). But in the middle of this sentence Paul inserts a lengthy parenthesis about the gospel—as if he can't help but repeat the essence of it one last time.

So he reminds his readers first of the content of "his" gospel: "the preaching of Jesus Christ"—not the preaching Jesus did, but the preaching Paul did about Jesus. The gospel is the good news about Jesus Christ and his saving work on the cross.

Next, Paul states the goal of the gospel: "so that all the Gentiles might come to the obedience that comes from faith" (v. 26 NIV). The gospel is for the whole world, and every person in it. It's not just for Jews but for Gentiles too; not just for Westerners or whites or the middle class, but for all races, all classes, all ethnic groups. If the gospel is true, then it must be true for everyone. If it isn't for everyone, then it isn't true.

Furthermore, the goal of the gospel won't be reached when everyone hears it or even when everyone believes it. The goal is "the obedience of faith for the sake of his name among all the nations" (Rom. 1:5). It will only be reached when the whole redeemed people of God live Christlike lives of holiness, love, and service, for his name's sake.

That will indeed result in glory for God.

PRAYER: May it be so!

Series: *The Mission of God*

READ: Isaiah 54:1-8

Pitching a Bigger Tent

Lengthen your cords and strengthen your stakes. (Isaiah 54:2)

I was once invited to preach in a historic Baptist church in Calcutta, India, where I was shown the evangelical equivalent of a holy relic: William Carey's pulpit chair. Needless to say, I didn't dream of trying to sit in it!

As a young lay-preacher in England at the end of the 18th century, William Carey began to argue for what was then a novel idea: obedience to the Great Commission. The churches of the English-speaking world at that time had almost no missionary outreach. They were content to tend their own flocks, and perhaps add to them from their own communities. Once when Carey advocated taking the gospel to the nations an older minister admonished him: "Young man, sit down! When God is pleased to convert the heathen, he will do so without your help or mine." Hmmm. That's an interesting theology. "Young farmers, sit down. When God is pleased to feed the hungry, he will do so without your help or mine." "Young doctors, sit down. When God is pleased to heal the sick . . ." God doesn't really work that way, does he?

William Carey helped organize the first Protestant mission society in 1792, and then went to India as one of its missionaries. At that inaugural meeting he preached a sermon on Isaiah 54:2. God restores Israel, his wife, and promises that she will be mother to more and more children. She needs a bigger tent to house them all, and we're the ones who need to pitch it. It's a picture of the church and its mission.

PRAYER: Father, help us lengthen our cords and strengthen our stakes so more can come in to your tent.

Series: *The Mission of God*

READ: Psalm 136:1-3, 23-26

Gratitude as Motive for Mission

. . . the Son of God, who loved me
and gave himself for me. (Galatians 2:20)

Paul never got over the wonder of Christ's love for him. He had been a persecutor of the church, an enemy of the Lord Jesus, "the worst of sinners" (see 1 Tim. 1:15 NIV). Yet the risen Christ revealed himself to Paul, transformed him, and commissioned him for gospel ministry as a missionary to the Gentiles. As a result of his own experience of the Lord's mercy, Paul felt a never-ending debt of gratitude to share the grace and love of Christ with others (see Rom. 1:15). It continued to motivate his missionary service to his dying day.

John Newton was a latter-day Paul. He too was the worst kind of sinner. Newton captained a slave ship on the African coast. When he wrote his famous hymn about the amazing grace "that saved a wretch like me," he wasn't exaggerating. But grace transformed Newton as it had the apostle, and turned him from a slave trader into a servant of the gospel.

Newton labored to the end of his long life in gratitude and love for the one "who loved me and gave himself for me." And when he died he left this epitaph:

> John Newton, Cler[ic], once an infidel and libertine, a servant of slaves in Africa, was, by the rich mercy of our Lord and Saviour Jesus Christ, preserved, restored, pardoned, and appointed to preach the faith he had long labored to destroy.

PRAYER: "Give thanks to the Lord, for he is good." (Psalm 136:1)

Series: *The Mission of God*

READ: Isaiah 49:14-21; Revelation 7:9-17

Who Are These?

I looked, and behold, a great multitude that no one
could number, from every nation, from all tribes
and peoples and languages. (Revelation 7:9)

It's difficult for us to imagine how devastating the Babylonian captivity was for the people of Judah. They were exiled from the land—Israel, the Promised Land! Jerusalem had been destroyed—Zion, the City of God! The Temple lay in ruins—God's house, once filled with his glory! It was easy to believe God had abandoned and forgotten them (Isa. 49:14).

I could never forget you, says the Lord, any more than a mother could forget the baby at her breast. "Behold, I have engraved you on the palms of my hands" (v. 16). What, God has hands? They're tattooed with the names of his people? It's a shocking image, and meant to be. And, of course, one day he would have hands, and they would be permanently marked with the nail-print scars that prove how much he loves.

So we can trust him not to forget us, never, ever, no matter what. And one day Zion, who thought she was bereaved and barren, will look in wonder and ask, "Where did all these children come from? Who are these?" "They came from every tribe and tongue and nation," John answers. "These are those who have been washed in the blood of the Lamb. They came out of great tribulation, but now their God has wiped away all tears, and they will praise him forever and ever."

PRAYER: God, I praise you for that
great multitude. May I be part of it.

Series: *The Mission of God*

READ: Revelation 21:1-7; Revelation 22:1-5

Mission Accomplished

I saw the holy city . . . prepared as a bride
adorned for her husband. (Revelation 21:2)

In AD 410, St. Augustine received the news that Rome had been sacked by barbarians. Augustine found comfort in thoughts of another city. The cities of man rise and fall, he wrote, but the City of God is everlasting.

The earthly Jerusalem was merely a symbol of that eternal city—the heavenly Jerusalem where God will dwell with redeemed humanity forever and ever. God's salvation mission will culminate in a new creation, "a new heaven and a new earth" (21:1), where he will be eternally with his people and where all sin, sorrow, and suffering will be forever gone.

As John describes it in his vision, he offers images that can barely begin to suggest the joys of our eternal inheritance—the garden of Eden *inside* the City of God . . . trees with healing leaves and the river of life . . . the perpetual light of God . . . riches and wisdom and strength and honor and glory and blessing to Him who sits on the throne and to the Lamb, forever and ever.

I can't imagine it: beauty that never fades, strength that never diminishes, blooms that never wither, music that never stops, pleasures that never cloy, bodies that never grow old or die, relationships that never are broken. This is how the story ends for all who love the Lord Jesus Christ.

Only it isn't really the end; it's just the beginning.

PRAYER: To Father, Son, and Holy Spirit
be praise, now and forever.

Series: *The Mission of God*

READ: Psalm 1

The Way of Wisdom

Wisdom is better than jewels, and all that you may desire cannot compare with her. (Proverbs 8:11)

The book of Proverbs is the treasury of the Old Testament's wisdom literature. To be wise in the biblical sense means thinking, acting, and speaking in ways that lead to human flourishing. There's a big difference between knowledge and wisdom. Knowledge is knowing that tomatoes are a fruit, not a vegetable; wisdom is knowing not to put them on an ice cream sundae. Knowledge is being able to recite the Ten Commandments; wisdom is devoting yourself to keeping them.

Psalm 1 is all about wisdom, though the word doesn't occur there. The psalmist describes the "blessed" or "happy" person (Ps. 1:1), which is what living wisely makes us. Wisdom begins with the negative—rejecting the ideas and actions and attitudes of those who have turned away from God. Positively, wisdom is delighting in God's Word and making it the daily focus of our life. Those who live this way are like trees "planted by streams of water." Though everything around them may be dry and barren, they will always be flourishing and fruitful.

People somehow have the idea that sin is fun and godliness is boring. The truth is exactly the opposite. It's the wicked whose lives end up being as dry and empty and unsubstantial as chaff. But the "way" of the righteous leads straight to the Lord and membership in "the congregation"—the great community of those who are his own. Meanwhile there is abundant life all along it.

PRAYER: Lord Jesus, I take delight in you who are the Way, and I want the abundant life you promise.

Series: *Walking in the Way of Wisdom*

READ: Proverbs 7

Lady Folly

All at once he follows her, as an ox goes
to the slaughter. (Proverbs 7:22)

The opposite of knowledge is ignorance. The opposite of wisdom is folly. Whether or not you are foolish doesn't depend on how much you know. As C. S. Lewis remarked, "A man may be a Master of Arts and still be a fool." Folly isn't not knowing; it's knowing and not doing.

Proverbs 7, like several other of the book's early chapters, is written in the form of a father's advice to his young adult son, warning him against being taken in by the seductive come-on of an adulterous woman. But this chapter isn't meant to be read literally as much as allegorically. The "forbidden woman" is Lady Folly; the path she beckons us toward—the road that leads to death—is the way of life that rejects God and his Word and follows sin to its inevitable destination (vv. 25-27).

John Newton, the pastor best known for writing the hymn Amazing Grace, tells us what makes a fool:

> "A fool has no sound judgment; he is governed wholly by appearances . . . He pays no regard to consequences . . . Are these the characteristics of a fool? Then there is no fool like the sinner, who prefers the toys of earth to the happiness of heaven; who is held in bondage by the foolish customs of the world; and is more afraid of the breath of man, than of the wrath of God."

PRAYER: Lord, help me resist the voices that entice me to sin. Guide my steps into the way of life.

Series: *Walking in the Way of Wisdom*

READ: Psalm 119:97-112, 145-152

First Things First

Prepare your work outside; get everything ready for yourself in the field, and after that build your house. (Proverbs 24:27)

Recently I visited the historic sites of Abraham Lincoln's boyhood in Kentucky and Indiana. The Lincoln family led a hard life on a series of frontier farms. Everyone knows about the log cabins they lived in, but the first job was always felling the trees to clear the fields for planting and splitting rails for fences to protect the crops. (There was a reason young Abe was good with an axe!) First things first; crops before houses. Because it didn't do much good to have a cabin if there was nothing in it to eat when winter came.

Besides offering good advice for early American pioneers, the proverb has some practical wisdom for us. It tells us to make sure we put first things first and second things second in our lives. It's amazing how easily distracted we are, how readily tempted to do what we like rather than what needs to be done. It's true with our Saturday chores, our homework, our jobs—and our life's priorities. Jesus told us plainly what those priorities should be: God's kingdom and his righteousness. Put those first things first, and the secondary things have a way of working out for us.

What does that actually look like? It can be something as simple as beginning each day with Bible reading and prayer before turning to our daily business. My pastor has a good formula: "Scripture before screens." It's remarkable what cultivating daily godly habits can do.

PRAYER: Lord, help me be consistent in my daily devotions.

Series: *Walking in the Way of Wisdom*

READ: Daniel 4:28-37

Pride Goes Before a Fall

Pride goes before destruction, and a haughty spirit before a fall. (Proverbs 16:18)

According to the ancient Greek historian Herodotus, the walls of Babylon were so massive that a four-horse chariot could drive around the city on top of them. So when King Nebuchadnezzar looked out on his city at the height of its power and glory it's not surprising that his ego swelled to gigantic proportions: "Is not this great Babylon, which I have built by my mighty power . . . and for the glory of my majesty?" (Dan. 4:30). Watch out, king. You were warned. God has a way of putting puny mortals in their place when they start thinking like that. What Nebuchadnezzar needed to learn was that only God is great, and humans, however wealthy or powerful, are nothing compared to him.

It's a lesson God will teach the whole world one day. "The haughty looks of man shall be brought low, and the lofty pride of men shall be humbled, and the LORD alone will be exalted in that day. For the LORD of hosts has a day against all that is proud and lofty, against all that is lifted up—and it shall be brought low" (Isa. 2:11-12).

There's a simple way to avoid the pain of a fall and destruction. Get down now! Be humble! As John Bunyan's shepherd boy sang in the Valley of Humiliation, "He that is down, needs fear no fall, he that is low, no pride: he that is humble, ever shall have God to be his guide" (*The Pilgrim's Progress*, pt. 2).

PRAYER: God, you are great and I am small.
Help me always to keep that perspective.

Series: *Walking in the Way of Wisdom*

READ: Matthew 6:25-32

Don't Worry

The LORD does not let the righteous go hungry,
but he thwarts the craving of the wicked. (Proverbs 10:3)

Are you a worrier? I'm not usually, but I can fall into that trap at times—the one where you let fears about the future spoil your peace in the present. Jesus said that excessive anxiety about the necessities of life—food, drink, clothing—is the hallmark of people who don't know God. As his followers, we have better things to worry about.

In this passage about the nagging worries of daily existence, Jesus uses one of his favorite arguments—the "how much more" line of reasoning. If God feeds the birds each day and clothes the flowers in such splendid raiment, how much more will he do for us, his dear children?

It's important, though, not to draw the wrong conclusion from Jesus' teaching. He wants us to dial down our anxiety, not to sit back and do nothing. The Lord will take care of our needs, but that doesn't mean we just open our mouths and expect him to fill them. After all, he gives the birds their food, but they still work pretty hard getting it, as anyone who has ever watched a robin pulling a worm out of the lawn knows. Daily bread was given to the children of Israel in the wilderness because of special circumstances; the rest of us have to earn it. "A slack hand causes poverty, but the hand of the diligent makes rich" (Prov. 10:4).

PRAYER: Thank you for my daily bread,
and for giving me the means of securing it.

Series: *Walking in the Way of Wisdom*

READ: 1 Peter 4:7-11

Amor Omnia Vincet

Hatred stirs up strife, but love covers all offenses. (Proverbs 10:12)

The Roman proverb used in the title of this devotional is translated "Love conquers all." It's an ancient statement of contemporary bumper sticker theology: "Love Wins." But I wonder: Whose love? Conquers what? Wins how? Every wedding includes mutual promises to love, but that doesn't stop divorces from happening. You can love a child with all your heart, but that won't conquer his addiction or her agnosticism. How often does it happen in our experience that love, far from being all-conquering, is powerless to stop the destructive or hurtful behavior of our loved ones? All too often, love fails.

Better to say, with Proverbs and Peter, that love *covers* all. Note: it says cover, not cover up. Love isn't blind (contrary to another popular saying). Love sees the offenses and acknowledges that they are wrong, that they are in fact *offenses*. But it can also cover them—with forgiveness. When someone wrongs us, rather than allowing anger to fester into hatred, we can choose a better way: "Put on then, as God's chosen ones, holy and beloved, compassionate hearts, kindness, humility, meekness, and patience, bearing with one another and, if one has a complaint against another, forgiving each other; as the Lord has forgiven you" (Col. 3:12-13).

As Christians we have the power to forgive one another because God's forgiveness covers us; and God has the power to forgive our sins because he has covered them with the blood of Jesus.

PRAYER: God, please give me strength today to put up with the little offenses I experience and to forgive the big ones.

Series: *Walking in the Way of Wisdom*

READ: Psalm 73

Where Are They Now?

*When the tempest passes, the wicked is no more,
but the righteous is established forever. (Proverbs 10:25)*

It's tempting to envy the prosperity of those the Bible calls "the wicked" or "the ungodly"—that is, people of the world. These aren't necessarily extremely evil people; rather they are, in the psalmist's words, "those who are far from [God]" (Ps. 73:27). They live as though God doesn't really matter, as if this world is all there is—and some of them live very well indeed. Their lives and possessions, their mansions and super yachts, their doings and sayings, are all over our social media. We may look at it all and think, wouldn't it be nice to be that rich, or even a fraction of that rich?

The psalmist sometimes thought like that. In the first part of his prayer he confesses his resentment of the godless rich. He shared the common attitude of his day, that good people should be blessed and bad people punished—in this life. He was disturbed by the sight of bad people who never had a care in the world and died rich and satisfied. But then one day he went into the temple and gained an eternal perspective.

One of the biggest mistakes we make in thinking about the justice and goodness of God is jumping to premature conclusions. Who wins and who loses, who's had it good and who's had it bad—that's not decided in this life. Only the final judgement will reveal all.

PRAYER: Lord, there is nothing on earth
that I desire more than you.

Series: *Walking in the Way of Wisdom*

READ: Luke 12:13-21

Rich Toward God

Honor the LORD with your wealth . . . then your
barns will be filled with plenty, and your vats will be
bursting with wine. (Proverbs 3:9-10)

Jesus' story is known as the parable of the rich fool. This farmer was a fool because he thought his prosperity was all for himself—notice how many times he uses the words "I" and "my." He also thought he would have many years to enjoy his goods, but he didn't even have another day. The parable asks a pertinent question: "the things you have prepared, whose will they be?" (v. 20). The ironic answer is seen in verse 13. The money and property we care so much about and work so hard for may sadly be our kids' to fight over.

Our proverb today seems to draw a straight cause and effect relationship between financial giving and financial getting. If you offer your wealth to God, he will make sure you receive even more in return. But we know the truth is not that simple. The farmer in Jesus' story didn't honor the Lord at all, yet his barns were overfull. Yes, there is a connection between giving and being blessed, but it's not necessarily a financial one. The important question is how do we honor the Lord with our wealth? In Jesus' terms, how can we be rich toward God? The answer is by giving to those in need. When God blesses us financially it's so that we can bless others. As St. Ambrose commented on the rich fool, "His barns should have been the mouths of the poor."

PRAYER: God, I want to be rich toward you.
Help me to budget accordingly.

Series: *Walking in the Way of Wisdom*

READ: John 8:23-32

What to Buy

*Buy truth, and do not sell it; buy wisdom,
instruction, and understanding. (Proverbs 23:23)*

I happened to be browsing in a jewelry store one day while my wife was getting a new battery to put in her watch. A nicely dressed salesman politely asked if there was something I was interested in. Looking at all the glitter and sparkle in the display cases, I smiled and said that we had reached a point in our lives where we really didn't need or want to buy any more gifts for ourselves. The salesman smiled back and said, "I understand."

There is one thing we all should buy though. As John Bunyan's pilgrims, Christian and Hopeful, replied when asked what they wished to buy in Vanity Fair, "We buy the truth" (*The Pilgrim's Progress*, pt. 1).

These days, however, the very notion of "truth" has become controversial. Depending on where you get your news and information, the truth can be elusive. What are we supposed to believe? Whom should we listen to? The government? The media (which ones)? Our Facebook feed? The guy who tweets links to alarming stories and videos? How about listening to Jesus? "I am . . . the truth" (John 14:6). Or this: "You will know the truth, and the truth will set you free" (John 8:32). We buy truth—and wisdom—when we believe in Jesus, the Son of God, Savior of the world, and Lord of our lives. He sets free from sin and death, and from excessive fear about the future.

PRAYER: Thank you, Father, for the eternal
security that is ours in Christ.

Series: *Walking in the Way of Wisdom*

READ: Judges 21:20-25

Where There Is No Vision

Where there is no prophetic vision the people cast off restraint. (Proverbs 29:18)

Around the time of our church's 100th anniversary, the congregation decided to remodel and expand the building. Outside the new entrance they built a substantial sign engraved with the words, "Where there is no vision, the people perish"—quoting Proverbs 29:18 in the King James Version. The quote suggests the idea that we need to expand our view of the possible, that we should imagine what could be, rather than merely settle for what is. Because if you can see it, you can achieve it. But if you have no vision, you're doomed to decline.

That may very well be true, but it's not what our proverb is saying. A more accurate translation helps in understanding the meaning. What the proverb is saying is that without the Word of God, people will do whatever they please. No "prophetic vision" in Old Testament terms means no biblical preaching and teaching, no Bible reading, Bible hearing, Bible believing, Bible obeying. When a society casts away God's revelation, it casts off all restraint. The result is social chaos. It's like the book of Judges—everybody does what seems right in their own eyes (21:25).

Is there a more accurate description anywhere of the world we live in? When people do whatever they please, things don't get better, they get worse. People don't become happier, they grow bored, disillusioned, and depressed. They turn on each other. If you think following your own way instead of God's way is the path to personal happiness, just look around.

PRAYER: Lord, I love your Word. Help me to follow it always.

Series: *Walking in the Way of Wisdom*

READ: Psalm 33

Victory Belongs to the Lord

The horse is made ready for the day of battle,
but the victory belongs to the LORD. (Proverbs 21:31)

In the psalmist's day, horses and chariots were the weapons of superpowers, the tanks and missiles and aircraft of the ancient world. When Pharaoh pursued the escaping Israelites into the wilderness, what made their position seem hopeless was the Egyptians' chariot army that was pinning them against the sea. But we know how that turned out. "The king is not saved by his great army" (Ps. 33:16).

A quotation variously attributed says that "God is on the side of the big battalions." It does seem like the strong usually win the battle. Very rarely does a David defeat a Goliath. But our proverb is asserting the truth of the biblical doctrine of providence. God really does rule the world. His will, not human might, determines the outcome. The issues of victory or defeat, success or failure, life or death, actually are in the hands of the Lord.

Victory belongs to the Lord, yes. But there are two opposite errors we can fall into. One is believing that all you need is a big enough horse, as if human knowledge or technology is enough to win whatever battle you are facing. The other error is believing you don't need any horse at all. Read the proverb again. Victory belongs to the Lord, but the horse is still made ready for the day of battle. Because God works his providential will through human means and human agents.

PRAYER: Lord, thank you for all the human means (medicine, governments, families) you use to help us win our battles.

Series: *Walking in the Way of Wisdom*

READ: Hebrews 13:8-14

Sweeter than Honey

Eat honey, for it is good, and the drippings of the honeycomb are sweet to your taste. Know that wisdom is such to your soul; if you find it, there will be a future, and your hope will not be cut off. (Proverbs 24:13-14)

The creed of the stoic is expressed in the saying "This too shall pass." It's meant to be both a comfort and a warning. Are you suffering, down in the dumps, filled with pain? Hang on! It will pass. Nothing lasts forever. Are you riding high, on a roll, on top of the world? Watch out! It will pass. The wheel will turn, your downfall will come. Nothing lasts forever.

In a sense the Bible agrees with this point of view. All physical things do pass away. Ecclesiastes says that everything under the sun is vanity, a striving after the wind. Hebrews asserts that "here we have no lasting city" (13:14). It's not just our cities; all our achievements, our possessions, our youth, our beauty, our strength—none of it can last, because nothing earthly lasts forever.

But that isn't the ultimate truth. Some things do last forever. God's wisdom is one; finding it gives you a future and a hope. God's Word is another. It's sweeter than honey, more precious than gold. Jesus said, "Heaven and earth will pass away, but my words will not pass away" (Matt. 24:35). Above all, Jesus himself is "the same yesterday and today and forever" (Heb. 13:8). That's why "we seek the city that is to come" (Heb. 13:14), our forever home with himself that Jesus has promised us.

PRAYER: Lord, help me to focus on the things that are eternal.

Series: *Walking in the Way of Wisdom*

READ: 2 Samuel 18:24-33

Train Your Child

Train up a child in the way he should go; even when
he is old he will not depart from it. (Proverbs 22:6)

Every Christian parent wishes there were a surefire formula for passing their faith on to their children. Proverbs seems to promise that: just train your child properly and all will be well. But life is often more complicated. We all know someone who raised their child "in the way he should go," only to see him or her walk away from the Lord. Maybe that someone is you. We also know people who grew up in a home where there was very little interest in the church but who were wonderfully converted and are now following and serving Christ. Grace is a mystery, and in the end as parents we should neither shoulder the blame nor take the credit for our children's spiritual lives.

Listen to King David's heart-wrenching cry upon hearing of the death of his wayward son: "O my son Absalom, my son . . . Would I had died instead of you" (2 Sam. 18:33). The Bible says that David was a man after God's own heart. He was also a lousy husband and father. Perhaps he blamed himself for Absalom's rebellion, which came within a whisker of costing David both his kingdom and his life. Whether he did or not, he never stopped loving his child. Nor do we. And we can continue to pray that lessons of faith and love learned in childhood will finally return to our children in the end. It's never too late for grace.

PRAYER: Lord, bless the children of my own and my church family.

Series: *Walking in the Way of Wisdom*

READ: Matthew 26:47-52

Friend or Foe?

Faithful are the wounds of a friend; profuse
are the kisses of an enemy. (Proverbs 27:6)

As an illustration of the wisdom of this proverb, consider the interactions between Jesus, Judas, and Peter on the night before the crucifixion. In the upper room, Jesus had told Peter bluntly that Satan would sift him like wheat (Luke 22:31). Ouch! When Peter protested that he would willingly die for him, Jesus cut him short. "I tell you, Peter, the rooster will not crow this day, until you deny three times that you know me." (v. 34). Then in Gethsemane Judas approached Jesus with all the apparent devotion of a true disciple. "And he came up to Jesus at once and said, 'Greetings, Rabbi!' And he kissed him" (Matt. 26:49). "Friend," Jesus replied, "do what you came to do" (v. 50).

I wonder about that word "Friend." Maybe Jesus was speaking ironically; some friend Judas turned out to be! And Jesus knew all about what Judas was up to. But could it be that he addressed Judas with real sorrow in his voice, for the friendship that might have been? I don't know which it was, but I do know that it's important to be able to distinguish our friends from our enemies.

A true friend may tell us—in the right time and way—something about ourselves that wounds us; the truth often hurts. An enemy may offer profuse verbal kisses. The difference between them isn't in what they say (criticism vs. flattery), it's in the motive behind what they say. The friend hurts in order to help; the enemy flatters in order to betray.

PRAYER: Give me the humility to receive
criticism graciously when I need it.

Series: *Walking in the Way of Wisdom*

READ: Matthew 25:1-13

Look at the Ants!

*Go to the ant, O sluggard; consider her ways,
and be wise. (Proverbs 6:6)*

One of the themes Proverbs returns to again and again is the importance of hard work. Solomon clearly had a fear of sloth. "A little sleep, a little slumber, a little folding of the hands to rest, and poverty will come upon you like a robber, and want like an armed man." That's a saying he repeated verbatim, as though one warning about the dangers of taking it easy wasn't enough (see Prov. 6:10-11 and 24:33-34).

Proverbs also has a thing for nature in general, and ants in particular: "the ants are a people not strong, yet they provide their food in the summer" (Prov. 30:25). I don't know if you pay much attention to ants—except for trying to rid your house of them—but the thing is, you never see an ant standing still. They're always going someplace, often carrying a bit of food back to the nest. The opposite of the ant is the sluggard, the lazy person who procrastinates getting ready or puts off the work until it's too late.

So what do ants have to do with the parable of the wise and foolish maidens? Well, the point of Jesus' story is the importance of always being ready for his appearing, whether at the end of time or of your life. Only a fool (or a sluggard) would think that there will always be time to repent and believe when the moment arrives. As the spiritual says, "Keep your lamps trimmed and burning."

PRAYER: Jesus, I want to be watching and working for you when you come, whether at the end of my life or of the whole world.

Series: *Walking in the Way of Wisdom*

READ: Amos 5:11-24

Who Speaks for the Poor?

Open your mouth for the mute, for the rights
of all who are destitute. (Proverbs 31:8)

What does Proverbs mean when it tells us to open our mouths for the mute? Here we might remember an important principal of Hebrew poetry: parallelism. In both Psalms and Proverbs, the writer often emphasizes a point by saying essentially the same thing in a slightly different way in both halves of a verse: "Bless the LORD, O my soul, and all that is within me, bless his holy name!" (Ps. 103:1). Sometimes the parallelism is progressive, when the second phrase in the verse advances the thought of the first. So here, the mute aren't physically unable to speak, they're the poor whose cries for justice aren't listened to.

In our society those with a lot of physical and social capital—money in the bank, a good education, a strong extended family, a wide circle of friends, a decent job or career, insurance, retirement benefits, easy access to legal advice and medical care—have the means of protecting themselves and defending their rights. But there are many who lack those advantages. It may be because they are literally destitute, or it may be because they are socially marginalized.

So who will advocate for the rights of the defenseless among us: the immigrant who doesn't speak the language, the poor person who can't afford to pay for help, or the most voiceless and defenseless of all— the unborn? Who will speak for those who can't speak for themselves? Amos did. Will we?

PRAYER: Lord, show me how I can speak
for those who need a voice.

Series: *Walking in the Way of Wisdom*

READ: Matthew 18:21-35

Do You Want to Be Forgiven?

Whoever closes his ear to the cry of the poor will himself call out and not be answered. (Proverbs 21:13)

You're familiar with the concept of poetic justice. We call it "poetic" because it's kind of sweet and fitting, like a poem. It appeals to our aesthetic sense; it just seems right. Like Haman being hanged on the gallows he had built for Mordecai. Like the unforgiving servant being jailed for debt after refusing to cancel his friend's little loan. You get what you give. So if we turn a deaf ear to our neighbor's plea for help, we shouldn't expect God to come running when we cry out to him in need.

This is especially true when it comes to forgiveness. There is only one petition in the Lord's Prayer with a condition attached to it: "Forgive us our debts as we forgive our debtors." Jesus went on to reinforce this point, just in case we weren't paying attention while reciting the prayer. "For if you forgive others their trespasses, your heavenly Father will also forgive you, but if you do not forgive others their trespasses, neither will your Father forgive your trespasses" (Matt. 6:14-15). In Luke's account, Jesus expands on the positive side of this principle: "Give, and it will be given to you. Good measure, pressed down, shaken together, running over, will be put into your lap. For with the measure you use it will be measured back to you" (Luke 6:38). I don't know about you, but this makes me want to do a lot of forgiving, so I can receive a whole lot more.

PRAYER: Is there someone I need to forgive? Show me how, Lord.

Series: *Walking in the Way of Wisdom*

READ: Luke 14:7-11

True Humility

Toward the scorners he is scornful, but to the humble he gives favor. (Proverbs 3:34)

The apostle Peter quoted this proverb, then drew a practical lesson from it: "Humble yourselves, therefore, under the mighty hand of God so that at the proper time he may exalt you" (1 Peter 5:6).

In Philippians 2 Paul urged the Philippian Christians to submit to one another in humility, citing the example of Jesus. Though he was God, Jesus didn't cling to his divine status and prerogatives, but lowered himself all the way to a criminal's death. That's the essence of humility—to get lower. "Humble" comes from *humus*, which is Latin for "earth, or soil." Humility means getting lower with respect to our neighbor so that we can't look down on them. It means lowering our estimate of our own rights in order to serve the needs of others. It means forsaking our privilege and focusing on raising up the down-and-out. It's important to do this voluntarily, because if we insist on being high and mighty, God will bring us down.

That's the point of Jesus' parable of the guests at the wedding feast. His advice was to take the least important seats at the table so as not to be embarrassed by the host moving you lower. You want to be pleasantly surprised by God's treatment of you, rather than being humiliated by it. Think how much nicer it will be when he lifts you up instead of casting you down.

PRAYER: Lord, give me the gift of humility.

Series: *Walking in the Way of Wisdom*

READ: James 3:1-12

Keep Your Hand on the Tiller

When words are many, transgression is not lacking,
but whoever restrains his lips is prudent. (Proverbs 10:19)

Have you ever wished you could take back something you said? Of course you have. So have I.

Another of Proverbs' themes, echoed by the New Testament wisdom book of James, is the power of the tongue, both for good and ill. Some examples:

- There is one whose rash words are like sword thrusts, but the tongue of the wise brings healing. (12:18)
- The tongue of the wise commends knowledge, but the mouths of fools pour out folly. (15:2)
- A gentle tongue is a tree of life, but perverseness in it breaks the spirit. (15:4)
- Death and life are in the power of the tongue, and those who love it will eat its fruits. (18:21)
- Whoever keeps his mouth and his tongue keeps himself out of trouble. (21:23)

So how do we learn to control our tongues, to restrain our lips as Proverbs says? It takes a steady hand on the tiller! Perhaps the first step is recognizing the importance of our speech. Our words can be powerful, powerfully good or powerfully bad. Then we might also remember that restraint is a sign of true wisdom. And if we want wisdom, James tells us what to do: "If any of you lacks wisdom, let him ask God, who gives generously to all without reproach, and it will be given him" (James 1:5).

PRAYER: God, give me true wisdom.

Series: *Walking in the Way of Wisdom*

READ: Hebrews 12:3-11

"Spare the Rod, Spoil the Child"

My son, do not despise the LORD's discipline or be weary of his reproof, for the LORD reproves him whom he loves, as a father the son in whom he delights. (Proverbs 3:11-12)

The book of Proverbs is famously big on parental discipline, including discipline that seems unduly harsh to us. Remember "Spare the rod and spoil the child"? That's based on Proverbs 23:13: "Do not withhold discipline from a child; if you strike him with a rod, he will not die." Well, maybe he won't. But there are better corrective alternatives. For many families today, much corporal punishment has been replaced by the "time out," and that's a good thing. Don't use Proverbs as an excuse to beat your child.

But discipline isn't just for kids. Hebrews quotes this passage in Proverbs to describe God's fatherly treatment of us. Discipline is teaching; it is not the same as punishment. God does not punish us for our sins; Christ has taken all that upon himself, draining the cup of God's wrath (John 18:11). Our cup, wrote John Newton, is not penal, judgmental; it's medicinal. God disciplines us in order to draw us closer to himself. We all sometimes need God's tough love to help us turn from the world towards him, the source of all that is good and true and beautiful. So how does God do that? When Hebrews 12 says "discipline," what it's referring to is suffering. Terrible as it may be, God can use suffering to make us more Christlike. Experiencing suffering offers us a choice: to run from God or run to him, in faith and trust.

PRAYER: God, draw me closer to yourself today.

Series: *Walking in the Way of Wisdom*

READ: Romans 12:9-21

Don't Get Even, Get Generous

If your enemy is hungry, give him bread to eat, and if he is thirsty, give him water to drink, for you will heap burning coals on his head, and the LORD will reward you. (Proverbs 25:21-22)

Have you ever thought about the difference between Proverbs and proverbs—God's wisdom versus the human sayings that have been around forever and that offer advice for everyday life? The book of Proverbs comes from heaven. Human proverbs sometimes come from the other place. For example, when someone insults you or cheats you, the human response is: "Don't get mad, get even." Proverbs says don't get even, get generous.

Paul quoted this verse in a section of Romans devoted to Christian ethics. Sounding very much like Jesus in the Sermon on the Mount, the apostle told us to "Bless those who persecute you . . . Repay no one evil for evil . . . [and] never avenge yourselves" (Rom. 12:14, 17, 19). Instead of vengeance, we must show kindness to our enemy, offering help instead of harm. And here's the reason: doing that will heap burning coals on the head of the one who has hurt us.

I wonder how that works. Does it mean that the wrongdoer will really get it in the neck when the Lord of vengeance finally judges everyone? Or could it be that the "fiery coals" means that our gracious response causes this person to burn with shame at the thought of their shabby behavior? If that's the case, perhaps we'll have turned an enemy into a friend.

PRAYER: Lord, give me the grace not to pay back evil for evil.

Series: *Walking in the Way of Wisdom*

READ: Luke 6:27-36

An Eye for an Eye?

Do not say, "I will do to him as he has done to me; I will pay the man back for what he has done." (Proverbs 24:29)

Speaking of payback, let's listen to Jesus: "Turn the other cheek," "Go the extra mile," "Give him your cloak too." In these famous examples in Luke 6, Jesus is modifying what was known as the *lex talionis*—the principle of "an eye for an eye and a tooth for a tooth" (Matt. 5:38). That Old Testament law was actually a moderating influence. Human nature being what it is, people have a tendency to adopt escalating acts of retaliation. As mobster Jim Malone said to federal agent Eliot Ness in the movie *The Untouchables*, "[Al Capone] sends one of yours to the hospital, you send one of his to the morgue." The Law said no, you can't do that. You can't take an eye for a tooth. The penalty must match the offense.

But even that is too much for Jesus, at least when it comes to our personal quarrels. Thankfully, in North America, we live in democracies that have legal systems and police forces. When functioning properly, these are God's means of protecting our lives and property. Jesus isn't saying we mustn't go to court to defend our rights. Turning the other cheek is how we should respond to an insult, not to a criminal assault. Jesus is telling us that the little grievances or demands that may come our way shouldn't provoke us to violence. Just let them go, he says. Leave it to the Lord.

PRAYER: Holy Spirit, I pray that this day your fruit may ripen in my life. (see Galatians 5:22-23)

Series: *Walking in the Way of Wisdom*

READ: James 4:13-17

Lord Willing

Do not boast about tomorrow, for you
do not know what a day may bring. (Proverbs 27:1)

When I was growing up, it was customary for the church bulletin to feature the letters "D.V." in the schedule of events for the coming week—as in, "The Ladies Missionary Society will meet on Thursday afternoon at 2 p.m. D.V." The letters stood for a Latin phrase, *Deo volente*, "God willing." It seems a quaint, bygone custom now, and I suppose it did become a bit ritualistic, but there was real wisdom behind those little letters. That wisdom came straight from this proverb, as expanded upon in the book of James.

Whenever we make plans, even if it's just where we plan to have lunch tomorrow, our plans must always be conditional. We will do this or that or the other *if the Lord wills*. Because we're not really in control of the future. We live as if we were, and most of the time it's true. Until suddenly it's not. We might not have tomorrow, let alone next year, to "trade and make a profit" (v. 13). Tomorrow belongs to the Lord, not to us. Nothing is guaranteed us beyond today.

Of course, we can and should still make our plans. By all means make your business plans and vacation plans and retirement plans; block out your week, schedule your meetings, write down your appointments. But as you do, always—mentally if not out loud—add "If the Lord wills" (v. 15). I'm not suggesting we need to put D.V. back in our calendars and bulletins; just that we should always bear it in mind.

PRAYER: Father, thank you so much
that I can trust you for the future.

Series: *Walking in the Way of Wisdom*

READ: Acts 9:36-42

A Good Name

A good name is to be chosen rather than great riches, and favor is better than silver or gold. (Proverbs 22:1)

When Proverbs talks about choosing a good name it's not referring to expectant parents having lengthy conversations about what to call the baby. It's talking about caring in the right sense for your personal reputation. Our next devotion will address the problem of being overly concerned about your reputation in your community, whatever that community is (workplace, school, town, church, club). But today we're invited to reflect on what it means to want to have "a good name."

Eulogy literally means "good word." When someone dies, a eulogy is usually given at the funeral, focusing (one hopes) on the virtues of that person's life and character. When Dorcas fell ill and died, the eulogy at her funeral wasn't just verbal, it was visual. As Peter entered the upper room where the body was laid out, "All the widows stood beside him weeping and showing tunics and other garments that Dorcas made while she was with them" (Acts 9:39).

It has been pointed out that eulogy virtues are very different from résumé virtues. Résumé virtues are all about credentials and accomplishments; eulogy virtues are all about character. At your funeral, people probably won't talk about what you owned or how much money you made or what kind of house you lived in. But they are certain to talk about what kind of name you had. You can choose today to make it a good one. At your funeral that's all that will matter.

REFLECTION: How might I choose a good name rather than riches?

Series: *Walking in the Way of Wisdom*

READ: Matthew 10:16-33

The Fear of Man

*The fear of man lays a snare, but whoever trusts
in the LORD is safe. (Proverbs 29:25)*

In an earlier devotional I mentioned that we don't seem to pay enough attention to the fear of the Lord these days, especially considering how much the Bible says about it. But there's another kind of fear many of us worry about far too much—"the fear of man." This isn't the reasonable fear of what harmful people might do to us; it's the excessive fear of what critical people might say or think about us. The fear of man comes from worrying about our social standing. It can lead us to be embarrassed about being identified as a Christian at work or school. It can shame us into conforming to the world's values and behavior or make us keep silent when speaking the truth is unpopular.

When a gang came to arrest Jesus in the garden of Gethsemane, Peter pulled out a sword and fought, ready to make good his boast that he would die for Jesus. But just a few hours later, a serving girl's simple question caused him to deny all knowledge of his Lord. As Christians we probably won't be asked to lay down our lives for Jesus, but we will likely be asked to risk social ridicule and ostracism for following him.

The antidote to the fear of man is the fear of God, the only one who decides eternal issues (Matt. 10:28). So let's put things in perspective: "The LORD is on my side; I will not fear. What can man do to me?" (Ps. 118:6).

PRAYER: Lord, deliver me from the fear of man. May I fear only you.

Series: *Walking in the Way of Wisdom*

READ: Luke 18:18-30

Who Wants to Be a Millionaire?

*Give me neither poverty nor riches; feed me with the food
that is needful for me, lest I be full and deny you and say,
"Who is the LORD?" or lest I be poor and steal and profane
the name of my God. (Proverbs 30:8-9)*

I have an English friend who, when asked at the dinner table if he would like another helping, often replied, "No thank you. I have an elegant sufficiency." That's a fine thing to have in life—an elegant sufficiency. Not to have so much that we become possessed by our possessions. Not to be stuffed so full of the world and its things that we have no room for God in our lives. John D. Rockefeller, at the time the richest man in America, was asked, "How much is enough?" "Just a little more," he famously replied. It's difficult to find your satisfaction in God when you're always wanting just a little more.

On the other hand, it's certainly no fun being poor, to be in such need that you worry constantly about paying the bills, having enough to eat, buying clothes for your children, and keeping a roof over your head. That's not just hard, it's dangerous. If I'm deprived of life's necessities, I will be tempted to take desperate and dangerous steps to get what I need.

Following Jesus is costly, as the rich young ruler learned to his sorrow. If we put anything ahead of him, it has to go. But the rewards for discipleship are out of this world. Meanwhile, may the Lord grant us an elegant sufficiency of all we need.

PRAYER: Lord, thank you for your promise
that you will meet all my needs.

Series: *Walking in the Way of Wisdom*

READ: Psalm 32, James 5:13-16

What to Do with Your Sins

Whoever conceals his transgressions will not prosper, but he who confesses and forsakes them will obtain mercy. (Proverbs 28:13)

Both David and Solomon (Psalms and Proverbs) knew long ago what modern psychology has confirmed. Suppressed guilt produces serious side effects. The psalmist's spiritual struggles resulted in physical symptoms (Ps. 32:3-4). Unconfessed sin is hard on us.

But confession is hard too. It's one thing to confess our sins to God. This, of course, is the place to begin. But we may also need to go on with James' directive to confess to one another—perhaps to a trusted pastor or counselor, an accountability partner, a spouse, or a victim. That's when it gets really hard. It's embarrassing to own up to the wicked or foolish things we have done, thought, and said. It's also possible that acknowledging our sins will have real consequences for us relationally or even legally. No matter how much carrying guilt may hurt, it often seems like keeping silent (Ps. 32:3) or covering up our iniquity (v. 5) is the easier option.

Except that confession is the only way to find forgiveness (v. 5). As long as we cover up rather than confess, guilt just keeps gnawing away inside. Oh, and there's one more thing we must do. The person who confesses *and forsakes* their sins will find mercy: "But if we walk in the light, as he is in the light . . . the blood of Jesus his Son cleanses us from all sin" (1 John 1:7).

PRAYER: Spend some time in confession.
Then ask, is there someone I need to talk to?

Series: *Walking in the Way of Wisdom*

READ: Psalm 119:89-112

A Lamp to Our Feet, a Light to Our Path

Trust in the LORD with all your heart, and do not lean on your own understanding. In all your ways acknowledge him, and he will make straight your paths. (Proverbs 3:5-6)

These words from Proverbs 3 send me back in time, and I can see Mr. Van Houten leading our junior high Sunday school department in the memory verse and hear my 12-year-old-self reciting them (in the King James Version). Like many others, this proverb with its exhortation and promise has guided me my whole life.

An exhortation: trust in the Lord with all your heart (positive) and don't rely on your own understanding (negative). Take God's Word as your truth, even when you can't fully understand it. Use it as your rule and guide, even when it's hard to follow. Acknowledge the Lord—his word, will, and way—in everything you do, believe, and say. Don't think you are smarter than the Bible. And then the promise: he will make straight your paths.

As always with Bible promises, this is not an ironclad guarantee that our paths will never be crooked or steep or hard or, for that matter, deadly. But it is an assurance that no matter how much the paths of our lives may twist and turn, in the end the Lord will straighten them all out and make sure they lead us straight—home to him. It includes the promise that he will be with us all the way: "Even though I walk through the valley of the shadow of death, I will fear no evil, for you are with me; your rod and your staff, they comfort me" (Ps. 23:4).

PRAYER: Lord, I trust your promise to leave me home one day.

Series: *Walking in the Way of Wisdom*

READ: Psalm 84

Songs of Ascent

My soul longs . . . for the courts of the LORD. (Psalm 84:2)

Psalms 120-134 are titled the "Songs of Ascent." This collection of psalms was composed for worshipers on their way to the temple in Jerusalem. These psalms were climbing songs, travel songs sung by Jewish pilgrims as they walked up the road toward Mount Zion.

Jewish worship in the Old Testament was seasonal, not weekly. Public worship took place at the temple in Jerusalem during the three great annual festivals. In the spring, Passover commemorated the Israelites' deliverance from slavery in Egypt. Then seven weeks later came Pentecost, marking the giving of God's Law to Moses on Mount Sinai. Finally, the fall festival of Tabernacles was held to give thanks for the harvest and to recall God's provision and guidance during the years of wilderness wandering before the children of Israel reached the promised land. Faithful Jews gathered in Jerusalem for worship: at Passover to remember God's salvation, at Pentecost to give thanks for his Word, and at Tabernacles to celebrate his providential care.

For the Old Testament believer, the temple was important not so much in itself, but because of the one who dwelt there. Longing for the place was really longing for the person, for intimacy with God through worship. For Christians, Jesus is the temple. He is the place where God can be met, the one through whom the Father is worshiped. Through his indwelling Spirit, the highway to Zion now lies within our hearts, and we are blessed indeed (v. 5).

PRAYER: Triune God, thank you that I have free access to the Father through the Son by the Spirit.

Series: *Psalms of Ascent*

READ: Psalm 120

I Am for Peace

I am for peace, but . . . they are for war! (Psalm 120:7)

"Sticks and stones may break my bones, but words can never hurt me." When was the first time you heard that? Probably many years ago, on a playground somewhere. Well, it wasn't true then, and it isn't true now—especially now, when hurtful words can be tweeted from a phone or posted online. Slander and accusations are like sharp arrows or glowing coals (v. 4). When aimed against us they hurt.

In the psalmist's case, the malicious speech was provoked by an unpopular stand taken among hostile strangers. He finds himself living far away from God's land and God's people (v. 5); Mesech in the far north and Kedar in Arabia are about as distant from the temple as one could imagine. The world's enmity is aroused by the psalmist's life and witness, which contradict the world's value system; he is for peace, but they are for war (v. 7). But the sharp, fiery words of his enemies will be paid back by sharp, fiery judgment from God (vv. 3-4). In the justice of God, people eventually will receive what they hand out to others. That should make us careful about how we talk.

Here's a wonderful alternative to negative, insulting, critical comments. "Let your speech always be gracious, seasoned with salt, so that you may know how you ought to answer each person" (Col. 4:6). In the Old Testament salt was added to the Temple sacrifices. If you want your speech to be gracious, think of your words as if they were being offered to the Lord.

PRAYER: God, please forgive me for hurting others with my words. May my speech always be gracious.

Series: *Psalms of Ascent*

READ: Psalm 121

My Help Comes from the Lord

The LORD will . . . keep your life. (Psalm 121:7)

When the psalmist lifts his eyes to the hills, we moderns might think he's simply admiring the view. Actually, it's a different matter entirely. I thought of this psalm when traveling in Bhutan, a small, beautiful country in the Himalayas. From the road that wound through Bhutan's steep valleys, I could see countless Buddhist prayer flags dotting the hilltops all around. Something like that sight greeted the psalmist as well. Ancient peoples believed the high places were closer to the gods, so that's where the pagan shrines were located. Thus the question: "From where does my help come?" (v. 1). Do I look to the idols of my culture or do I look to the Lord?

Our help comes from the Lord, the psalmist proclaims. God is constantly vigilant to care for us. Nothing can slip past him to harm us (v. 4). God's protection is comprehensive; he guards us from accidents (our foot will not slip), and from diseases both physical and psychological (the sun will not strike us by day or the moon by night).

But now comes the problem. This psalm seems to promise too much. Are we literally given such blanket protection? Obviously not. Christians go out to car crashes and come in to cancer diagnoses every single day. So then, is the psalm false? Obviously not! Generations of believers have found wonderful comfort in the truth of the psalmist's testimony: "My help comes from the LORD" (v. 2). He does protect and preserve me—either from all ills or through them. Nothing "in all creation" can "separate us from the love of God in Christ Jesus our Lord" (Rom. 8:39).

PRAYER: Thank you, Father, for your providential care over my life.

Series: *Psalms of Ascent*

READ: Psalm 122

Jerusalem

Pray for the peace of Jerusalem! (Psalm 122:6)

To get to the temple, the worshipers had to climb. That was a simple fact of geography. The city of Jerusalem is set in the hill country of Judea. Traveling there, especially by the main road that goes up from Jericho in the Jordan River valley, meant a literal ascent, a long uphill hike. Try to picture that road, swollen with pilgrims on the eve of a festival. Imagine them straining to catch the first glimpse of the holy city, singing these songs to make the last weary miles go faster. And then, there it is. Jerusalem at last! What a sight!

Scripture often has multiple layers of meaning. Take "Jerusalem," for example. Literally, it was, and still is, a city on the map. But in the Bible, the city also represents God's dwelling place on earth, where God was known and worshiped. Then symbolically, Jerusalem or Zion is the City of God, standing for all the people of God in all ages of the world who belong to the Lord. Finally, the eschatological meaning: the heavenly Jerusalem (Revelation 21-22) represents the new creation and the world to come.

So how do we pray for the peace of Jerusalem? We do that literally, of course, praying for peace in the Middle East. But we also pray for the peace of the church, for the blessing and security of all who love the Lord. And we pray ultimately for the coming of the promised new creation, when God's work of salvation is finished and his kingdom is complete.

PRAYER: Lord, I pray for the peace of Jerusalem—literal Jerusalem and spiritual Jerusalem.

Series: *Psalms of Ascent*

READ: Psalm 123

Our Eyes Look to the Lord

As the eyes of a maidservant to the hand of her mistress,
so our eyes look to the LORD our God. (Psalm 123:2)

Arrogance is hard to take, isn't it? I can put up with a lot from people, but not from people I know are looking down on me. The psalmist was the same way. He's had more than enough of scorn and contempt from those who thought they were better because they had more money than he did (v. 4).

So what does he do about it? It's easy to take a wrong turn here. When we feel the scorn of others, we're tempted to make ourselves feel better by finding someone even lower on the social scale and heaping scorn on them. We vent our anger and humiliation by channeling it downwards: the father punishes the son, the son hits his younger brother, and the little boy kicks the cat. But the psalmist finds healing not by looking down but by looking up. "To you I lift up my eyes, O you who are enthroned in the heavens" (v. 1).

Compared to God, we're all low, way down among the servants. The vast difference between us mortals and the one who is enthroned on high makes all our human distinctions of class or race or wealth or accomplishment seem trivial by comparison. Because whoever we are, or whatever we have done, we still have the same fundamental need. "So our eyes look to the LORD our God, till he has mercy upon us" (v. 2).

PRAYER: Lord, today I humble myself before you. You are infinitely great, and I am amazed that you care about me.

Series: *Psalms of Ascent*

READ: Psalm 124

Our Help

Our help is in the name of the LORD,
who made heaven and earth. (Psalm 124:8)

"I don't *need* any help!" Have you ever heard that cry from a stubborn child? Have you ever said it yourself? Of course, it's true that we all have to learn to do things for ourselves. But we all do need help, all the time. No one can make it on their own.

Consider when enemies rise against us (v. 2), when floods threaten to sweep us away (v. 4) and the raging waters engulf us (v. 5), then we realize how weak and vulnerable we are. We lose a loved one, and we're devastated. We experience financial reversals or the loss of a job, and we can't see how we'll make it. Accident or disease strikes us down, age and infirmity make us feeble and unable to care for ourselves. And then comes death. Where can we find help to face all this?

"Our help is in the name of the Lord," believers confess. (In my home church, we start each service that way.) God's name—his character, his steadfast love, his omnipotent power and gracious mercy—that's what we depend on. When trouble comes, people look for help from many sources—from savings, technology, medicine, family, friends, the government. Many never even think of looking to the Lord. Yet God himself and God's help through secondary means are not mutually exclusive options. Just remember that wherever or whomever it comes from, the ultimate source of your help and strength is the Lord.

PRAYER: Lord, as you have used others to help me,
use me to help others.

Series: *Psalms of Ascent*

READ: Psalm 125

From This Time Forth and Forevermore

The LORD surrounds his people, from this time forth and forevermore. (Psalm 125:2)

For most of human history, ordinary people have been vulnerable to sudden attack. If you were a simple farmer who one day saw an armed band of enemies galloping toward your village, you had only one option: to run for it. Your only hope of survival was to reach a safe hiding place or defensible position.

The Bible, and the Psalms in particular, are full of images like that for God. He is "our refuge and strength . . . our fortress" (Ps. 46:1, 7, 11). "The LORD is my rock and my fortress and my deliverer, my God, my rock, in whom I take refuge, my shield, and the horn of my salvation, my stronghold" (Ps. 18:2). "You are a hiding place for me; you preserve me from trouble" (Ps. 32:7).

That's the thought behind the psalmist's words here in Psalm 125. As he makes the climb up to the city, the writer's thoughts focus on Mount Zion, the main hill on which Jerusalem was built. All who trust in the Lord are able to stand like a mountain amid all the storms of life and assaults of the enemy. It's not that we are so strong in ourselves. It's that, now and always, we are surrounded by the Lord.

The Lord's protection does not mean trouble can never reach us. But it does mean that in order to get to us, it has to go through him first.

PRAYER: God, I bless you for the promise that you make all things work together for my good.

Series: *Psalms of Ascent*

READ: Psalm 126

Sowing in Tears, Reaping with Joy

He who goes out weeping . . . shall come home with shouts of joy. (Psalm 126:6)

Psalm 126, like the other Psalms of Ascents, is set against the backdrop of Israel's return from exile. It's all about an unexpected turn of events, an unimaginable reversal of fortune, an impossible dream actually coming true. For the survivors of the Babylonian captivity, coming back to the city of Jerusalem was a sort of resurrection from the dead.

But what is this about weeping while going out to plant seeds? Why would anyone do that? In a subsistence agricultural society like the psalmist's, planting season was the hungry time. The grain you had reserved as seed for next year's crop may well have been the last food in the house. You faced a choice between planting it, and going hungry for a while, or eating it now and starving later. The exile was a hard time, a season of weeping for Israel. But out of that sowing, God brought a harvest of new life for his people.

For many years, Words of Hope broadcast the gospel in Russian to the Soviet Union. Rev. John Sergey faithfully proclaimed God's Word despite the difficulties. He loved Psalm 126:6; I heard him quote it often. And eventually he had the joy of seeing much fruit spring from the precious seed of the Word that he had sown. So "let us not grow weary of doing good, for in due season we will reap, if we do not give up" (Gal. 6:9).

PRAYER: Lord, give me the stamina to keep on sowing good seeds of obedience and witness, trusting that they will bear fruit.

Series: *Psalms of Ascent*

READ: Psalm 127

The Work of the Lord

Unless the LORD builds the house, those who build it labor in vain. (Psalm 127:1)

Nisi Dominus frustra is an old motto of the Reformed Church in America: "without the Lord, all is in vain." It's the main point of Psalm 127. Unless God is working in us, with us, and through us, all our efforts at building his kingdom will end in failure and futility. As Jesus would later say, "Apart from me you can do nothing" (John 15:5).

Okay, got it. But what does this have to do with having lots of children (vv. 3-5)? Well, imagine what life was like in the psalmist's day. No insurance companies, no pension plans, no social services, no welfare programs, no police forces or fire departments. The only thing standing between you and ruin or destruction was your family. So you had better have lots of children and have them when you're young, so that by the time you are old they will have grown into adults who can provide for and protect you.

A key point to remember is that God uses *us* to do his work. Yes, the Lord has to build the house and keep watch over the city, but he does that through our efforts! It's true that without him nothing we do matters, but it's not true that we need to do nothing. So remember the flip side: *with* the Lord, nothing we do is in vain. "Be steadfast, immovable, always abounding in the work of the Lord, knowing that in the Lord your labor is not in vain" (1 Cor. 15:58).

PRAYER: Lord, show me what work you have for me to do for your kingdom.

Series: *Psalms of Ascent*

READ: Psalm 128

God-Fearing People

*Blessed is everyone who fears the LORD,
who walks in his ways! (Psalm 128:1)*

I've said this more than once, but we need to think more about the fear of the Lord. Our picture of God tends to downplay those elements in his character that might be upsetting. If we do mention the fear of the Lord, we hasten to add that it doesn't mean we should be *afraid* of God. It just means feeling awe. Awe for God is great, but maybe there should also be "a little bit of afraid" in our fear of God. Afraid as in fear of offending him, fear of dishonoring him, fear of treating sin lightly and assuming God will forgive. The psalmist equates the fear of the Lord with obedience. The 18th century English writer William Law wrote a devotional book entitled *A Serious Call to a Devout and Holy Life.* God-fearing people respond to that call.

Psalm 128 describes the blessings God-fearing people can expect. They will enjoy the fruits of their own labor, rather than seeing it seized by some robber or invader. They will rejoice in their large families, gathered around the dinner table. They will experience the prosperity of the whole community throughout their long and happy lives and live to see their grandchildren growing up.

The psalmist pictured God's blessings in terms of the only world and life he knew. Our world is different, and our experiences may be different too, but our outlook is also longer. We know that since Jesus died and rose again, those who walk in his ways will see blessing far beyond anything this world can offer.

PRAYER: God, teach me how to fear you properly.
I want to walk in your ways.

Series: *Psalms of Ascent*

READ: Psalm 129

Greatly Have They Afflicted Me

May all who hate Zion be put to shame. (Psalm 129:5)

Picture yourself at the temple along with a congregation of pilgrims. The worship leader begins a song with a call and response. A leader sings, "Greatly have they afflicted me from my youth," then the congregation is cued ("Let Israel now say") and repeats the refrain. So the song is really about the story of the people of God, not just the psalmist's individual suffering. For almost its whole history, Israel had been mistreated and abused, going all the way back to its "youth" in Egypt. But her enemies have not prevailed (v. 2). The Lord is righteous (v. 4). He remembers his covenant promises. He cuts the cords that bind his people and delivers them from their enemies.

The people of God are still persecuted in many places today. Why are some people so hostile toward believers? What have the Christians of Egypt or Pakistan or Nigeria or India done that makes some want to blow them up or shoot them in their churches? Why do Chinese officials bulldoze the buildings where believers do nothing except gather to pray for them? Why is it a criminal offense in North Korea to confess faith in Jesus? Why such fear, such hatred?

Perhaps the only explanation is the one Jesus gave: "If the world hates you, know that it has hated me before it hated you . . . because you are not of the world . . . therefore the world hates you" (John 15:18-19). But be aware: the day is coming when all who hate Zion will be put to shame.

PRAYER: Lord Jesus, I pray today for believers
who are suffering for their faith in you.

Series: *Psalms of Ascent*

READ: Psalm 130

Out of the Depths

But with you there is forgiveness,
that you may be feared. (Psalm 130:4)

We all know what it's like to cry out to God for help when we're in the depths of sickness or sorrow. But here the pit is one the psalmist has dug for himself through his own sin. And we're all in there with him. God could show us things about ourselves that would make us collapse in shame. If the Lord chose to mark our iniquities, if he published a report card detailing every one of our sins—every nasty thought, every angry or hurtful word, every misdeed and failure—it would flatten us, utterly destroy us.

"But with you there is forgiveness . . ." (v. 4). Has there ever been a more beautiful statement of the gospel? Yet there is a twist: ". . . that you may be feared." There it is again, the response that's so important for biblical believers. Not "that you may be praised" (though we do), not "that we may be thankful" (though we are), but "that you may be feared." We must never treat forgiveness lightly or in a matter-of-fact way.

The psalmist knew that God would somehow erase all the bad marks against us and enable us to stand before him, justified and forgiven. What he couldn't know is how God would do that. For that we turn to the apostle: "And you, who were dead . . . God made alive together with [Christ], having forgiven us all our trespasses, by canceling the record of debt that stood against us with its legal demands. This he set aside, nailing it to the cross" (Col. 2:13-14). Thanks be to God!

PRAYER: I bless you, Lord, for your wonderful forgiveness.

Series: *Psalms of Ascent*

READ: Psalm 131

Like a Quieted Child

O Israel, hope in the LORD from this time forth
and forevermore. (Psalm 131:3)

This little psalm offers a most beautiful metaphor of faith. The image is of a child of two or three, nestled quietly in her mother's lap. Picture yourself as that child, and the mother's lap as the loving embrace of God. What are you doing there? Or rather, what *aren't* you doing there? The child isn't thinking about anything. "I do not exercise myself in great matters: which are too high for me" (v. 1, *The Book of Common Prayer*). At some point we turn away from the restless thoughts that keep us awake at night, we give up trying to solve life's deep mysteries, we let go of the troubling questions that undermine faith, and we leave it all with the Lord.

The child isn't saying anything. The psalmist doesn't say his soul is quiet; he says it has been quieted (v. 2). The child has been crying—toddlers get a lot of "owies"—but now she has calmed down. A mother's comfort has hushed her fretfulness. Faith doesn't mean we'll never be hurt, but it does mean we have the wonderful comfort of belonging to the Lord.

Finally, the child isn't asking for anything. Notice: she has been weaned. She's not there just to be fed. The child has learned to see her mother as more than an automatic responder to her every cry. The child's relationship with her mother is no longer simply instinctive dependence and demand; it is growing toward real love.

PRAYER: Spend some time being quiet before the Lord,
picturing yourself being held in his arms.

Series: *Psalms of Ascent*

READ: Psalm 132

The Lord Has Chosen Zion

The LORD has chosen Zion; he has desired it
for his dwelling place. (Psalm 132:13)

King David wanted to do something nice for God. After all, God
had blessed him in so many ways. The Lord had given David a new
kingdom, a new capital city, and a grand new palace. So David decided
to build God a new house, too. "Not so fast," said the Lord. "It's not
for you to build me a house. Instead, I will build you a 'house'—an
everlasting dynasty."

The sons who followed David were mostly disappointments, and
the royal line was eventually extinguished. After Judah went into exile,
no descendant of David ever ruled again as king. But that didn't mean
the Lord's promise came to nothing. Jesus is the true Son of David. His
kingdom is eternal, his reign will never end.

Jesus is also the true house of God. His body is the dwelling place
for God on earth, the one in whom God can be known personally
and through whom God can be truly worshiped. A Samaritan woman
once asked Jesus a question about where the right place to worship
God was. Was it in Samaria or Jerusalem? Jesus replied, "The hour
is coming when neither on this mountain nor in Jerusalem will you
worship the Father . . . True worshipers will worship the Father in
spirit and truth" (John 4:21, 23).

Since Jesus came into the world, worship is no longer about a place
or a building. It's only about a person.

PRAYER: Father, I come to you in worship
through the Son and by the Spirit.

Series: *Psalms of Ascent*

READ: Psalm 133

Beautiful Unity

Behold, how good and pleasant it is when brothers dwell in unity! (Psalm 133:1)

Brothers don't always dwell together pleasantly in unity. The first brothers, you may recall, were Cain and Abel. Brothers (and sisters!) sometimes don't get along at all. Families fight, siblings have rivalries, people living together disagree with and aggravate one another. It's the same in our spiritual family, the church. But when, despite our differences, faults, and failures, we actually live together in unity—well, that's a beautiful thing.

Beautiful, says the psalmist, like the oil flowing down Aaron's beard and onto his collar; beautiful like the dew of Hermon falling on Zion. The oil was the anointing oil used to ordain Aaron to the priesthood and consecrate his sacred vestments (Leviticus 8). It symbolizes the Holy Spirit, who has been poured out on us so we can be priests to one another, bearing each other up before the Lord in prayer. Mount Herman in Lebanon was proverbial for its abundance of water, in contrast to dry Mount Zion. The unity of God's people is like water falling on a parched land.

A practical question: how do we achieve such unity? In Colossians 3:12-13, Paul lists three key qualities: patience, forbearance, and forgiveness. Patience is longsuffering, being slow to take offense. Forbearance is putting up with the small stuff that annoys us. And if it's more than small stuff, that's where forgiveness comes in. The church that lives out Colossians 3 will experience the blessing the Lord has commanded.

PRAYER: God, show me how I could be like the healing oil of the Spirit in my family and church.

Series: *Psalms of Ascent*

READ: Psalm 134

Come, Bless the Lord

Come, bless the LORD, all you servants . . . who stand
by night in the house of the LORD! (Psalm 134:1)

I love the hymn "The Day Thou Gavest:"

We thank Thee that Thy Church unsleeping,
While earth rolls onward into light,
Through all the world her watch is keeping,
And rests not now by day or night.

What I love here is the thought that the worship of God is perpetual. It keeps on going right around the world. While we are going to bed, Christians somewhere on the other side of the globe are getting up to praise the Lord.

The psalmist was also thrilled by that idea. Leadership of the temple worship was entrusted to the Levites, the tribe the Lord had set apart for liturgical duty. Only the descendants of Aaron were priests, but the other Levites served as musicians and singers, gatekeepers, craftsmen, caretakers, guards, and the like. And they served in shifts, day and night, so that, as another stanza of the hymn says, "The voice of prayer is never silent, nor dies the strain of praise away."

Imagine you were one of the Levites pulling the midnight to 4 a.m. shift. Maybe as your eyelids droop and your head nods, you hear the encouragement: "Lift up your hands to the holy place and bless the LORD!" So you suck it up, and in response sing right back, "May the LORD bless you!" Amen to that!

PRAYER: Lord, I give you thanks for your church here and around the world, now and through the ages; and especially that I am part of it.

Series: *Psalms of Ascent*

READ: Psalm 19:1-4

Revelation

Lift up your eyes and look to the heavens. (Isaiah 40:26 NIV)

How did you come to know about God? That's easy—someone told you. And that, in a nutshell, is what revelation means. No one can find out about God on their own, by their own unaided reason. Someone has to tell them, and ultimately that Someone must be God himself. People cannot discover the truth about God through investigation, the way they solve a mystery or make a scientific discovery. People can only learn about God through revelation, God's self-disclosure.

God first tells us about himself in the general (general in that it is available to everyone everywhere) revelation of the created world. The wonders of the earth around us and the heavens above us are stunning evidence of the glory, wisdom and power of the creator God.

> *"And what is this God?" I asked the earth . . . I asked the sea and the deeps . . . and they replied, "We are not your God. Look above us." I asked the heaven, the sun, the moon, and the stars, and "No," they said, "we are not the God for whom you are looking." And I said, "Tell me something about my God, you who are not he. Tell me something about him." And they cried out in a loud voice: "He made us."*
>
> *(St. Augustine, Confessions)*

What single cause produced this unimaginably great world? Did everything simply evolve on its own from nothing as the materialists say? "Lift up your eyes and look to the heavens." What do you think?

PRAYER: Thank you, Lord, for showing us the truth about yourself through the glories of your creation.

Series: *What to Believe*

READ: Psalm 19:7-14

Scripture

. . . in your light do we see light. (Psalm 36:9)

I blamed it on the light. I began to notice that I was having trouble reading the fine print on a page and the little date number on my watch. It was simply amazing how many places had bad light! Of course it wasn't really the light. So I swallowed my pride and bought a pair of reading glasses. What a difference! What was previously blurred jumped sharply into focus. What was dim became clear.

John Calvin compared the Bible to eyeglasses. The self-revelation of God in creation is no longer sufficient to teach us about God because we have turned away from God and suppressed the truth. As a result, our thinking has been impaired (Rom. 1:18-23). Our spiritual vision is blurred. We can no longer see God clearly, unless we "put on" his Word and "read" the world through it.

The Bible is our source for the full truth about God. The psalmist describes it as, perfect, trustworthy, right, radiant, sure and altogether righteous, more precious than gold, and sweeter than honey (Ps. 19:1-11). It will revive us, make us wise, give us joy, enlighten us, warn us, give us great reward.

> *I want to know one thing, the way to heaven: how to land safe on that happy shore. God himself has condescended to teach the way; for this very end he came from heaven. He hath written it down in a book. O, give me that book! At any price, give me the book of God!*
>
> *(John Wesley)*

PRAYER: Thank you, Lord, for your Word

Series: *What to Believe*

READ: Romans 8:18-24

Sin

For the wages of sin is death. (Romans 6:23)

Creation's splendors proclaim the Creator's greatness. When we read the book of creation alongside the Bible, we learn much about the God who made everything from galaxies to sub-atomic quarks.

But that's not the whole story. God's creation is not all beauty and light. There is also darkness, cruelty, suffering, and death in the world. Creation, as someone has remarked, speaks out of both sides of its mouth. If a star-studded sky tells us that God is great, the sight of a child undergoing chemotherapy might lead us to question whether he is good—or even if there is a God at all. I recently read a book by a man who had been raised in a Christian family but abandoned the faith as an adult. The prehistoric record of mass extinction events and the insignificance of human beings in a vast universe made it all seem meaningless to him.

Can we as believers make sense of this? The apostle tells us that the creation itself is suffering the after-effects of humanity's sin. Creation is groaning in pain; you can even hear it. You hear it in the dreadful screams of a wounded animal, in the shriek of the destroying wind or the roar of the flood waters, in the moans that fill a nursing home's corridors. But the creation's suffering is neither senseless nor purposeless. It's like the pain of childbirth, leading to better things. We can look forward someday to a new heaven and earth, in which righteousness will dwell (2 Peter 3:13).

PRAYER: "When I look at your heavens, the work of
your fingers . . . what is man that you are mindful of him . . . ?
Yet you have made him . . ." (Psalm 8:3-5)

Series: *What to Believe*

READ: Romans 7:15-25

Flesh

All have sinned and fall short of the glory of God. (Romans 3:23)

What is wrong with us? We know we aren't what we ought to be. Very few of us are what we would like to be. We know what is right; it's just that we can't seem to figure out how to do it.

And what about the human race? How do you explain a species that is capable of producing both the works of Mozart and the killing fields of Pol Pot? Human beings are God-like, able to create and appreciate beauty, to explore truth, to love and be loved, to seek God and to know him. Human beings are also dishonest, cruel, corrupt, and capable of the worst atrocities. So which is it? Angels or demons?

The truth is, we're a bit of both. Scripture says that we were created in the image of God (Gen. 1:26-27). Even though fallen, some of that image remains, like embers in the ashes of a fire. That is why we have so much capacity for good, and also why we have such a deep, inborn longing for God. But Scripture also says we are sinners. We have turned away from God, putting ourselves at the center of things instead of God. The result is that our human nature has become twisted, curved inward upon itself. This is what the apostle means by the "flesh"—our fallen human nature. We're no longer able to love God and others, or even love ourselves as we ought. And we find it all too easy to do truly terrible things.

Who can deliver us from the mess we're in?

PRAYER: Thanks be to God for the victory that is ours through our Lord Jesus Christ.

Series: *What to Believe*

READ: Ecclesiastes 2:1-11, 1 John 2:15-17

The World

*If anyone loves the world, the love
of the Father is not in him. (1 John 2:15)*

What do you think of when you hear the word "*world*"? World record? World news? World Series? Similarly, the word *world* can mean different things in the Bible. It can mean the physical earth, the world of nature—"their voice goes out . . . to the end of the world" (Ps. 19:4). It can mean the people who live on earth, the world of humanity—"For God so loved the world" (John 3:16). But it often means something bad—human society in rebellion against God, the world of sin and evil, the place where God's truth is despised and God's laws are trampled and God's people are persecuted and God's son was crucified. "Do not love the world or the things in the world" (1 John 2:15). While we should admire the world of nature, and love the world of people, we must hate and reject the world of sin.

In his masterpiece *The Pilgrim's Progress*, John Bunyan calls the world "Vanity Fair." Village fairs in his day were places of buying and selling, of amusement and entertainment. But it's all vanity, empty of eternal significance (see Eccl. 1). As Bunyan says, there is no avoiding it—"the way to the Celestial City lies just through this town." And if we maintain our distinctive Christian identity as we pass through the world we will arouse its wrath. But we need not be afraid—"In the world you have tribulation. But take heart; I have overcome the world" (John 16:33).

PRAYER: Lord, help us to stand firm for you
when the world tries to squeeze us into its mold.

Series: *Walking with Christian: Pilgrim's Progress*

READ: Acts 16:25-34

Awakening

What must I do to be saved? (Acts 16:30)

Many contemporary churches describe themselves as "seeker sensitive" and plan their services in ways they assume will appeal to non-Christians. But there's something important we need to recognize. People aren't naturally seekers. Left to oneself, no one is looking for God. The New Testament is pretty blunt on this point. Unbelievers' hearts are darkened (Rom. 1:21), their minds are hardened against the truth (2 Cor. 3:14). They are blind to the glory of Jesus (2 Cor. 4:4). They are "dead in trespasses and sins" (Eph. 2:1).

Among some, there's a belief that everyone is going to heaven. Unless someone is incredibly evil—Hitler-grade evil—they will end up in the right place. You'll be saved as long as you don't do anything very, very bad. But according to Scripture it's just the opposite. If you do nothing, if you just drift through life indifferent to God, you will perish. You have to do something to be saved.

And what is that? When you seriously ask that question, you will discover that God has already begun to work in you. We were spiritually dead, but God graciously made us alive. We were blind, but God has shone the light into our hearts. Has God awakened you? Are you interested in him, attracted to him? If you are a seeker, that didn't come naturally. It's a sign of grace, an indication that God's Spirit is working in you.

Do you wonder how you should respond to his gracious love? "Believe in the Lord Jesus, and you will be saved" (Acts 16:31).

PRAYER: Lord God, awaken me to your love.

READ: Psalm 35:1-10

Salvation

*. . . salvation is nearer to us now than when
we first believed. (Romans 13:11)*

In its original Old Testament sense, the term *salvation* had a physical meaning. It was not a spiritual, other-worldly concept. Salvation was very much a matter of escaping death in this world. For David, salvation meant first and foremost getting away from all the nasty people who were chasing him to kill him (Ps. 35:3, 8-10).

As God's revelation progressively unfolded, salvation came to take on deeper layers of meaning. Once when the noted New Testament scholar B. F. Westcott was riding on a train, he was approached by a young Salvation Army worker who asked if he was saved. "I have been saved, I am being saved, and I shall be saved," he replied.

It was a very biblical answer. Believers have been saved (past tense) in the sense that all our sins were forgiven the moment we trusted in Christ (justification). We are being saved (present tense) as we are increasingly delivered by our obedience in the power of the Spirit from the presence of sin in our lives (sanctification). We shall be saved (future tense) when the Lord returns to raise our bodies from the grave and complete his work of salvation for the whole universe (glorification). Salvation in that sense is nearer now than when we first believed, and one day nearer today than yesterday.

PRAYER: Thank you, Lord, for saving me; for pardoning me in the past, delivering me now, and for the hope of one day sharing your glory in the world to come.

Series: *What to Believe*

READ: Romans 8:31-38

Justification

. . . justified by faith, we have peace with God. (Romans 5:1)

The Bible uses numerous pictures to convey the rich shades of meaning in God's saving work through the cross of Jesus Christ. Justification is a legal image, drawn from the court room where the accused stands before the judge charged with capital offenses.

Imagine that's you there, standing before the judge, on trial for your life. There's not much question about the facts. The evidence against you is overwhelming and unanswerable; in fact, you have been forced to admit your guilt. Now the moment has come for sentence to be passed. The gavel snaps down with an awful crack. You wait to hear the words of your doom. But instead, the judge cries, "Not guilty!"

That's justification. To be justified is to be declared righteous by God, even though we are *not* righteous in ourselves. Justification is a different kind of righteousness, given to us as a gift through faith in Christ. We are not made right with God by anything we do; instead, Christ's perfection is credited to us. Justification is instantaneous. The moment we trust in Christ we are completely righteous in God's sight. Justification is permanent. The supreme judge, God himself, is the one who acquits us. No power in all creation can possibly reverse his sentence. "It is God who justifies. Who is to condemn?" (Rom. 8:33-34).

> PRAYER: Heavenly Father, I thank you for clearing me of my guilt when I did not deserve it. All praise to you!

Series: *What to Believe*

READ: Romans 3:21-26

Atonement

*. . . making peace through his blood,
shed on the cross.* (Colossians 1:20 NIV)

"Will not the Judge of all the earth do right?" asked Abraham long ago (Gen. 18:25 NIV). The answer is an emphatic yes! God will always do only what is right.

But how can it be right for God to justify (accept as righteous) people who are sinful? After all, we are indignant when an obviously guilty criminal gets off scot-free. As a proverb says, "The judge is condemned when the guilty is acquitted." So the question is not just how can God justify sinners, but how can he justify sinners *justly*.

In Romans 3 Paul addresses this question. He is explaining how God can justify those who have faith in Jesus while still remaining just himself (v. 26). The answer lies in the death of Christ on the cross, "whom God put forward as a propitiation" (v. 25; "sacrifice of atonement" NIV).

The root meaning of the biblical word for atonement is to "cover." Christ's sacrificial death "covers" the sins of those who trust in him. It also "covers" (*propitiates* is the technical term) the wrath of God against sin. Here is a staggering thought: God himself satisfies the demands of his own justice. The Son lovingly offers, and the Father willingly accepts, the payment of sin's penalty: death. That is why God can remain righteous as he pardons all who are joined to Christ through faith.

PRAYER: "Look, Father, look on his anointed face,
and only look on us as found in him."
(*And Now, O Father, Mindful of the Love*)

Series: *What to Believe*

READ: 1 Peter 1:17-21

Redemption

. . . you were bought with a price. (1 Corinthians 6:20)

One of the little memories I retain from childhood is shopping one afternoon with my mother at Herpolsheimer's Department Store in downtown Grand Rapids. We went down into the basement to the "Redemption Center" where my mother exchanged some green stamps for a small appliance.

Redemption is the acquisition of one thing in exchange for another. When the New Testament writers speak of salvation as redemption, they are using a commercial image, drawn from the world of buying and selling. Specifically, the world of slavery, the buying and selling of people. In the Roman empire, a kind master would sometimes choose to free a slave. To do so he would take the slave to the marketplace and publicly "redeem" him by paying a ransom price to the local gods.

That is an illustration of what God does in saving us. We are redeemed from slavery, our bondage to sin, not by the payment of silver or gold but by the most precious substance in the universe—the blood of Jesus Christ (1 Peter 1:19). Such a costly redemption puts us in debt to the Lord. "You are not your own," writes Paul. "You were bought with a price. So glorify God in your body" (1 Cor. 6:19-20).

PRAYER: Thank you, Lord, that I am not my own,
but belong to my faithful savior Jesus Christ, who has
fully paid for all my sins with his precious blood.

Series: *What to Believe*

READ: John 3:1-8

Regeneration

You must be born again. (John 3:7)

Automotive engineers have spent millions of dollars and years of effort to improve the efficiency of car engines. Their work has led to better gas mileage and less pollution. But it's not enough. Environmentalists continue to draw attention to the polluting effects of the internal combustion engine. What is ultimately needed is not more efficient cars, but an entirely different kind of vehicle with a new propulsion system and a new energy source.

What do human beings need in order to be saved? Do we need to be made just a little better? Would a 10 percent improvement in morality be enough? 50 percent? 100 percent?

The Bible says that what we need is not improved spiritual efficiency but a new birth by the power of the Holy Spirit. In order to be saved, increased effort on our part is not enough. Moral exhortation, self-help books, motivational programs—none of those can sufficiently change us. By nature, we are spiritually dead. Regeneration is the miraculous act by which the Spirit makes us inwardly alive, alive toward God. We become a new creation in Christ Jesus! Nothing less than that will do. John Wesley was once asked why he preached so frequently on John 3:7. "Because you must be born again," he replied.

PRAYER: I praise you, Lord, as the God who brings life from death. Thank you for new birth in Christ Jesus.

Series: *What to Believe*

READ: Titus 3:4-8

Grace

He saved us, not because of works done by us in righteousness, but according to his own mercy. (Titus 3:5)

At the heart of our faith lies the message of salvation by *grace*. Grace isn't a substance; it can't be packaged or dispensed. It isn't available in book form or on video. It's one thing you can't buy at Amazon (or anywhere else). Grace is God's love in action.

God's grace acts supremely in a particular Person. Earlier in this letter, Paul had written that "the grace of God has appeared, bringing salvation for all people" (Titus 2:11). Here he says "the goodness and loving kindness of God our Savior appeared" (3:4). When Paul says that grace appeared what he means is that *Jesus* appeared. If you talk about grace or love "appearing," you're really saying that someone who embodies those qualities has arrived on the scene. Abstractions don't walk on stage to enter the play, characters do. If God's grace and love have appeared in the world, that can only be through a particular person. Jesus Christ is God's grace personified: in his holy incarnation, perfect life, saving death, and hope-giving resurrection.

Receiving this grace-of-God-in-Christ is what saves us, not any good works we do. This is for sure, says the apostle Paul (v. 8); you can take it to the bank. If you know Christ the Savior, you have eternal life!

PRAYER: Thank you, Lord, for your incredible grace.

Series: *Trustworthy Sayings*

READ: Acts 27:13-44

Work

So take heart. (Acts 27:25)

Medieval monks had a saying: *Ora et labora*, "pray and work." Those two activities are not mutually exclusive. It's been said that we should pray as if everything depended on God, and work as if everything depended on us.

Luke's account of his and Paul's voyage and shipwreck on the way to Rome is one of the most exciting stories in the Bible. Two things stand out. The first is that God is always in control. Storms may come, we might even have to go through a shipwreck, but God is managing it all. The Lord says, "Don't worry, I've got this. You'll make it." "Do not be afraid, Paul; you must stand before Caesar" (v. 24).

The second great truth is that our actions matter. We may be tempted to think that because God is sovereign and is working out his purposes, it doesn't really matter whether we do anything or not. We can just sort of sit back and let God do his thing. But that's not what we see in Acts 27. When the sailors try to steal the lifeboat and sneak off to shore, Paul grabs the centurion. He knows that without the crew to man the ship, they won't last the night. So he tells the Roman soldier, "Unless these men stay in the ship, you cannot be saved" (v. 31). Wait, didn't God assure Paul everyone would be saved? Yes. But if the sailors leave, they won't be saved? Yes, again. Here's the point. God works his will *through us*. God's purpose is invincible, but our efforts are indispensable. Maybe those old monks were on to something.

PRAYER: Lord, help me to do my part
in what you are doing in the world.

Series: *Acts*

READ: Hebrews 12:1-3

Discipleship

You have need of endurance . . . (Hebrews 10:36)

Bennett Cerf, founding publisher at Random House, employed two people full-time just to read unsolicited manuscripts. In more than thirty years he published exactly two books of the thousands received "over the transom," as they used to say. When asked why he persisted in such an obviously inefficient practice, Cerf replied, "Because one of the two I published was the great novel *Cry, The Beloved Country.*"

A masterpiece is worth the effort. A thing of great value is worth waiting and working for. Patience is rewarded when the long-sought prize is finally attained.

"You have need of endurance," wrote the author of Hebrews. "Let us run with perseverance the race before us" (see 12:1). That race is a marathon, not a sprint. It is the race of Christian discipleship, of following and imitating Jesus. Discipleship is a long journey, from sin to wholeness and holiness, from lostness to life, from earth to heaven. It's hard, and it takes a lifetime

Remember, there is no prize for beginning the Christian life, only for finishing it.

PRAYER: Lord, give us grace to "see Thee more clearly, to love Thee more dearly, to follow Thee more nearly, day by day."
(Richard of Chichester)

Series: What to Believe

READ: John 10:22-30

Perseverance

Who shall separate us from the love of Christ? (Romans 8:35)

Our patient endurance in the life of Christian discipleship is sustained by God's gracious covenant love. In theology it's called "the perseverance of the saints." A better expression might be "the preservation of the saints."

Some friends recently visited Ireland. They told about their stay on a sheep farm deep in the green countryside. It was spring, lambing season. The sheep spent the night out in the hillside pastures. When day dawned, the shepherd went out to call his sheep. At the sound of his voice the sheep came running, streaming into the fold from every direction.

Those who are Christ's recognize his voice in the promise and call of the gospel. They respond. They come to him and follow him. But it is really the Lord who gathers and protects the flock. He holds them in his hands.

Our belief in the preservation of the saints is based on God's faithfulness to us, not our faithfulness to him. It is God's "stick-to-it-iveness"—or better, his "stick-to-us-ness." We know that if we belong to Christ, we will not fall away or be lost in the end because he will not let us go.

PRAYER: Thank you, Father, that even when my hold on you is weak, your hold on me is strong and unbreakable.

Series: What to Believe

READ: Ephesians 1:3-6; Ephesians 2:1-5

Predestination and Election

You did not choose me, but I chose you. (John 15:16)

Predestination and Election: not the easiest doctrines in Christian theology. Many of the problems we have thinking about these things stem from the fact that we live in time (past, present, future) and God does not.

These terms underscore the determinative factor of God's decisions in human affairs. What happens, happens because, in the final analysis, God decides it should. God *predestines* (predetermines) all that comes to pass, although in the mystery of his sovereignty he allows humans the freedom that makes them responsible for their actions. If he is the kind of God the Bible says he is (the Ruler of all things), then he must exercise ultimate control.

Election is the particular part of predestination that has to do with salvation. The Greek word from which "elect" comes means "to choose." God chose those whom he will save in Christ even before the creation of the world. This is what the Bible says. "We love him because he first loved us." "You did not choose me; I chose you so that you would bear fruit."

The fact is, unless God chooses us we cannot choose him. According to Scripture we are spiritually dead by nature—incapable of even believing in him on our own. Our salvation is God's doing, from first to last. As John Newton once remarked of those who rejected the biblical doctrine of election, "Maybe you contributed something to your salvation, but that was more than I could do!"

PRAYER: All praise to you, Lord God, now and forever.

Series: What to Believe

READ: Romans 10:5-17

Faith

Let the one who is thirsty come. (Revelation 22:17)

The famous Danish physicist Niels Bohr once said: "The opposite of a small truth is a falsehood; the opposite of a great truth is another great truth." Reality is like that, in both the physical and spiritual realms.

The great truth opposite election is faith. In a sense it's not hard to be saved, says Paul. You don't have to climb up to heaven or descend into hell. All you have to do is believe and call on the name of Jesus. Whoever does that *will* be saved. God so loved the world that he gave his son so that *whoever*—anyone, everyone—believes in him will not perish. The same opportunity is open to all, regardless of who they are: everyone who calls on the name of Jesus will certainly be saved. And, as Paul goes on to say, if any are lost it will be because of their refusal to believe and obey the gospel (Rom. 10:16). No one will be able to blame anyone but themselves for that.

The Tzeltal Indians of Chiapas State in Southern Mexico have a beautiful definition for faith. In their language the word for faith literally means "holding on to God with your heart." I once saw another beautiful definition that treated the word "faith" as an acronym: **F**orsaking **A**ll, **I** **T**ake **H**im." That is exactly what each of us must do, and keep on doing. If we hold on to Christ with our hearts, we will be saved. The gospel is the power of God to save everyone who believes (Rom. 1:16).

PRAYER: Jesus, I call on you today,
to hold on to you with all my heart.

Series: What to Believe

READ: Acts 10:1-16, 34-43

Inclusion

God shows no partiality. (Acts 10:34)

The Roman soldier Cornelius, though a Gentile, was "a devout man who feared God . . . gave alms generously . . . and prayed continually" (v. 2). So what's the problem? Most people would conclude that he's good to go. What more does he need?

He needs Jesus. Apparently being good and kind and devout is not enough. But Jesus promised that those who seek will find, and those who ask will receive, so Cornelius' prayers will be answered. It just so happens there is a man not far away who can introduce Cornelius to the Lord. God sends two visions, one to Cornelius telling him how to find Peter, and one to Peter telling him not to refuse Cornelius. In case Peter didn't get the point, a voice from heaven spells it out for him more than once: Don't call unclean anything (or anyone) God has made unclean.

Peter goes, though it isn't easy for him to overcome his lifelong aversion to gentiles. But he goes! And he preaches—the same gospel message he's been repeating since the day of Pentecost: "They killed him, but God raised him!" The gospel is good news about what God has done in the life, death, and resurrection of Jesus Christ to save the world. And it's for everyone. God shows no partiality, he doesn't play favorites. He doesn't mean the gospel to be just for his ancient covenant people of Israel; it's for the whole world. It's not that the gospel is for nice, clean people, but the unclean need not apply. As a matter of fact, there are no unclean people out there, only people waiting to be cleansed with the blood of Christ.

PRAYER: Lord, teach me to see no one as unclean.

Series: *Acts*

READ: Acts 1:1-7

Kingdom

Will you at this time restore the kingdom to Israel? (Acts 1:6)

Jesus' preaching focused on the kingdom of God (Matt. 4:17). His mission was God's mission: to bring the kingdom—God's reign of shalom—to earth. God's kingdom exists wherever Jesus is reigning as Lord. Jesus spent three years—plus forty days—talking to them about it, but the disciples still didn't get it. "Lord," they asked, "are you going to give the kingdom back to Israel now?" As the great biblical scholar N. T. Wright observed, the answer to this—like so many of the disciples' questions—was, "Yes, but not the way you think." They still thought Jesus was a nationalistic Messiah. But Jesus' triumph over death spelled good news for all people everywhere.

Eventually the disciples would get it, and they came to understand these truths about the kingdom:

- It is universal in scope. The kingdom is being restored to Israel, but "Israel" now includes people from every nationality and race. Christ is the hope of all.
- It comes through the work of the Holy Spirit who uses our witness to bring people to Christ.
- It is gradual in its growth. From those first believers in Jerusalem, the kingdom would slowly spread throughout the whole world. Wherever the church of Jesus Christ is growing, the kingdom is on the move. Wherever Christians are living out their faith in love and service the kingdom is coming.
- It is God's to complete. He alone can bring it in fullness, and he will do so at the time he has set by his own authority.

PRAYER: Your kingdom come.

Series: *The Mission of God*

READ: Psalm 2

Judgment

We die only once, and then we are judged. (Hebrews 9:27 CEV)

Ours is an age that rejects the idea of limits and consequences. Accountability is out; freedom is in. Tell someone he has to pay a penalty for breaking the rules, and you'll likely have an argument. Judgment is not a popular concept. People like to believe that in the end, no one gets punished, no one has to pay for anything, there are no consequences for sin.

The Bible says otherwise. The God who raises up the humble also resists the proud; in fact, he laughs at their arrogant pretensions. "He who sits in the heavens laughs; the Lord holds them in derision" (v. 4). God's love compels but his wrath terrifies (v. 5). "God's patience is not placidity, any more than his fierce anger is loss of control, his laughter cruelty, or his pity sentimentality. When his moment comes for judgment . . . it will be by definition beyond appeasing or postponing" (Derek Kidner).

So what to do? Well, here is a word to the wise, literally (vv. 10-12). Be warned, see the truth. It is a very dangerous thing to believe that actions have no eternal consequences simply because we would like it to be that way. Be humble; serve the Lord with "fear and trembling." Be reconciled to the Holy Judge through his Son, the King. "Blessed are all who take refuge in him" (v. 12).

PRAYER: Holy and righteous God, I bow to you in humility and repentance, and kiss the Son.

Series: What to Believe

READ: Romans 13:8-14

Obedience

Faith without deeds is useless. (James 2:20 NIV)

"Deeds are the fruits of love," said William Tyndale, "and love is the fruit of faith." "Owe no one anything," Paul urged, "except to love each other" (Rom. 13:8). "Dear children, let us not love with words or speech but with actions and in truth," added John (1 John 3:18 NIV). As followers of Jesus Christ, we are pledged to obey him by practicing his precepts and obeying his commands. His principal command is to love others through lives of sacrificial service.

Several years ago a book came out titled, *The Altruistic Personality: Rescuers of the Jews in Nazi Europe.* The authors, a pair of sociologists, attempted to determine what kind of people were most likely to risk their lives to help save Jews from Hitler's gas chambers. Their conclusion: What most distinguished the rescuers was that they lived in "embedded relationships," shaped by the teaching of "normocentric communities." Translated from "sociologese," that means most rescuers came from strong families who were committed to the church. "It's not because I have an altruistic personality," said Dirk, a Dutch resistance worker interviewed for the study. "It's because I am an obedient Christian. The Lord wanted us to rescue these people, and we did it." That's what real faith looks like. Faith that doesn't affect your behavior isn't worth anything.

PRAYER: Father, help me to love with actions and in truth, as you do.

Series: What to Believe

READ: 1 Corinthians 12:14-21, 26-27

Church

. . . now you are God's people. (1 Peter 2:10)

In the New Testament the church is the *ekklēsia*, the company of those who have been "called out" of the world to be the people of God. The New Testament church is the counterpart to the Old Testament congregation of Israel. It is the assembly of all those who have heard and responded to God's call to join the community of believers who belong to the Lord Jesus.

As Christians, we need the church. "The New Testament knows nothing of solitary Christians" (John Wesley). The church is the true home of every Christian. Trying to be a Christian without belonging to a flesh-and-blood Christian community is like trying to be a hand or a foot without belonging to a human body.

But the church also needs us in order to fulfill its mission. The church is meant to be distinctive, even revolutionary. It is Christ's body on earth, charged with fulfilling his mission to the poor, the lost, the alienated. The church is God's new community of reconciliation—multi-racial, multi-national, multi-cultural. The church needs to be a power for good in the world. An ancient Christian manuscript dating from the time when the church was turning the whole Roman empire upside down states: "If you say, 'I am a Jew,' nobody will be moved. If you say, 'I am a Roman,' nobody will be upset. If you say, 'I am a Greek, a barbarian,' nobody will be disturbed. If you say, 'I am a Christian,' the whole heaven will shake."

PRAYER: I want to say I am a Christian, today and every day.

Series: What to Believe

READ: Psalm 96

Worship

To him . . . be praise . . . for ever and ever! (Revelation 5:13 NIV)

Of all the things we do, worship is the only thing that will last forever. The Jewish Talmud, the collection of rabbinical commentary on the Hebrew Bible, puts it this way: "In the future all sacrifices will cease, but the offering of thanks will not cease to all eternity. Similarly all confessions will cease, but the confession of thanks will not cease to all eternity."

Worship is what we were made for. The chief purpose of human beings, as the Westminster Catechism states, is "to glorify God and enjoy him forever." The redeemed will spend eternity engaged in the one activity that can never be completed: to "ascribe to the Lord the glory due his name" (Ps. 96:8). Because however much glory we give to God, he always deserves more!

When the Lord Jesus returns, many things that are essential now will no longer be necessary. No more law, medicine, or government. No preaching, teaching or evangelism. No helping the poor (no more poor!), no striving for justice (no injustice!). Just worship. If that's the case, the smart thing is to start practicing now, so that worship—our eternal life's work, the one thing for which we were created—becomes more natural to us.

PRAYER: "Since I am coming to that holy room, where, with thy choir of saints for evermore, I shall be made thy Music; as I come I tune the instrument here at the door, And what I must do then, think here before." (John Donne, *Hymn to God in My Sickness*)

Series: What to Believe

READ: 1 John 1:1-4

Joy

We are writing these things so that our joy
may be complete. (1 John 1:4)

The Scottish philosopher and sceptic David Hume once asked an English bishop why religious people always looked so dour. Replied the bishop: "The sight of you, Mr. Hume, is enough to make any Christian melancholy." That was a monumental put-down. But even though Mr. Hume was so thoroughly put in his place, he does have a point. Sometimes Christians can be terribly joyless and dismal.

C.S. Lewis titled his autobiographical account of his conversion *Surprised by Joy*. From childhood he longed for an experience that he could hardly describe or define. He called it "joy." It wasn't merely pleasure; it went deeper than that. It wasn't just happiness; it lasted longer than that and was less based on circumstances. Unexpectedly, when he came to Christ Lewis experienced the joy he had long sought. True joy is found in God ("He's a hedonist at heart," as Lewis' fictional devil Screwtape sneers).

If it isn't exactly happiness and it isn't exactly pleasure, what exactly is joy? It's a deep sense of wellbeing and security that comes from having life—real life, "eternal life," as the apostle John calls it (v. 2). This life comes through a faith relationship with the Father and the Son. Sharing in this new life also unites us in fellowship with the church, making us one with all who believe in Jesus. John says that this is the reason he wrote down the story of Jesus, of which he himself had been a prominent eyewitness. Not just so that we would believe, not just so that we could be saved, but so that we would have joy.

PRAYER: Father, in your presence there is fullness of joy,
at your right hand are pleasures forevermore. (see Psalm 16:11)

READ: Isaiah 43

Death

When you pass through the waters, I will be with you; and through the rivers, they shall not overwhelm you. (Isaiah 43:2)

My father was a great trout fisherman, and he occasionally (alas unsuccessfully) tried to teach me the sport. I never caught many fish, but I have strong memories of wading the streams. It's rather nerve racking, even with waders on, to walk into a fast-flowing river and grope with your toe through cloudy water for the bottom. And there's a very special kind of shock awaiting you when you step into a hole and go in over your head.

In *The Pilgrim's Progress*, John Bunyan's pilgrim, Christian, faced many difficulties and dangers during his progress to the Celestial City. His last obstacle was the River of Death. Here it was Hopeful who took the lead and lent his brother strength. When Christian began to sink, Hopeful cried, "Be of good cheer, my brother, I feel the bottom, and it is good."

One of the solemn but holy privileges of pastoral ministry is visiting Christians as they face death. Not all of them pass through the river easily, for they "find it deeper or shallower, as (they) believe in the King of the place," but all are taken safely across in the end if they stand on Christ, the Solid Rock. As the great Dutch theologian Herman Bavinck said during his last illness, "Now my scholarship avails me nothing, nor my dogmatics: it is only my faith can save me."

PRAYER: "O holy and merciful Savior, Thou most worthy Judge eternal, suffer us not, at our last hour, because of any pains of death, to fall from thee." (*Book of Common Prayer*)

Series: *Walking with Christian: Pilgrim's Progress*

READ: 2 Corinthians 4:16-18

Glory

When he appears we shall be like him. (1 John 3:2)

What do you say to someone with an incurable degenerative disease? To a person in the last stages of cancer? Or to a nursing home patient whom advancing age is robbing of the use of body or mind?

If the person is not a Christian, there is very little to say in the way of comfort or encouragement. "The decay of the outward man in the godless is the most melancholy spectacle in the world, for it is the loss of *everything*" (James Denney).

It's a different story for those who know Jesus Christ. I have often met face to face with people in situations like the ones above. Whenever I am speaking with a Christian, I find myself drawn to 2 Corinthians 4:16-18. Though outwardly we are wasting away, inwardly we are renewed. Though our bodies are running down toward death, spiritually we move forward to life. The afflictions that trouble us here are momentary. What they are leading to is glory, and glory is forever.

The future of every believer is to be glorified, freed completely from sin, suffering and death, made over into the likeness of Christ himself. Glorious thought!

PRAYER: "When we've been there ten thousand years,
bright shining as the sun, we've no less days to sing
God's praise than when we've first begun." (*Amazing Grace*)

Series: What to Believe

READ: Hebrews 12:22-29

Heaven

*But you have come to Mount Zion and to the city
of the living God, the heavenly Jerusalem. (Hebrews 12:22)*

We seem to hear very little about heaven in church these days. For past generations of Christians, heaven was a subject that was never very far from their thoughts and conversation. Just look, for example, at many of the old hymns and gospel songs we used to sing. Today heaven is almost a forgotten subject. Why?

One reason for that is fear of escapist thinking that neglects the needs of this world. Fair enough. But consider also how most of us live. As our personal worlds have grown increasingly prosperous and comfortable, we feel less and less desire to trade them for a better world on high. When life is pretty good here, there's not much incentive to look forward to life there. How can heaven be better than our comfortable Laz-E-Boy in front of the big-screen TV? Besides, why should you want to go to heaven when you can go to Italy or Hawaii almost anytime you want?

Well, consider this about heaven: God is there. Christ is there. All the glorified saints, the redeemed of the Lord, are there. "When I get to heaven," wrote old John Newton, "I shall see three wonders there: the first wonder will be to see many people there whom I did not expect to see; the second wonder will be to miss many people whom I *did* expect to see; and the third and greatest wonder of all will be to find myself there."

Will you be there too?

PRAYER: For the means of grace and the hope
of glory, dear Lord, we thank you.

Series: What to Believe

READ: Revelation 5:6-14

Eternity

And he shall reign forever and ever. (Revelation 11:15)

This devotional was originally published on December 31, 1999.

And so, at last, we come to it. After all the hype, all the predictions and dire warnings, the last day of the last year of the 1,000's. A century gone, a millennium finished. (Technically, 2000 is the last year of the 20th century. The 21st century begins on January 1, 2001. But let's not be pedantic. Everybody is worked up about the calendar flipping to years beginning with "2".)

In a few hours we will know whether the much-ballyhooed Y2K problem is real, or is simply more millennial hysteria. Well, right here and now, I want to make a prediction. What is going to happen tonight at the instant when the clock changes to 00:00:01? I can absolutely assure you what will happen: God will still be ruling his world! Blessing, honor, glory and power will all belong to him. Jesus Christ, the Lamb that was slain for the sins of the world, will still be Lord! He will continue to hold in his hand the scroll of human history and destiny, which he alone directs.

No, I don't know whether lights will go out tonight, or if planes will crash and chaos be unleashed. But I do know that nothing will happen to me or my world without the will of my Father in heaven, not this night or any night. I don't know whether Christ will return in the year 2000. But I do know that his coming, and the eternal reign it will usher in, is closer today than yesterday.

PRAYER: "O God, our help in ages past,
our hope for years to come, our shelter from the stormy blast,
and our eternal home." (*O God, Our Help in Ages Past*)

Series: What to Believe

READ: Habakkuk 1:1-4

It's a Small World

*O LORD, how long shall I cry for help,
and you will not hear? (Habakkuk 1:2)*

You have probably had one of those "It's a small world!" experiences, like bumping into an acquaintance from back home when you're traveling in a distant country. I have a similar feeling of shocked recognition when I come to the Book of Habakkuk. Here we are, among the twelve Minor Prophets of the Old Testament. It's sort of a strange place, really. There are a lot of books here that aren't read very often, written by people with odd-sounding names like Obadiah and Haggai. They are talking about problems and issues in civilizations that have been dead for 2,500 years. And then, just as we're tempted to leave, we turn a corner and bump into somebody we know. We recognize this man Habakkuk! He's asking the very same questions we ask.

Listen to what Habakkuk is saying to God: "How long must I keep praying?" "Why don't you listen?" "Why don't you answer me?" "Why don't you do something about this problem?" "How could you let that happen?" Does any of that sound familiar? Have you ever prayed that way? Of course you have, and so have I. Let's spend some time with Habakkuk over the next few days and see if he finds any answers to his anguished questions.

PRAYER: God, thank you that when I am hurting or angry or just plain perplexed, I can still come to you and you hear and understand.

Series: *Habakkuk*

READ: Habakkuk 1:1-4

Why Doesn't God Act More Like God?

Why do you tolerate wrongdoing? (Habakkuk 1:3 NIV)

The Hebrew prophet Habakkuk was an ancient man with a modern problem. Habakkuk believed in God. He served God. He prayed to God. But he didn't understand God. He could not fathom why God allowed so many terrible things to occur. In the end, all the prophet's questions could be boiled down to this one: Why doesn't God act more like God?

Think of it this way. What would you do if you were God? It seems to us that if God really acted like God, there wouldn't be any more fatal accidents, no more birth defects, no more cancer or AIDS, no more wars, no more suffering or pain. The whole world would flourish with peace and happiness, faith and goodness. We could understand that, that would make sense to us.

What doesn't make sense to us is the world we live in, if it truly is ruled by a God of love. When we as believers experience tragedy or sorrow, and even more when God seems silent in response to our cries for his help, we are confronted with the issue of trust. It comes down to the question of whether or not we are willing to believe that the Lord knows what he is doing in our lives and in the world. If we really trust in a loving, sovereign, all-wise God, shouldn't we be willing to give him— can we say this believingly?—the benefit of the doubt?

PRAYER: Lord, when it's hard, help me go on trusting you.

Series: *Habakkuk*

READ: Habakkuk 1:12-13

The Problem of Evil

Your eyes are too pure to look on evil. (Habakkuk 1:13 NIV)

A few years ago a book was published with the intriguing title, *All I Really Need to Know I Learned in Kindergarten.* Similarly, you could say that everything we need to believe we learned in Sunday school. Recall the little prayer we—at least I did; I hope you did too—said as young children: "God is great and God is good." If you can just hold on to both parts of that prayer you have all the basic theology you need.

Here's the problem: Habakkuk believed that God was great and God was good, too. The trouble was, what Habakkuk thought about God seemed to be contradicted by what he saw happening around him. That's what caused his distress. As the evangelist Leighton Ford said after the death of his twenty-two-year-old son, Sandy: "Our problem is reconciling our faith with our experience." How do you do that?

Not quickly or easily. At the end of chapter 1, Habakkuk is left dangling, so to speak. But he continues to struggle with God. When your faith seems to be contradicted by your experience, the easy thing to do is to give up your faith. Just walk away from God in disappointment and anger. But it is far better to keep on wrestling with the problem like Habakkuk did, refusing either to surrender your faith or to deny your experience.

PRAYER: God, when I'm struggling
to hang on to faith, give me strength.

Series: *Habakkuk*

READ: Habakkuk 2:1-4

Waiting for God

I will stand at my watchpost . . . and look out to see what he will say to me. (Habakkuk 2:1)

One of the most powerful artistic expressions of modern atheism is the play *Waiting for Godot* by Samuel Beckett. The play consists mostly of a dialogue between two characters who are waiting for a man called Godot to show up. But nothing much happens. And in the end, a messenger arrives to announce that Godot isn't coming.

The point of the play is that God isn't coming. The message is that there is nothing to wait for—no meaning of life, no purpose to existence, no loving Father in heaven, no heaven (or hell); nothing beyond the bare stage of this world.

Habakkuk too was waiting for someone. "I will stand at my watch," he said, "and station myself on the ramparts; I will look to see what he will say to me" (v. 1). Here's the picture: troubled Habakkuk metaphorically standing up there on a watchtower like a sentinel in a besieged city looking for the approach of the relief column, waiting for God to answer his questions. Some may think that questioning God like that is wrong. Not at all. What's wrong is to question him without waiting for him to answer us. Waiting for God is different than waiting for Godot, because we know God will show up in the end—with answers!

PRAYER: Father, I wait and watch for you today in faith.

Series: *Habakkuk*

READ: Habakkuk 2:1-4; Psalm 27

Standing on the Ramparts

I will stand at my watchpost and station
myself on the ramparts (Habakkuk 2:1 NIV)

The Bible speaks often of the importance of waiting for the Lord—of standing, so to speak, on the ramparts alongside Habakkuk. "Wait for the LORD; be strong, and let your heart take courage; wait for the LORD!" (Ps. 27:14).

Waiting is a function of hoping. To wait for the Lord is to confidently expect God's deliverance—from pain or suffering, from sin, from poverty, from sorrow, from loneliness, from all the troubles and evil that blight our life in this world (see Rom. 8:24-25). To wait is to refuse to give up on God, no matter how bleak our circumstances are. "I wait for the LORD," cried the psalmist, ". . . and in his word I hope!" (Ps. 130:5). Waiting is persistent trust in both the goodness and power of God, and that equals hope—no matter what!

Notice where Habakkuk is waiting and keeping watch. He's up on the city wall. Cities in Bible times were always enclosed by walls, for the same reason our houses and cars have locks on the doors and our countries have navies and air forces patrolling the borders. There are a lot of bad actors out there who will hurt us if they get a chance. We need protection because we live in a fallen world. So in one sense Habakkuk's stance is a reminder of how much we need God to come to rescue and restore the world. In another sense, his waiting is an expression of his faith that God will do just that.

PRAYER: Come, Lord Jesus!

Series: *Habakkuk*

READ: Habakkuk 2:2-4

And the Answer Is . . .

For still the vision awaits its appointed time . . . If it seems slow, wait for it . . . (Habakkuk 2:3)

Habakkuk's basic problem, like ours, is the struggle to reconcile faith with experience. If God is good, if he's so holy he can't even bear to look on evil (1:13), and if he's also watching over and governing the world, then what is going on? What's wrong with this picture? Because the world, in case you haven't noticed, is chock-full of bad stuff.

God's answer to Habakkuk's agonizing questions about suffering and evil is that . . . well, that there is an answer. But, the Lord adds, you're going to have to wait for the details. "At the time I have decided, my words will come true. You can trust what I say about the future. It may take a long time, but keep on waiting—it will happen!" (2:3 CEV). It's like the old gospel song says: "Farther along we'll know all about it, farther along we'll understand why."

Meanwhile, there's faith. "The righteous shall live by . . . faith" (v. 4). Faith is proved under the pressure of suffering. It is only when we are faced with circumstances tempting us to reject God that we are in a position to demonstrate whether or not we will trust God and go on waiting for him—or just give up. The promise is that if you don't give up, if you keep trusting God to the end, you will live.

PRAYER: Father, I thank you that again and again you have proved yourself worthy of trust.

Series: *Habakkuk*

READ: Habakkuk 2:4; Romans 1:16-17

Just by Faith

The righteous shall live by . . . faith. (Habakkuk 2:4)

Habakkuk 2:4 may just have been the apostle Paul's favorite Bible verse. Here's why. In Paul's understanding, this basic insight about faith can be read in two ways. First of all, the righteous person will live because of his or her faith. The proud are going to disappear. They won't endure. But the righteous who are living by faith—who go on trusting God even when they don't understand what he's doing—they will live forever. As Paul once said, we walk by faith, not by sight (2 Cor. 5:7).

But it also works the other way around because the reverse is equally true: Those who live by faith are righteous. It is just this attitude of faith, this willingness to believe in God when there is little else to go by, that makes us acceptable to God, even when the evidence might seem to be against him. God is pleased to count as righteous those who trust in him—specifically, who trust in Christ's death on the cross for their sins. This message about the way of salvation (that is, about a way of being counted as righteous before God on the basis of faith in Jesus) constitutes the core of the Christian gospel. It is what we mean by the theological expression, "justification by faith." It is the gospel, and it is the power of God for salvation to everyone who believes it. Do you?

PRAYER: Thank you, Lord, for the gospel, and your gift of forgiveness and righteousness in Christ.

Series: *Habakkuk*

READ: Romans 5:6-8

The Bible Way

The righteous shall live by . . . faith. (Habakkuk 2:4)

While surfing across television programs one day, I happened upon a talk show that made me pause in my channel-hopping. The question they were discussing—or, to put it more accurately, shouting over—was this: "Is Jesus Christ the only way of salvation?" One of the guests said politely, "Well, yes, actually. He is." At which point the host jumped in and yelled, "You can't make that claim! You don't have enough information!" But if the Bible is true, we do have enough information.

According to the Bible, there are only two ways people attempt to be saved. One is the way of religion. The way religion understands salvation is neatly summed up in one of America's favorite texts: "God helps those who help themselves." Religion teaches that in order to be saved it's up to us to do what is required—with a little help from God, of course.

But "God helps those who help themselves" is not a biblical text. The Bible way of salvation is just the opposite. The gospel message is that "Christ died for the ungodly . . . While we were still sinners, Christ died for us" (Rom. 5:6, 8). Religion says, "God saves the righteous." The gospel says, "God saves the unrighteous." "Christ died for the ungodly." God helps those who *can't* help themselves. Believe that good news, and you will live in peace.

PRAYER: Thank you, Lord Jesus, for showing your love
by dying for sinners and making them your friends.

Series: *Habakkuk*

READ: Habakkuk 2:6-19

Woe to the World

Woe to him who piles up stolen goods and makes himself wealthy by extortion! How long must this go on? (v. 6 NIV)

We love to sing "Joy to the world, the Lord is come." But in connection with the Lord's coming, the Old Testament is more likely to say, "Woe to the world." Habakkuk's second chapter, for example, consists mostly of a series of "woes"—warnings about God's approaching judgment upon a wide variety of evildoers.

Do these words of woe apply to our contemporary society? Does God still mean to judge the sins of the world? The answer, thankfully, is yes. I say, "thankfully" because judgment is actually a good thing. To see why, just picture a world without it. The innocent would suffer and no one would care. The guilty would profit, realizing that crime does pay. The powerful would take whatever they wanted, and nothing would stand in their way. So, yes, the message of God's judgment is good news for those who hear it and respond appropriately.

Still, judgment is not God's last word. There will come a time when the door of salvation will be shut (see Matt. 25:10-13). But that time has not come yet. A warning of judgment is also an invitation to repent. Habakkuk's woes are really an expression of God's mercy, intended to turn us from our sin and cause us to seek the Lord.

PRAYER: "Seek the LORD while he may be found; call upon him while he is near" (Isaiah 55:6). I call upon you today, Lord.

Series: *Habakkuk*

READ: Isaiah 11:1-9

The Coming Flood

*For the earth will be filled with the knowledge of the glory
of the LORD as the waters cover the sea. (Habakkuk 2:14)*

Habakkuk foretells a time when "the earth will be filled with the knowledge of the glory of the LORD as the waters cover the sea" (Hab. 2:14). What a glorious prospect! How full of water is the ocean? That is how full of God the creation will be! Every hill and tree and stream, every home and family, every tribe and nation, every person left on earth will be filled with the life of God, reflecting his glory.

The Old Testament word that best sums up the wonders of the new creation is the word shalom, or "peace." Biblical peace is much more than merely the absence of war. Instead it is well-being, wholeness, fruitfulness, delight. Where shalom is, all is right and all is well.

Humankind will never succeed in bringing peace on earth. Isaiah's prophecy speaks of a great Prince, a descendant of the house of David, who will arise like a fresh shoot from a dead stump. This mighty King is the One who will establish shalom in the earth. And we now know his name—it is Jesus Christ.

Meanwhile, ask yourself, does my life add at least a trickle to swell the coming flood, when the earth will be filled with the knowledge of the glory God as the waters cover the sea?

PRAYER: Make me a blessing to someone today;
out of my life may Jesus shine.

Series: *Habakkuk*

READ: Habakkuk 2:18-20

Where Is God?

The LORD is in his holy temple; let all the earth keep silence before him! (Habakkuk 2:20)

When I was a boy, the Sunday morning service in our church often opened with the choir singing softly in reverent tones these words from the second chapter of the book of Habakkuk: "The LORD is in his holy temple; let all the earth keep silence before him" (v. 20). Habakkuk suggests that we stop our own noise-making for a bit—all the wrangling, the jarring discord, the complaining, the boasting, the hype, the sales pitches, the endless "spinning"—and fall silent before the sovereign God who reigns as Lord over all. For the Temple isn't just a building in Jerusalem; the whole creation is his temple.

What does it mean to keep silent before God? First of all, our silence is a token of our humility and reverence before God, of our awe and—to use the biblical word—fear. But silence can also be an expression of faith. Let's face it. The fact that a good and loving God rules the world is not always obvious, as Habakkuk makes clear. This is one reason why the Bible so strongly proclaims that, in fact, God is in his holy sanctuary, reigning on the throne. There comes a point when we should put an end to our cries and complaints, our doubts and anger with God, and fall silent before the Lord in quiet trust. "Let us learn," said the great theologian John Calvin, "to glorify God by our silence."

PRAYER: Spend time in silence, glorifying God.

Series: *Habakkuk*

READ: Habakkuk 3:17-18

Singing in Hard Times

Though the fig tree should not blossom . . . yet I will rejoice in the LORD; I will take joy in the God of my salvation. (Habakkuk 3:17-18)

Habakkuk paints a picture of hard times here. There are no buds on the fig tree, no grapes on the vine, no produce from the fields, no cattle in the barns. That's his situation. No income, no resources, no prospects; the cupboard is bare, the paycheck is gone. What then? What do you say when you pray and trust God, but the doctor tells there's nothing more they can do for you? What do you do when your boss says he's sorry but you no longer fit in with their plans for the future? What do you say when your fig tree does not bud?

A lot of people say, "Forget it," and turn their backs on God. But Habakkuk says that even though things are lousy, "yet I will rejoice in the LORD" (v. 18). Habakkuk is singing his faith, even his joy, not because of his circumstances but despite them. He's singing in a minor key, but he's still singing. It's easy to sing praises to God when everything is great: "I sing because I'm happy, I sing because I'm free." A better test of faith is how you meet loss. Can you still sing when life stinks, when you're hurting? Habakkuk can because he knows God. "I will take joy in the God of my salvation" (v. 18).

If you can say that, you can face anything.

PRAYER: Lord, no matter what, I will praise you.

Series: *Habakkuk*

READ: Psalm 103

Thanksgiving

Bless the LORD, O my soul, and all that is within me,
bless his holy name! (Psalm 103:1)

I'm always puzzled by those who say they don't believe in God, but then say they are thankful for this or that good thing in their lives. What does that mean, exactly? To whom are they thankful? To truly give thanks there has to be someone to give them to. I suppose what such people mean is that they're glad nature dealt them a winning hand, or they "thank their lucky stars" for their prosperity and good fortune. They're happy that, at least compared to many, they seem to have won life's lottery. But feeling lucky isn't really thanks-giving. If you are a Christian, think what a blessing it is just to be able to bless the Lord for his healing, salvation, forgiveness, and protection with "all that is within us."

What do you give thanks for today? I think the thing I'm most thankful about is that I know whom to thank for all I have received. How sad when people realize they have been given much but don't really know the Lord who is the giver. So they say things without thinking that actually contradict their beliefs. I guess it must be hard to know you have been blessed, that you haven't earned or deserved your blessings, but you're not able even to say a proper thank-you. Before anything else, give thanks to God first of all for this: that in Christ he has made himself known to us as the Father who loves us, saves us, makes us his children, forgives us, and faithfully cares for us every step of our way.

PRAYER: For salvation and for all
your other gifts, we thank you, Father.

Series: *Walking with Christian: Pilgrim's Progress*

READ: 1 Peter 2:13-25

What Did Jesus Do?

*Christ also suffered for you, leaving you an example,
so that you might follow in his steps. (1 Peter 2:21)*

Some years ago, a phrase enjoyed popularity among young—and some not-so-young—Christians: "What Would Jesus Do?" If memory serves, it started in a youth group discussion about ethical issues. When faced with a decision about right or wrong behavior, ask yourself, WWJD? That could be a helpful mental exercise, but it seems to me there's a better question to ask when trying to decide what we ought to do in day-to-day living: What *did* Jesus do? This is the rule of guidance offered by Mr. Stand-fast, a wonderful example of a mature Christian from part two of *The Pilgrim's Progress*. Knowing his days on earth were coming to a close, he said this: "I have loved to hear my Lord spoken of, and wherever I have seen the print of his shoe in the earth, there I have coveted to set my foot, too." Stand-fast didn't ask what Jesus would do, he looked at what Jesus actually did, and then tried to do the same.

Like someone walking single-file in the tracks of his leader, the Christian tries always to set his feet in the prints of the Lord's shoes. Where did Jesus walk, and what did he do? He went about doing good; he walked especially among the poor and outcast without ignoring the rich (remember Zacchaeus). Jesus healed the sick and cared for the suffering, he encouraged the downcast and welcomed society's rejects. Most of all, he "came . . . proclaiming the gospel of God" (Mark 1:14). What is something you can do today to walk in Jesus' steps?

PRAYER: We thank you, God, for the Lord Jesus, who serves us not only as sacrifice for sin but as pattern and example.

Series: *Walking with Christian: Pilgrim's Progress*

READ: 2 Corinthians 4:16-5:8

Paul's Great Desire

My desire is to depart and be with Christ. (Philippians 1:23)

For as long as there have been humans, humans have been wondering about what comes next. What happens to us when with die? Of course, if you are an atheist, the answer is simple: nothing. An inscription on many ancient graves went like this: "I was not, I was, I am not, I care not." So common was this, writes scholar N. T. Wright, that it was often abbreviated to just its initials.

Even believers wonder, though. Do we go right to heaven when we die? Do we fall asleep until Jesus returns? Are we with our loved ones who have gone before? The Bible is pretty clear on the subject of heaven and the life to come. While most of what it says about the future refers to the triumphant return of the Lord Jesus and the resurrection of the dead and creation of the new heaven and earth of the world to come, the New Testament tells us enough about the state of the Christian dead to kindle our hope and longing. When in prison facing possible execution, Paul wrote the Philippians to say that his desire wasn't to be acquitted and set free. It was to depart, like a ship slipping its moorings, and be with Christ. When believers "fall asleep in Jesus," to use another of the apostle's beautiful expressions, they go instantly to be with the Lord (2 Cor. 5:6-8). To be absent from the body is to be at home with the Lord.

So Christian, lift up your head! You're one day closer to heaven today than yesterday.

PRAYER: "Thanks be to God, who gives us the victory through our Lord Jesus Christ." (1 Corinthians 15:57)

Series: *Walking with Christian: Pilgrim's Progress*

Appendix

The Christian Year is organized around seasons, which invite the believer to reflect on Christ's birth, ministry, death, and resurrection, and our response to Christ. Each season varies in length and includes special feast days—some of which are familiar, others of which may be new to you. This summary will help you keep track of where you are in the year and find the entries for feast days.

ADVENT AND CHRISTMAS

The Christian Year begins with Advent. Advent starts with the fourth Sunday before Christmas, and ends on Christmas Eve. During Advent, we anticipate the birth of Jesus, and the longing of all creation for the redemption he brings. The Christmas season begins Christmas Day (December 25) and ends after 12 days, on January 5. During Christmas, we celebrate the miracle of Jesus' birth.

EPIPHANY

Epiphany starts on January 6, with the Feast Day of Epiphany. Some Christian traditions continue Epiphany until the start of Lent; in others it ends on February 2. We have included enough devotionals for the longer celebration. During Epiphany, we focus on the events of Jesus' life and ministry, starting with the visit of the Magi to the infant Jesus.

LENT

Lent marks the 40 days (not including Sundays) before Easter. In total, it is 46 days from Ash Wednesday to Holy Saturday. During Lent, we join Jesus on his journey to the cross, and reflect on his death.

EASTER

Easter, or Eastertide, lasts fifty days, including forty days from Easter Sunday to Ascension Day (based on the forty days during which the risen Lord appeared to his disciples, according to Acts 1:3) and ten more days up to Pentecost Sunday. During Easter, we focus on Jesus' time on earth with his disciples after his resurrection, the birth of the church, and the cosmic impact of his life, death, and resurrection on all creation.

ORDINARY TIME

Ordinary Time lasts for about six months, from Pentecost to the start of Advent. During Ordinary Time, we share the life of faith, lived in response to God's saving work in our lives.

Feast Days:

CHRISTMAS EVE	ADVENT & CHRISTMAS, DAY 28
CHRISTMAS DAY	ADVENT & CHRISTMAS, DAY 29
EPIPHANY	EPIPHANY, DAY 1
ASH WEDNESDAY	LENT, DAY 1
PALM SUNDAY	LENT, DAY 40
GOOD FRIDAY	LENT, DAY 45
HOLY SATURDAY	LENT, DAY 46
EASTER	EASTER, DAY 1
ASCENSION DAY	EASTER, DAY 40
PENTECOST	EASTER, DAY 50

About the Author

David Bast is a writer and pastor who served for 23 years as the President and Broadcast Minister for Words of Hope. In his more than 40 years of devotional writing and preaching, he has been encouraging believers around the world to be shaped by God and his Word.

Prior to his ministry and work at Words of Hope, Dave served as a pastor for 18 years in congregations in the Reformed Church in America. A graduate of Hope College and Western Theological Seminary, he is the author of nine devotional books and Bible studies, including *Why Doesn't God Act More Like God*, *Christ in the Psalms*, and *A Gospel for the World*.

Dave and his wife, Betty Jo, have four children and eight grandchildren. Dave enjoys reading, growing tomatoes, and avidly follows the Detroit Tigers.

Find more of Dave's work at woh.org/DavidBast

Good News. All Ways.

MANY LANGUAGES

Words of Hope provides gospel content in over 75 languages. Some have no existing Scripture translations. Others are spoken by small tribes of people in remote areas. All are the heart languages of people waiting to be introduced to Jesus for the first time.

MANY COUNTRIES

Words of Hope provides free daily devotional content in North America and around the world! We have ministry directors working in Albania, Niger, India, and more.

MANY FORMATS

Where Christian literature and churches are illegal, we evangelize through social media and host online discipleship classes. Where there are no Scripture translations, we partner with local pastors to create online teaching videos. Where people cannot read or write, we record audio devotionals. Because the good news must be shared in all ways possible.

ONE HOPE

Throughout the global network of Words of Hope, faith in Jesus is our one shared focus. He is our only hope for this life and the next, and the world needs to know!

MORE FROM WORDS OF HOPE

Subscribe to our daily devotional:
woh.org/devotional

Pray around the world with us:
woh.org/pray

Donate to share the good news:
woh.org/donate

"[Jesus] came and proclaimed
the good news of peace to you
who were far away and peace
to those who were near."

EPHESIANS 2:17

700 Ball Avenue NE
Grand Rapids, MI 49503
1-616-459-6181
www.woh.org

Made in the USA
Monee, IL
22 October 2024

68096610R00227